Real-World LEARNING FRAMEWORK

FOR SECONDARY SCHOOLS

Digital Tools and Practical Strategies
for Successful Implementation

Marge Maxwell **Rebecca Stobaugh** **Janet Lynne Tassell**

Solution Tree | Press

a division of
Solution Tree

555 North Morton Street
Bloomington, IN 47404
800.733.6786 (toll free) / 812.336.7700
FAX: 812.336.7790
email: info@solution-tree.com
solution-tree.com

Visit **go.solution-tree.com/instruction** to download the reproducibles in this book.

Printed in the United States of America

19 18 17 16 15   1 2 3 4 5

Library of Congress Cataloging-in-Publication Data

Maxwell, Marge.

Real-world learning framework for secondary schools : digital tools and practical strategies for successful implementation / by Marge Maxwell, Rebecca Stobaugh, and Janet Lynne Tassell.

pages cm

Includes bibliographical references and index.

ISBN 978-1-935249-44-3 (perfect bound) 1. Education, Secondary--United States. 2. Education, Secondary--United States--Computer network resources. 3. Education, Secondary--Curricula--United States. I. Stobaugh, Rebecca. II. Tassell, Janet Lynne. III. Title.

LA222.M39 2015

373.73--dc23

2015025043

Solution Tree
Jeffrey C. Jones, CEO
Edmund M. Ackerman, President

Solution Tree Press
President: Douglas M. Rife
Associate Acquisitions Editor: Kari Gillesse
Editorial Director: Lesley Bolton
Managing Production Editor: Caroline Weiss
Production Editor: Tara Perkins
Copy Editor: Ashante K. Thomas
Proofreader: Elisabeth Abrams
Cover Designer: Rian Anderson
Text Designer: Laura Kagemann

Acknowledgments

We would like to thank the teachers and educators who contributed projects for this book, including: Erica Cassady, Samantha McMahan, Kelli Ralston, Shelton Fisher, Jennifer Gonzalez, Shannon Lay, Lydia Renfro, and Sam Northern. We want to thank Wesley Waddle, Terri Stice, Matthew Constant, and Andi Paganelli for reviewing the book. We would like to thank Wesley Waddle and Hart County Schools for the lesson plan format used in the projects.

Solution Tree Press would like to thank the following reviewers:

Jerelyne Nemanich
Learning Technology Coordinator
Spring Lake Park School District 16
Spring Lake Park, Minnesota

Patrick Waters
Professional Educator
Monarch School
Houston, Texas

Beth Weeks
Campus Technology Specialist
Sherman Independent School District
Sherman, Texas

Visit **go.solution-tree.com/instruction**

to download the reproducibles in this book.

Table of Contents

Reproducible pages are in italics.

About the Authors

Marge Maxwell, **PhD**, is a professor of educational technology at Western Kentucky University. She has been helping teachers implement technology into teaching and learning for more than thirty years. Her focus is on real-world learning while incorporating critical thinking, high student engagement, and technology. She believes in planning for learning, not technology. Marge earned her doctorate in curriculum and instruction as well as a master's degree in exceptional education at the University of North Carolina at Chapel Hill. She has been a special education teacher, supervisor of exceptional children, director of instructional technology, and teacher trainer in public schools. She maintains the http://create-excellence.com website to support the Create Excellence Framework.

Rebecca Stobaugh, **PhD**, is a previous middle and high school teacher. In her position as a middle school principal, she focused on aligning curriculum, increasing the level of critical thinking in assessments and instruction, and establishing a schoolwide discipline plan. Currently, Rebecca serves as an associate professor at Western Kentucky University, teaching assessment and unit-planning courses in the teacher education program. She supervises first-year teachers and consults with school districts on critical thinking, instructional strategies, assessment, technology integration, and other topics. Rebecca has authored three books including *Assessing Critical Thinking in Middle and High Schools* and was an editor who designed mathematics challenge projects for a six-set mathematics series.

After several years as a mathematics teacher, **Janet Lynne Tassell**, **PhD**, spent fourteen years as the Director of Learning and Assessment working with K–12 teachers in curriculum and professional development. She is now an associate professor at Western Kentucky University, where she teaches Elementary Math Methods and directs the Elementary Mathematics Specialist Endorsement program. For the Gifted Master's program, she teaches Identification/Assessment and Current Issues in Gifted Education courses. In the Fall 2014 semester, she taught a semester abroad at Harlaxton College in Grantham, England. She has been the co-director of the Toyota Math and Technology Leadership Academy and the professional development coordinator for the Javits grant Project GEMS (Gifted Education for Math and Science) initiative for students in grades 3–6. She and her husband, Brad, published a book connecting reading and mathematics fluency titled *Speaking of Math: Fluency Poems for Partners—Addition*. She recently led a team of fourteen authors to design and author a six-book series, *Explore the Core,* for first- through sixth-grade students to delve deeper into the Common Core mathematics standards.

To book Marge Maxwell, Rebecca Stobaugh, or Janet Lynne Tassell for professional development, contact pd@solution-tree.com.

Introduction

Samuel walks into his middle school science class at the beginning of the year, excited to be entering a new grade level with more intensive science. However, he finds that "science" is packets of worksheets, outdated movies, and old textbooks. Samuel has never had an opportunity to perform an experiment or use the scientific process other than by memorizing the steps of the process from a simplistic experiment—one for which he already knew the conclusion before he started. He sees no connection to mathematics and technology that could help science come to life. Samuel now equates science to a reading comprehension exercise, and he thinks that technology is used only for taking quizzes, practicing mathematics skills, locating information, and typing papers. He watches the teacher use the interactive board to show a PowerPoint presentation or to have students come to the board one at a time to circle an answer. He had hoped to experience more real-world science such as his cousin at another school talks about. Instead, he finds science as dull and rote.

Students need to be excited about learning! Students naturally crave meaning when they have the opportunity to be inspired in a school that cultivates a real-world learning environment. Students desire assignments with dimensions and substance that make them crave more on the topic. Often, classrooms are riddled with worksheets that do not create authentic-learning connections for students. As an educator, planning quality curriculum may have left you considering the following questions.

- Have my students shown me what topics interest them? Have I incorporated their interests into my instruction and lesson planning?
- Do I find it difficult to incorporate curriculum standards in real-world activities?
- Do I find it difficult to challenge students with provocative questions?
- Are my students working on teacher-directed tasks and projects in isolation?
- Do my students work on technology that does not enrich their learning nor expand on the content?

This book helps you answer these questions and address the concerns they may reveal.

In a real-world environment, creation is not a formulaic set of steps but rather is a messy process. Often, creation of important work involves starting and stopping—revising all the while. If we consider an artist designing a masterpiece, we can envision the artist beginning with personal inspiration, addressing questions he or she asks him- or herself, working from a blank canvas, and then problem solving to come up with a pathway to brilliance. The masterpiece is the result of many experiences, revisions, and failures the artist experiences. The term *create* means bringing something unique into being that did not previously exist and would not evolve on its own. Based on this concept, the instructional framework this book introduces is termed the Create Excellence Framework. With this framework, teachers and students have the opportunity to plan project-based instruction that is comprehensive, pulling from the real world by utilizing cognitive complexity, student engagement, and technology integration.

As we consider the real world's meaningful impact on education, teachers and students need a tool to achieve the best-designed project. Teachers must be open to meaningful learning, remembering also that the learning will be a messy process, as it is in the complex and often chaotic real-world environment. What students produce will be personalized and unique. This requires teachers to have flexibility and focus as they plan, keeping in mind the ultimate goal is to support learning that leads to brilliance!

The Create Excellence Framework for Real-World Learning

Researcher Christopher M. Moersch (2002) developed the H.E.A.T Framework (higher-order thinking, engaged learning, authentic learning, and technology integration), and we have adapted it to further define each component, emphasizing the teacher's need to *create* an experience for the students (Maxwell, Constant, Stobaugh, & Tassell, 2011). The resulting Create Excellence Framework is a research-based, lesson-plan framework that can guide students, parents, and teachers in thinking about learning in a different, yet comprehensive, way (Tassell, Maxwell, & Stobaugh, 2013). The foundation of the Create Excellence Framework and chapter structure of this book provide readers a deep understanding of how real-world learning, supported by cognitive complexity, student engagement, and technology integration, can support student learning (see figure I.1). The purpose of this book is to help teachers improve instruction for students by designing instructional tasks that include these four key components. This framework gives us a new lens to look at how to plan instruction as well as helps teachers balance the needs of the new demands of rigorous standards. It incorporates the key components necessary to create engaging and meaningful lessons for student learning. The Create Excellence Framework is intended to be a tool to help with enhancing your current curriculum. Throughout the school year, teachers can utilize the framework to design tasks and projects at various levels. Throughout the book, we provide tangible examples of sample tasks and projects.

All the components important for adding depth to learning and planning comprehensive lessons are addressed through this framework. Each component covers the same five levels of increasing complexity to help the teacher target growth in his or her instructional development of tasks and projects: (1) Knowing, (2) Practicing, (3) Investigating, (4) Integrating, and (5) Specializing. The cognitive-complexity component also incorporates the revised Bloom's taxonomy higher-order thinking skills: Remember, Understand, Apply, Analyze, Evaluate, and Create. Table I.1 (pages 4–5) highlights this structure, clarifies the role of each component, and illustrates how all the pieces of the framework fit together. Chapter 1 explains these levels in depth. Levels 1–3 involve tasks while levels 4–5 involve projects. *Tasks* are small classroom activities while *projects* are more complex and use several instructional strategies, have open-ended solutions, involve more student choice and decision making, and take longer to complete. The lower levels of the framework are teacher directed (levels 1–3), whereas higher levels are more student directed (levels 4–5) with the teacher partnering with students to design projects and assignments (Tassell et al., 2013). The target levels for consistent student learning are levels 3 and 4, which are shaded in tables depicting the framework levels throughout the book. While level 3 is still teacher directed, students are engaging in higher cognitively complex tasks and

Real-World Learning Students learn from, interact with, and have an impact on the real world.		
Cognitive Complexity Level of critical thinking required by students for an instructional task or project	**Student Engagement** Level at which students take responsibility for their own learning, instruction is differentiated, and students partner or collaborate with the teacher, other students, or outside experts to guide their own learning	**Technology Integration** Level at which students use technology as a research tool, collaboration tool, design tool, and presentation tool; student-directed technology use is seamlessly integrated into real-world content; students' critical thinking with technology use is at Bloom's Analyze, Evaluate, or Create levels

Figure I.1: Structure of Create Excellence Framework and book.

projects. Students are beginning to take more responsibility for their learning in level 4. Level 5 is attained after consistent learning at levels 3 and 4 and could be accomplished a few times a year.

Real-World Learning

Real-world learning is where the student learns from, interacts with, and has an impact on the real world. The goal is for students to experience real-world, authentic learning by interacting with the real world to complete tasks and solve problems. The real-world learning component is the foundation for the other three components (cognitive complexity, student engagement, and technology integration), as it establishes an authentic context for learning.

Cognitive Complexity

The student's level of thinking with the real-world content is vital to creating a quality task. The cognitive-complexity component within the Create Excellence Framework is based on the revised Bloom's taxonomy (Anderson & Krathwohl, 2001). At the teacher-directed level of the framework, learners are engaged in learning experiences that the revised Bloom's taxonomy would classify as Remember, Understand, and Apply. The student-directed levels of the Create Excellence Framework embrace Bloom's top three cognitive processes (Analyze, Evaluate, and Create). At these top levels the students, instead of the teachers, are identifying the real-world questions, and generating projects while thinking like an expert focused on an open-ended, global learning emphasis. Chapter 2 provides an in-depth discussion of these levels and Bloom's cognitive processes.

Student Engagement

The student-engagement component of the Create Excellence Framework offers guidance in the degree to which learners (1) take responsibility for their own real-world learning, (2) partner or collaborate with the teacher, other students, or outside experts, and (3) use resources such as teachers and experts in the discipline. Teachers can help the students differentiate their interests and make choices in how they approach the task or project. Teachers can also support the students by helping them identify resources and collaboration opportunities.

Table 1.1: Create Excellence Framework

CREATE LEVELS	REAL-WORLD LEARNING	COGNITIVE COMPLEXITY (BLOOM'S COGNITIVE PROCESSES IN PARENTHESES)	STUDENT ENGAGEMENT	TECHNOLOGY INTEGRATION
				Teacher Directed
Level 1 Knowing	• Learning focuses on **non-relevant** problems using textbooks or worksheets	• Teacher directs student interaction with content or standard at Bloom's **Remember** level (Recognizing, Recalling)	• **Teacher lectures** or questions and students take notes OR • **One correct answer** is expected	(Level 0 for no technology) • **Teacher uses technology** for demonstration or lecture OR • Students use technology at Bloom's **Remember** level OR • Technology is a **student option** but is not required or is used for **keyboarding**
Level 2 Practicing	• Learning provides some application to the real world using **real objects or topics**	• Teacher directs student interaction with content or standard at Bloom's **Understand** level (Interpreting, Exemplifying, Classifying, Summarizing, Inferring, Comparing, Explaining) and Bloom's **Apply** level (Executing, Implementing)	• Students are engaged in a **task directed by the teacher** AND • **Multiple solutions** for one task are accepted	• Students use technology for Bloom's **Understand**- or **Apply**-level thinking tasks OR • Students use technology for **gathering information**
Lower Cognitive Complexity				

	Student Directed		
Level 3 Investigating	• Learning **simulates the real world** (such as a class store or assuming the role of a political commentator)	• **Teacher directs** student interaction with the content or standard at Bloom's **Analyze** level (Differentiating, Organizing, Attributing), **Evaluate** level (Checking, Critiquing), or **Create** level (Generating, Planning, Producing)	• **Students have choice for tasks** AND • **Tasks are differentiated** by content, process, or product (such as addressing learning preferences, interests, or ability levels)	• Technology use appears to be an **add-on** or alternative—not essential for task completion AND • Students use technology for Bloom's **Analyze-, Evaluate-,** or **Create-** level thinking tasks
Level 4 Integrating	• Learning emphasizes and **impacts the classroom, school, or community** AND • Learning is integrated across subject areas	• **Students generate** questions or projects with the content or standard at Bloom's **Analyze** level (Differentiating, Organizing, Attributing), **Evaluate** level (Checking, Critiquing), or **Create** level (Generating, Planning, Producing)	• **Students partner with the teacher** to define the content, process, or product AND • There is a student **inquiry-based** approach AND • Students **collaborate with other students**	Student technology use: • Is **embedded in content and essential** to project completion AND • Promotes **collaboration among students** and **partnership with the teacher** AND • Helps them **solve authentic problems** at Bloom's Analyze, Evaluate, or Create levels
Level 5 Specializing	• Learning has a positive **impact on a national or global** issue or problem AND • Students **collaborate with experts** in a field or discipline	• **Students generate** questions or projects with the content or standard at Bloom's **Create** level (Generating, Planning, Producing) AND • **Complex thinking like a content expert** occurs OR there is an open-ended, **global-learning** emphasis	• **Students initiate their own inquiry-**based learning projects; thorough immersion and full implementation from topic to solution occurs AND • **Students initiate appropriate collaborations** pertaining to their project	Student-directed technology use: • Is **seamlessly integrated in content at Bloom's Create** level AND • Has **several technologies** AND • Includes **collaboration with field experts** or **global organizations** to find solutions to an in-depth "real" problem
Higher Cognitive Complexity			

Technology Integration

Technology integration is relatively new to learning, and it is constantly evolving. However, it is also the component that gives a spark to how real-world learning can be discovered and conveyed. The technology-integration component emphasizes *student* use of technology, not teacher use of technology. Technology integration is more than just having the students go to the computer lab to watch a science video, take an online quiz, locate information on the web, or progress through levels of online mathematics activities or standards. The students are using technology to display their learning. At the highest level on the Create Excellence Framework, students design projects that are seamlessly integrated in content at the highest level of the revised Bloom's taxonomy, include several technologies, and involve collaboration with field experts or global organizations to find solutions to real, complex problems. Figure I.2 offers a sample project highlighting how Samuel's teacher (from the opening scenario) learned how to use each component of the Create Excellence Framework.

Learning in Today's World: Standards and the Create Excellence Framework

With national standards now available in the major content areas (mathematics, English language arts, science, social studies), it is critical to help teachers plan instruction with opportunities for students to learn at higher levels. Furthermore, teachers and students need to make connections to the real world while designing learning.

Many teachers and principals are highly concerned with the acquisition of content knowledge and skills in the standards, and we believe that the same knowledge and skills are promoted by purposefully designing learning experiences to be unified around real-world concepts and ideas. If teachers use real-world themes and essential or guiding questions to integrate their (otherwise separate) courses and align content standards to the real-world themes, students will have a coherent context for every assignment, classroom activity, field-work experience, and project they undertake. Students will also achieve a deeper level of understanding of what they are learning because of the integration of the standards in real-world themes and experiences. Students will begin to see that everything is relevant and related (Martinez, 2014).

The 21st century standards turn an eye toward authentic-learning opportunities—instruction that must be designed with a unique thread of real-world impact. The standards require a strong attention to appropriate levels of rigor, matching challenge level to the task or project and to the student, and are based on higher-level learning, which is connected to the Create Excellence Framework's cognitive-complexity component. No longer do students work in isolation with the new standards. There is an expectation of collaboration and mentoring, which incorporates engaged learning techniques. This connects with the framework's student-engagement component. Technology integration is a key element seen in many of the standards and is one that students expect and need.

Changing Teacher Standards

Teachers are faced with an ever-changing, ever-present challenge of keeping abreast of techniques that are best for student learning, all the while honing their instruction of content standards. There is a shift in conversation about the importance of ensuring highly *qualified* teachers in all classrooms to, instead, highly *effective* teachers for all students. As this conversation grows, many states are adopting the Danielson Framework for Teaching (Danielson, 2014) and using components of this model to develop professional growth systems. Teachers are now looking toward higher-level thinking strategies and boosting student learning. Table I.2 (page 8) illustrates how the Danielson Framework integrates real-world learning, higher-level learning, tools and resources, and differentiation into instruction. In table I.2 and other tables throughout this book that feature standards, words are italicized to show key phrases in the standards that align to the component.

Project Scenario: After learning how to plan a project using the Create Excellence Framework, Samuel's middle-grades teacher informs his class that the students' desks are being replaced due to being ineffective, unsafe, and old. Groups are assigned to develop the optimal student desk that would meet their needs.

	REAL-WORLD LEARNING	COGNITIVE COMPLEXITY	STUDENT ENGAGEMENT	TECHNOLOGY INTEGRATION
Student-Directed Task	The class is told that the desk-constructing groups are in competition for an award. The principal will select the best prototype and work with the winning group to investigate school desks that meet similar design qualities. The students are excited to influence the decision about the type of desks that could actually be chosen and purchased for their classroom. Level: 4	In groups, students identify what qualities a desk should have to meet the needs of students in their classroom. Students then brainstorm various conceptual designs and evaluate which concept is most likely to meet their needs and is cost effective. Using their engineering skills, students make calculations of size of the desk, cost of materials, and so on. They build prototype desks from supplies provided to the students by the school's PTO. Each group tests and evaluates its prototype; then it restructures and improves the original design. Level: 4	Throughout the design process, groups collaborate with the teacher to ensure they are progressing on their solution. Students Skype with a furniture designer to pose questions about their prototype and get feedback from the designer. Level: 4	As groups are formulating their conceptual designs, they use a free online program, Google SketchUp, to develop their desk designs. They create persuasive presentations for the principal in Animoto (an online presentation program). The process of designing the prototype also involves technology integration. Level: 4

Source: Adapted from Tassell et al., 2013.

Figure I.2: Student-directed project sample to complement the Create Excellence Framework.

Table I.2: Examples of Where Create Excellence Framework Components Connect to Danielson Teacher Standards

DANIELSON FRAMEWORK FOR TEACHING DOMAIN	SAMPLE STANDARD	CONNECTION TO CREATE EXCELLENCE FRAMEWORK COMPONENTS
1: Planning and Preparation	1A: Knowledge of Content and Pedagogy Distinguished: "The teacher displays extensive knowledge of the important concepts in the discipline and *how these relate both to one another and to other disciplines.* The teacher demonstrates understanding of prerequisite relationships among topics and concepts and understands the *link to necessary cognitive structures that ensure student understanding.* The teacher's plans and practice reflect familiarity with a wide range of effective pedagogical approaches in the discipline and the ability to *anticipate student misconceptions*" (Danielson, 2014, p. 9).	Real-world learning
1: Planning and Preparation	1E: Designing Coherent Instruction Distinguished: "The sequence of learning activities follows a coherent sequence, is aligned to instructional goals, and is designed to engage students in *high-level cognitive activity.* These are appropriately differentiated for individual learners. Instructional groups are varied appropriately, with some opportunity for *student choice*" (Danielson, 2014, p. 25) 1E Distinguished Critical Attributes "Learning experiences connect to other disciplines" (Danielson, 2014, p. 25).	Cognitive complexity Student engagement Technology integration Real-world learning
3: Instruction	3B: Using Questioning and Discussion Techniques Distinguished: "The teacher uses a variety or series of questions or prompts to challenge students cognitively, advance high-level thinking and discourse, and promote metacognition. Students formulate many questions, initiate topics, challenge one another's thinking, and make unsolicited contributions. Students themselves ensure that all voices are heard in the discussion" (Danielson, 2014, p. 63).	Cognitive complexity Student engagement
3: Instruction	3C: Engaging Students in Learning Distinguished: "Virtually all students are intellectually engaged in *challenging* content through well-designed learning tasks and activities that require *complex thinking* by students. The teacher provides suitable scaffolding and challenges students to explain their thinking. There is evidence of some *student initiation* of *inquiry* and student contributions to the exploration of important content; students may serve as resources for one another. The lesson has a clearly defined structure, and the pacing of the lesson provides students the time needed not only to intellectually engage with and reflect upon their learning but also to consolidate their understanding" (Danielson, 2014, p. 69).	Cognitive complexity Student engagement

The changes in the teaching standards are also reflected in other national and international standards. The International Society for Technology in Education (ISTE) standards for teachers (ISTE, 2008) and for students (ISTE, 2007) seek to integrate technology in a meaningful context so the students use technology to create, communicate, collaborate, and think critically. Similarly, the Partnership for 21st Century Learning (P21; formerly Partnership for 21st Century Skills) emphasizes promoting media literacy with students analyzing media and creating media products while engaging in critical thinking and collaborating. The Partnership for 21st Century Skills (2009) framework states that 21st century teaching "enables innovative learning methods that integrate the use of supportive technologies, inquiry- and problem-based approaches and higher order thinking skills" (p. 8). These expectations indicate that students are to use technology to collaborate as they engage in higher–cognitive learning tasks and projects about real-world topics. This philosophy connects to the Create Excellence Framework as the cognitive-complexity, student-engagement, and technology-integration components all circle around a real-world learning experience.

Changing Content Standards

In content standards for mathematics, English language arts, science, and social studies, one will note a trend calling for students to take more responsibility for their learning. This may play out in the classroom as students generating their own questions designing projects, facilitating discussions, peer-assessing work, and so on. Teachers will need a tool to help them support the intent of the standards. Without a planning framework to help organize and strive for a change in thinking, the fear is that the teachers will not have the structure and tools to make the changes necessary to their planning and, ultimately, instruction. These changes have caused us to re-examine how we develop curriculum.

It is no longer acceptable to plan and deliver content in isolation. The content must be done in a context. Teachers are stretched to involve their students at a new and heightened level of involvement in the classroom by applying the content in an interactive and authentic way. Through this interactive lesson experience, students will be engaged through their discussions. The instruction addresses the framework's student-engagement component as students interact in meaningful discussions, collaborate with their classmates, and partner with the classroom teacher in learning. The authentic changes in the standards require students to experience content through the real world. Levels 4–5 of the Create Excellence Framework emphasize the importance of the teacher designing instruction and provide support for teachers as they make this transition. See table I.3 (page 10) for examples highlighting how the Create Excellence Framework connects to the various student content standards.

In addition to these connections to standards that professional organizations propose, there are many more notable leaders in the field of education whose works and ideas align to the major components of the Create Excellence Framework. Visit **go.solution-tree.com/instruction** for a detailed table, "Publications With Elements That Align With the Create Excellence Framework," which illustrates the connection of several scholars' work and our framework.

Table I.3: Highlights of How the Create Excellence Framework Connects to Student Content Standards

CONTENT-AREA STANDARDS	STANDARD SAMPLE	CREATE EXCELLENCE FRAMEWORK COMPONENT
Common Core English language arts standards	SL.8.1 *"Engage effectively in a range of collaborative discussions* (one-on-one, in groups, and teacher-led) with diverse partners on grade 8 topics, texts, and issues, building on others' ideas and expressing their own clearly" (NGA & CCSSO, 2010a).	Student engagement
Common Core mathematics standards	Mathematics Practice 4: "Model With Mathematics—Mathematically proficient students can apply the mathematics they know to solve problems arising in everyday life, society, and the workplace. . . . They can analyze those relationships mathematically to draw conclusions. They routinely interpret their mathematical results in the context of the situation and reflect on whether the results make sense, possibly improving the model if it has not served its purpose" (NGA & CCSSO, 2010a).	Real-world learning Student engagement Technology integration Cognitive complexity
Next Generation Science Standards	HS-ETS1–3 *"Evaluate a solution to a complex real-world problem* based on prioritized criteria and trade-offs that account for a range of constraints, including cost, safety, reliability, and aesthetics as well as possible social, cultural, and environmental impacts" (Achieve, 2013).	Real-world learning
College, Career, and Civic Life (C3) Framework	D4.3.9–12 "Present adaptations of arguments and explanations that feature evocative ideas and perspectives on issues and topics to reach a range of audiences and venues outside the classroom using print and *oral technologies* (e.g., posters, essays, letters, debates, speeches, reports, maps) and *digital technologies* (e.g., Internet, social media, digital documentary)" (National Council for the Social Studies [NCSS], 2013, p. 60).	Technology integration

Structure of This Book

This book is presented in two parts. In part I, the chapters provide an in-depth look at each of the components of the Create Excellence Framework, highlighting how to classify levels within the framework and how they align with the standards. We provide descriptions of each component of the framework in chapters 1–4. Chapter 5 gives guidance for how to use the Create Excellence Framework in your classroom, school, and district. Examples of lessons covering a variety of subjects and framework levels for grades 6–12 are interwoven throughout the chapters in part I. Each chapter also includes discussion questions for readers to consider. Another section in each chapter, Take Action, provides readers with more in-depth activities and tasks, often including reproducibles.

In part II, we include several sample lesson plans from different content areas and spotlight real-world learning, cognitive complexity, student engagement, and technology integration. The projects specify grade levels, but they could be modified for higher or lower grades. Each project description includes the following.

- An assignment overview, including learning objectives, the standards they address, and resources, including technology, needed for the project
- A task or project description and scoring rubric, which can be copied and distributed to students to guide their creation of the project
- Sample student work is provided to show how a typical student might complete the project; the teacher may or may not decide to share this with students
- Create Excellence Framework rating that explains how closely the lesson fulfills the levels of the framework, with justification provided for the rating

You may also visit http://create-excellence.com to access many additional resources featuring web 2.0 tools and applications highlighted in the projects in this book as well as other resources that we have found to be outstanding in our work with teachers.

Conclusion

At a time when education is looking for answers, this book is needed! The Create Excellence Framework is a tool to design instruction with a research base. With the challenging environment of the new standards in many content areas requiring engaging and higher-level inquiry, the Create Excellence Framework can help you fill this need. The Danielson Framework for Teaching (2014) also reveals the importance of students driving instruction and making decisions involving their own learning. These manifestations drive and support the timely nature and need for the Create Excellence Framework—it can provide a guide and a target for student learning, encouraging students such as Samuel, the eager science student, who are hoping to experience deeper learning. Teachers can use the concepts from the Create Excellence Framework to inspire and reinforce their students' self-directed learning. While advocating for this type of real-world learning in the classroom, teachers can promote a vision for higher cognitive complexity, technology integration, and student engagement. In this type of learning environment, Samuel can realize his dreams and potential.

Discussion Questions

1. How can the Create Excellence Framework help you plan lessons that tap in to real-world and relevant learning?
2. Are there any components of the Create Excellence Framework in your current teaching?
3. How do you see the framework components embedded in the teaching standards for your school?
4. What has been missing from your instructional-planning tools? What struggles have you been having? How would the Create Excellence Framework help you with these struggles?
5. Are the tasks and projects you design more teacher driven or student driven?

Take Action

1. Consider a student in your classroom or school who wants to engage in higher levels of real-world learning than he or she currently has the opportunity to do. Have a discussion with the student about aspects of the current curriculum's cognitive complexity, student engagement, and technology integration as related to real-world learning in the Create Excellence Framework. Ask the student to share specific topics or issues that affect him or her that can be explored in class projects.

2. Have your class complete the survey provided in the "Personal Learning Survey" reproducible. What did you learn about your class that you did not know before? How can you use this information to design better learning experiences for your students?

3. Examine the content standards for your discipline. Find the elements within the Create Excellence Framework components that you want to develop in your classroom instruction. Discuss this with a colleague.

Personal Learning Survey

Name: _____

1. What would designing your own learning look like for you? Would you decide what you learn? Would you determine how it is measured or graded? Explain.

2. If you could have more opportunities to design your own learning, what would you keep the same? What would you change? Explain.

3. Do you prefer working alone, with a partner, or in small groups? Explain.

4. What do you want to study in the current content that connects to something in the real world? Explain.

5. What technology tools would you like to use that support your learning? Explain.

PART I

CHAPTER 1

Real-World Learning

A seventh-grade classroom has a door leading outside, and bees built a hive in the doorway. The students asked questions such as, What will we do about the bees? Why did they choose to live here? How do bees make honey? How do you move them? How do they help people?, and How can we capture them and put them in a hive so we can get the honey? The class decided that they wanted to capture the bees and maintain them in a beehive on the corner of the large school property (with permission of the principal). Teams of students researched a different aspect of this authentic problem. One team worked with a parent-teacher organization to raise money to purchase a beehive. A second team called a local beekeeper to help the students capture the bees and put them in the beehive. Another team researched how to maintain the bees and keep other students at the school safe. The fourth team researched how to extract honey from the hive, process it, and sell it. This opened another opportunity for the class as entrepreneurs!

Real-world learning involves the degree to which a student learns from, interacts with, and has an impact on the actual real world. Real-world learning involves challenging and messy problems. These problems are open to multiple interpretations, are multifaceted and interdisciplinary, and cannot be easily solved by applying an existing algorithm. In the course of solving an authentic problem, students will learn skills and curriculum in multiple subjects to augment the real-world application of those skills. For example, students may learn letter-writing skills when they want to write a letter to their senator urging him or her to support water conservation near their town. Real-world solutions may not always work, may not always please everyone, and may have consequences beyond the problem or discipline.

Real-world learning is not a new concept. Psychologist Jerome Bruner (1960) discusses constructivism based on the theme that learners construct new ideas or concepts on existing knowledge where learning is an active process. Philosopher and psychologist John Dewey (1938) also believes that learning is a social and interactive process, which students should experience and interact with the curriculum, and that all students should have the opportunity to take part in their own learning. For instance, apprenticeships have been a primary method of learning a trade for thousands of years and are still popular in the 21st century to learn some skilled trades as well as earn professional credentials. The state of Virginia still has a Law Reader Program whereby under the approved supervision of a licensed lawyer, one can study law, do some of the work of a lawyer, and become a licensed lawyer upon passing the bar exam (Virginia Board of Law Examiners, 2006).

Real-world applications of knowledge are critical for students to possess deep understandings of content. There are many levels of real-world learning.

Create Levels of Real-World Learning

The five levels of real-world learning are described in the following sections. (Visit **go.solution-tree.com /instruction** for a reproducible that outlines these levels and lists examples of tasks or projects for each level.)

Create Level 1: Knowing

Level 1 tasks focus on problems that are *irrelevant* to the real world, using textbooks and worksheets. Students are learning foundational knowledge or skills outside of a real-world context. Examples of level 1 tasks include reading sight words, filling in multiplication facts on a worksheet, or memorizing the periodic table of elements.

Create Level 2: Practicing

Level 2 tasks provide some application to the real world, using real objects or topics. For example, students may demonstrate mathematics problems with real marbles or write a paragraph about Mount Everest. Another example of a level 2 task would be to have students compare ocean-related terms, tell how they are related, and show the relationships in a Venn diagram.

Create Level 3: Investigating

In level 3, learning involves simulation of the real world in a teacher-directed task. Some examples include creating and operating a class store or assuming the role of a political commentator. Teachers can ask students to predict the weather by assuming the role of a weatherperson or to analyze crime data like a police detective. A detailed example of a level 3 activity would be to have students determine whether it is easier to swim or float in saltwater or in freshwater. In this activity, teachers give the students two large glasses, salt, water, and two eggs and instruct students to use the scientific method to experiment and discover in which water the egg will float and how much salt it takes. Students write each step of the scientific method during their experiment to answer the question.

Create Level 4: Integrating

In level 4, there is an emphasis on how student actions have a real impact on the classroom, school, or community. Learning is integrated across subject areas, including language arts, mathematics, science, and technology. Student learning is student directed as teachers give them the opportunity to decide the direction of their own projects and learning. Students may investigate electricity costs and document how much electricity the school is wasting each week. Students may prepare a spreadsheet with their data, create a plan to save electricity at the school, and give a presentation to the principal and the school-based, decision-making team to persuade them to adopt their plan. Another example of a lesson at this level is a teacher presenting the following scenario and assignment to a class: Since your school is only one-half mile from the ocean and you and your classmates have been concerned about saving sea turtles on the beach in your town, design and implement a campaign to preserve part of your beach to save the turtles. How will you present your findings to and persuade the city officials? This project involves subject areas such as science, technology, language arts, art, and public speaking.

Create Level 5: Specializing

In level 5, students collaborate with an expert in a field or discipline, and their learning and projects have a positive impact on a national or global issue or problem. For example, Common Cents' Penny Harvest program grew from one student's desire to feed the homeless, and students' penny collections have resulted in $8.1 million in matching grants for the homeless (Common Cents, 2013). Another example of a level 5 assignment is as follows: Many dead fish have washed up on the beach in your town. Upon investigating the cause of their death, a veterinarian tells your class that the fish ingested a toxic chemical. How can your class work with a national or international organization to help stop chemical dumping in the ocean? Table 1.1 introduces the five levels of real-world learning in the Create Excellence Framework.

Table 1.1: Real-World Learning Levels of the Create Excellence Framework

CREATE LEVEL	DESCRIPTION	SAMPLE TASK OR PROJECT
1: Knowing	• Learning involves problems irrelevant to the real world, using textbooks or worksheets.	Students look up and define Chinese terms on a worksheet.
2: Practicing	• Learning provides some application to the real world, using real objects or topics.	Locate a chart of China's twenty-five most populous cities. Classify them according to land types and regions.
3: Investigating	• Learning simulates the real world (such as a class store or assuming the role of a political commentator).	Select any of the Chinese royal dynasties, dress up in a traditional Chinese costume for that time period, and produce your own original play depicting a day in the life of your selected royalty.
4: Integrating	• Learning emphasizes and impacts the classroom, school, or community. • Learning is integrated across subject areas.	After studying transportation in China, it is obvious that bicycles are used extensively as a means of transportation as well as to carry a load. The students decide to redesign the bicycle to be effective and efficient for transporting people or heavy loads. They complete their designs in a CAD (computer-assisted drafting) drawing program and narrate the details of the design, emphasizing numerous points that make it effective and efficient. Students create a real prototype of their design and a marketing plan to sell their product to other students at their school.
5: Specializing	• Learning has a positive impact on a national or global issue or problem. • Collaboration occurs with experts in a field or discipline.	Your class has a pen pal class in China. A majority of the students from both classes are from farming families. After discussing the effects of GMOs (genetically modified organisms), pesticides, and poor water quality, both classes decide to partner together to create a non-GMO and clean water campaign for their farming communities. They consult with experts from national farming organizations in both countries to include ideas and recommendations for their campaigns. They capitalize on the joint efforts and advertise the partnership with the other country.

Beginning instruction with the real world not only grabs students' attention but also engages them much more than traditional lecture and textbook learning. Students need learning to be "real" to them; they need involvement *in* the real world; and they need to collaborate with other students, the teacher, and outside experts.

Real Versus Relevant

Students prefer real, not just relevant, learning. Relevant means that students can relate, connect, or apply the content you are teaching to something they know about (for example, sports, music, social networking, movies, or games). The problem with relevance is it does not go far enough to make learning meaningful and engaging. As education innovator Marc R. Prensky (2010) asserts, "Real means that there is a continuous perceived connection by the students between what they are learning and their ability to use that learning to do something useful or impact the real world" (p. 72). For students to actively attend to and retain information, it must be relevant to their interests or foreseeable future needs (Sousa, 2006). In fact, traditional learning will usually fall under level 1 or 2, relevant learning under level 2 or 3, and real learning will fall under level 4 or 5, depending upon the level of impact. Table 1.2 provides a sample topic to illustrate the differences among traditional, relevant, and real learning.

Table 1.2: Comparison of Traditional, Relevant, and Real Learning

TRADITIONAL LEARNING	RELEVANT LEARNING	REAL LEARNING
A teacher tells the class, "Read this article about going green and write a report about what it means to go green." (This is a level 2 real-world learning task because it involves talking about a real-world topic.)	A teacher tells the class, "We have been studying about how a city can go green. How green is our city? Assume the role of a politician who is promoting green activities for his city. Create a Voki video to give your campaign speech promoting a green city." (This is a level 3 real-world learning task because it is a simulation of the real world.)	After studying about ways to go green, students brainstorm activities. One team decides to investigate how the city can save water. It visits the city's water-treatment facility and works with the director to design posters using Glogster (www.glogster.com) to encourage citizens to save water. The mayor and water-treatment director judge the posters and select one to duplicate and display around the city. (This is a level 4 real-world learning project because students made a real contribution to their city.)

Elements of Real-World Learning

Elements of real-world learning incorporate learning integrated across subject areas, learning as close to the real world as possible, and collaborating with experts in the field or discipline being studied.

Learning Integrated Across Subject Areas

Educators Keith C. Barton and Lynne A. Smith (2000) state that interdisciplinary learning "provide[s] authentic experiences in more than one content area, offer[s] a range of learning experiences for students, and give[s] students choices in the projects they pursue and the ways they demonstrate their learning" (p. 54). Interdisciplinary units enable teachers to use classroom time more efficiently and address content in depth while giving students the opportunity to see the relationship between content areas and engage in authentic tasks and projects.

Students immersed in authentic-learning activities cultivate the kind of portable skills that are applicable in new and different situations, settings, or connections. These skills include judgment to distinguish reliable from unreliable information, patience to follow longer arguments and assignments, ability to recognize relevant patterns in unfamiliar contexts, and flexibility to work across disciplinary and cultural boundaries to generate innovative solutions (Jenkins, 2006).

In problem-based learning, students work for an extended period of time to investigate and respond to a complex question, problem, or challenge. Problem-based learning is the center of medical students' training as they develop work skills—collaborating, chairing a group, listening, recording, cooperating, respecting colleagues' views, critically evaluating literature, self-directing learning and use of resources, and presenting on and engaging in real medical tasks and projects (Wood, 2003). Within the real-world learning component, this learning would be considered level 3 if they are simulating the medical world, level 4 if they are having an impact on a small scale such as their class or school, or level 5 if they collaborate with medical experts and have an impact on a national or international scale. An example of problem-based learning in a high school setting might be students attending a town council meeting where the mayor points out the shortage of oil and the need for alternative energy for the town. She states that our young people will be the ones to live their lives with this new world of energy. So the high school students investigate current alternative energy sources and work with local engineers to devise a method of turning the town's waste into energy. They present their ideas to the town council and work with these engineers to implement their plan. This is a level 4 project on the Create Excellence Framework because students are making an impact on a community level.

Students involved in authentic learning are motivated to persevere despite initial frustration, as long as the project embodies what really counts to them—a social structure they enjoy, topics and activities of personal interest, and a feeling that what they are doing is important and valued (Herrington, Oliver, & Reeves, 2003; Prensky, 2010). By confronting students with uncertainty, ambiguity, and conflicting perspectives, instructors help them develop more mature mental models that coincide with the problem-solving approaches experts use. Be aware that the balance of challenge and uncertainty must be just right so that students are sufficiently engaged but not overwhelmed. Authentic-learning exercises expose the messiness of real-life decision making, where there may not be a right or a wrong answer per se, although one solution may be better or worse than others depending on the particular context or consequences. Such a nuanced understanding involves considerable reflective judgment, a valuable lifelong skill that goes well beyond the memorization of content (Briggs & Keyek-Franssen, 2010). For example, in a year-long service-learning project, a class may work with senior citizens at a local assisted living home. Students might survey residents' needs, make regular visits to read to residents or play music, make a greeting card for a special occasion, and so on. Students can plan a special field trip for themselves and their senior pals at the end of the school year. This project would involve language arts in reading and analyzing passages, mathematics in analyzing the survey data, and social studies in analyzing the issues of senior care. Planning a field trip involves many skills such as researching trip opportunities, collaborating with the assisted living staff, making arrangements for the trip, calculating costs and who will pay for what, and evaluating the trip afterward. This would be a level 4 real-world learning project since it is student directed and they are having an impact on their community.

Learning in the Real World

When a student learns from, interacts with, and has an impact on the real world, higher retention of learning will occur. Real-world learning is organized around complex activities built on multiple themes and academic disciplines and requires multiple steps over an extended duration of time. Students have a real audience for their work. They use real data and learn content through working on projects and real problems that interest them (Schools We Need Project, 2013). Take, for example, the seventh-grade class featured in the opening vignette of this chapter that decided to study the honeybees that were living outside its room and developed projects focusing on several different aspects, depending on students' interests. This would be a level

4 real-world learning project in which learning impacts the school and community. Learning is integrated across subject areas such as language arts, mathematics, science, economics, and social studies.

As another example, students may investigate and create projects to solve community issues such as by developing a local walking trail, promoting the inclusion of girls in community athletics, or endorsing stricter policies on littering in the community. This would also be a level 4 real-world learning project since it is student directed and they are having an impact on their community.

Such service projects can be instrumental in promoting relevant learning in many ways, including development of important personal and social skills; stronger ties to their schools, communities, and society; exploration of various career pathways; and promotion of community support for schools (Learn and Serve America's National Service-Learning Clearinghouse, 2007). Parents see service learning at all schools as a way to connect students to real-life issues and as a vehicle for better learning (Rasicot, 2006).

Collaborating With Field or Discipline Experts

Real-world problems comprise complex tasks to be investigated by students over a sustained period of time. Students locate their own resources and are not given a finite list of resources. Collaboration is integral to authentic learning where teamwork is critical to making decisions, solving problems, creating products, and even the social aspects of learning with a team. Collaboration between the teacher and students is essential to select the content, design the tasks or projects, and construct the assessment. Finally, authentic learning usually culminates in the creation of a whole product; however, the process was just as valuable to student learning as the product. For example, in a conservation unit, each student may document how much water his or her family uses each week, study personal water use habits, and make recommendations to his or her family about water conservation at home. The process of studying one conservation method at home could lead to other conservation efforts at home. It shows students that they can learn about topics that affect them and make informed decisions about many aspects of their lives.

True collaboration with experts in the field is invaluable in student acquisition of the knowledge, skills, and dispositions necessary to develop discipline, work ethic, and collaboration proficiencies. Collaboration with these experts could occur in person at the school, through a field trip to the expert's work location, or via video conferencing with Skype. Teachers of a specific discipline may find themselves collaborating with other teachers and experts from other disciplines. See table 1.3 for examples of experts that teachers may engage in various fields and activities that can be applied to those fields. In these examples, experts could perform any of these activities with students.

Table 1.4 (page 24) provides some sample projects for real-world learning and collaboration with experts.

The Teacher's Role in Facilitating Real-World Learning

Instructional methods evoke feelings in students that reinforce, support, or detract from knowledge and skill construction. Since even the cleverest team of students dealing with complex, sustained investigations may have difficulty making good judgments in the absence of appropriate scaffolding, it is the teacher's responsibility to design appropriate comprehension checks and feedback into the authentic-learning exercise (Lombardi, 2007). For example, students engaged in publishing a peer-reviewed online journal will evaluate each other over the course of the project and may receive additional guidance from the teacher, who assumes the role of publisher or editorial board member. The teacher may provide feedback on writing skills, communication skills, and publishing or reviewing skills. Don't abandon real-world projects if students fail to produce

Table 1.3: Sample Collaboration With Experts

FIELDS	PRACTITIONERS	TYPES OF COLLABORATION ACTIVITIES
Graphic design	• Local graphic designer • University graphic design professor or graduate student	• Teach pupils graphic design principles. • Collaborate and assist pupils in projects. • Judge pupil projects. • Co-assess projects with teacher and other pupils.
Technology and software design	• Local software designers • University technology and software design professors or graduate students	• Teach software design principles. • Collaborate and assist pupils in projects. • Judge pupil software designs.
Entrepreneurship and business planning	• Successful business person • University business professor or graduate student	• Teach business principles and how to design a business plan. • Judge business plan. • Guide pupils in developing a small business.
Local food production	• Local farmer • University agriculture professor or graduate student • County farm extension agent	• Teach local farming options and techniques. • Guide pupils in designing a new farm. • Guide pupils in developing a real garden at the school or setting up a local farmers' market.
Service learning	• Local nonprofit organization employee • Boy or Girl Scout leader • Nurse or doctor • Nursing home director	• Teach pupils about service learning opportunities. • Arrange volunteer opportunities with any of these organizations. • Guide students in making products for nursing home residents, reading to them, or writing letters for them.
Animals	• Local dog or horse trainer • Local veterinarian • University professor of equestrian or veterinary medicine	• Teach pupils about animal care and training. • Guide pupils in training an animal or designing a housing or nutrition plan.
Government	• Local government official • University political science or history professor	• Teach pupils government principles and role of politics. • Guide pupils in writing a position paper or letter to a senator about an issue that concerns the pupils.
Crime scene investigation	• Local police detective • Private detective • University crime investigator	• Teach pupils about crime investigation. • Guide pupils in a crime investigation project.

the level of work you expect. If students are not accustomed to real-world projects, they may need coaching and continuous feedback about the process in the beginning. Students need guidance in setting goals and learning strategies. The teacher acts as a partner and facilitator in group discussions. This will assist students in becoming more independent and ready to assume the responsibility for their own learning. See chapter 5, page 87, for ideas on monitoring Create Excellence Framework projects.

Table 1.4: Sample Projects for Real-World Learning

PROJECT	LEARNING INTEGRATED ACROSS SUBJECT AREAS	LEARNING *IN* THE REAL WORLD	COLLABORATE WITH FIELD OR DISCIPLINE EXPERTS
Honey bees outside a classroom (chapter's opening scenario)	Arts: write persuasive letters to PTA, communicate with beekeeper, use research skills Mathematics and economics: calculations of amount of food needed, honey sales Science: research about bee anatomy and behavior, beehive maintenance, collaboration with beekeeper	Bees are indeed in the real world; bees provide an opportunity for pupils to study and make decisions about a real-world problem, collaborate with an expert about bees, and manage this problem by turning it into an entrepreneurial opportunity.	Students in this class can collaborate and learn from a real beekeeper. He or she can help the pupils move the bees, start a new beehive, and maintain it on the school property.
Waterwheel Project at Ferryway School in Malden, Massachusetts (see www.edutopia.org/ferryway-iron works-integrated -studies-video)	Language arts: writing assignments, reflections, descriptions of pictures, publishing Science: simple machines, power tools, waterwheels Engineering: construct original waterwheel Mathematics: geometry, measuring History: history of waterwheels, related U.S. history Art: design and create historical outfits Technology: conduct research, create wiki, take digital pictures, publish writing	Students learn how to operate a real waterwheel; engineering concepts and practice.	Students collaborate with a waterwheel operator or university engineering intern.

Teaching Authentic Lessons

Integrated assessment is not merely summative in real-world learning but is woven into the tasks and projects, products, and teamwork. When genuine real-world learning occurs, it is highly unlikely that multiple-choice tests (that seek one "right" answer) will be adequate as they only capture lower-level knowledge. The embedded assessment in authentic projects analyzes multiple forms of evidence to measure student performance, including student engagement; collaboration with the team, teacher, and outside experts; artifacts produced throughout the task or project (including, for example, students' online journals or blogs); and the final product (Reeves, 2006).

Some teachers may want to teach authentic lessons but are not convinced that they can manage it. John F. Cronin (1993), project director for school transformation for the Loess Hills Area Education Agency, says that teachers do not have to jump in over their heads but can work toward more authenticity through a gradual but steady approach. Over time, a teacher can develop instruction that builds in complexity, such as by beginning with simulating the real world and later immersing students in the real world. Look for available opportunities for authentic learning. Many textbooks suggest "real-world" connections, most of which are level 2 or 3 on the Create Excellence Framework. Rarely do textbooks provide activities that are *in* the real world or that could be rated level 4 or 5 on the Create Excellence Framework. A teacher can transform these suggestions into activities that can be immersed in the real world. For example, a life-science textbook asks students which orange juice contains the most vitamin C and proceeds to provide four pictures: (1) freshly squeezed orange juice, (2) orange juice from concentrate, (3) canned orange juice, and (4) dairy carton orange juice. Students are asked to hypothesize the vitamin C content and then look it up on the Internet. While this is about a real-world topic, students are just looking up facts about a product with which they are already familiar. Using a real-world object makes the topic relevant (level 2), but it does not necessarily constitute a real-world task or project.

There are two methods for making this textbook activity about orange juice more real-world based. First, a teacher can have students bring in samples of the four types of orange juice and conduct an experiment in the lab to test the vitamin C content. Students can create a spreadsheet and graph as they test the samples, and then share their findings with the class. This would place the activity at level 3 because it is still teacher directed. A second option is that, while studying about vitamins, the students begin to discuss edible plants that have the most vitamin C. Students look up the vitamin C in these plants on the Internet. Students decide that they want to bring in samples of different fruits or plants and test the vitamin C content of each in the lab. Students form questions they want to answer through their experiments: Which plant or fruits contain more vitamin C? Does this confirm or refute findings on the Internet? Which form of the plant or fruit contains more vitamin C (fresh whole fruit, juice, dried, or from the bottle)? Which one is more easily absorbed and used by the human body? Students create a spreadsheet to record data as they test the plants and fruits and create graphs after completion. This would be a level 4 activity because of the higher-thinking level and because students are directing their own learning.

Teachers will likely have questions about how to plan a successful real-world learning project. Writer Kathy Baron (2010) outlines the following six steps.

1. Develop a compelling topic that:
   - Targets the standards that students need to know at their grade levels
   - Engages students
   - Addresses community issues or is meaningful to the community
   - Provides opportunities for in-depth investigations by all students
   - Provides opportunities for students to identify with or consider multiple perspectives (on gender, race, ethnicity, social class, or controversial scientific issues)
   - Has guiding questions that synthesize the big ideas and require students to engage in complex thinking

2. Design a comprehensive final product that:
   - Requires each student to create representations of the targeted knowledge and skills
   - Addresses the guiding questions
   - Includes accommodations for differentiation
   - Has an exemplar model and product descriptors created by the house or by other houses that can evolve during the expedition
   - Is adapted from a current professional product
   - Includes high-quality writing and craftsmanship from each student
   - Includes a plan for students to archive their finished pieces and reflections digitally for a portfolio

3. Choose the professional role(s) that students will assume during the expedition so:
   - Professionals can be scheduled to work with students
   - Students can develop the skill set(s) associated with the profession(s) and expedition
   - Students can present their final product to the appropriate audience

4. Identify and organize the major learning resources for the expedition that:
   - Are developmentally appropriate for all learners
   - Provide opportunities for all students to pursue independent research
   - Are made available in an online index, in the classroom, or in the library

5. Get the expedition on a shared team calendar to:
   - Schedule major learning activities and due dates
   - Block out a number of days in the final weeks of the expedition for student and teacher critiques and revisions
   - Schedule school specialists and community experts
   - Share school resources
   - Block out testing dates and other events
   - Book two to three field experiences
   - Block out additional time for the expedition manager

6. Plan for a culminating event that:
   - Includes the exhibition or evidence of high-quality work and writing from each student
   - Provides opportunities for every student to talk about his or her learning with a significant adult or audience
   - Includes a narrative of the expedition produced by students

Guiding Learning

The teachers' awareness of the classroom composition and ability to draw on real-life experiences to connect the content to learners' needs improve learning (Lin, 2006). Therefore, the teacher's role is transformed from sole source of information in the classroom to informed guide and expert facilitator of authentic-learning experiences (Renzulli, Gentry, & Reis, 2004). The teacher's role as facilitator is not passive. Yes, the learning is student centered, but a true facilitator must plan, be actively engaged with students as they learn, and have the awareness and finesse to adjust the learning task or project, environment, situation, and so on as needed.

When planning instruction for real-world learning, the primary considerations are as follows.

1. How close to the real world does learning occur?
   - If all learning is in the classroom and students are talking about the real world or pretending to be in circumstances or roles from the real world, then it can be classified as a simulation.
   - If some or most of the learning occurs in the real world and by interacting with the real world (outside of the classroom), then learning is more authentic.

2. Are students having any real impact on or changing something in the classroom, school, community, nation, or world?

Standards and Real-World Learning

Many of the new standards include wording such as *real world* or *authentic learning*. Table 1.5 lists some examples of real-world learning in specific teaching and student content standards. The Create Excellence Framework provides an organized approach to determine levels of student learning that align with the Danielson Framework for Teaching (Danielson, 2014) and curriculum standards like the Common Core State Standards, C3 Framework, and the Next Generation Science Standards.

Table 1.5: Real-World Learning in Standards

SOURCE OF STANDARDS	STANDARD INDICATORS
English Language Arts: Common Core English language arts	SL.8.1 *"Engage effectively in a range of collaborative discussions* (one on one, in groups, and teacher led) with diverse partners on grade 8 topics, texts, and issues, building on others' ideas and expressing their own clearly" (NGA & CCSSO, 2010a).
Mathematics: Common Core mathematics	HSS-MD.B.7 "Analyze decisions and strategies using probability concepts (e.g., *product testing, medical testing, pulling a hockey goalie at the end of a game)"* (NGA & CCSSO, 2010b).
Social Studies: College, Career, and Civic Life (C3) Framework	D2.Civ.2.9–12 *"Analyze the role of citizens in the U.S. political system,* with attention to various theories of democracy, changes in Americans' participation over time, and alternative models from other countries, past and present" (NCSS, 2013, p. 32).
Science: Next Generation Science Standards	MS-LS4–5 "Gather and synthesize information about the technologies that have changed the way humans influence the inheritance of desired traits in organisms" (Achieve, 2013).
Teacher Standards: Danielson Framework for Teaching	Domain 1: Planning and Preparation—1f Designing Student Assessments • "Teacher-designed assessments are authentic, with real-world application as appropriate" (Danielson, 2014, p. 29). Domain 3: Instruction—3a Communicating With Students • "The teacher invites students to explain the content to their classmates" (Danielson, 2014, p. 57). • "Students suggest other strategies they might use in approaching a challenge or analysis" (Danielson, 2014, p. 57).

Above and Beyond the Standards

The curriculum's goal should not be just the coverage of content but rather the discovery of content (Kwit, 2012). We do not want students to simply mimic or discuss real-world connections as part of a task. Students are already conditioned to sitting and completing tasks, but students who are busy are not necessarily engaged with the content. Even when the task or project has some connection to the real world, it can still just be that—a task or project *somewhat* related to, relevant to, or connected to the real world. The Create Excellence Framework proposes that standards can be discovered and taught *in* the real world as students solve real (not just relevant) problems.

For example, see the Common Core mathematics geometry standards in table 1.6. These standards are much less specific about the topic or what this might look like in the classroom, which leaves them ripe for innovation with real-world application. Ways to apply these standards in imaginative, real-world scenarios are included in table 1.6. Notice the learning progression from elementary to high school using the geometry strand for real-world learning projects.

Table 1.6: Real-World Learning With the Common Core Mathematics Geometry Standards

ELEMENTARY SCHOOL	MIDDLE SCHOOL	HIGH SCHOOL
4.GA.1 "Draw points, lines, line segments, rays, angles (right, acute, obtuse), and perpendicular and parallel lines. Identify these in two-dimensional figures" (NGA & CCSSO, 2010b).	6.GA.4 "Solve real-world and mathematical problems involving area, surface area, and volume" (NGA & CCSSO, 2010b). 6.GA.1 "Find the area of right triangles, other triangles, special quadrilaterals, and polygons by composing into rectangles or decomposing into triangles and other shapes; apply these techniques in the context of solving real-world and mathematical problems" (NGA & CCSSO, 2010b).	HSG.MG.A.3 "Apply geometric methods to solve design problems (e.g., designing an object or structure to satisfy physical constraints or minimize cost; working with typographic grid systems based on ratios)" (NGA & CCSSO, 2010b).
Elementary students are in charge of creating an organic garden to sell certain products at the local farmers' market. (Level 4 since it has a school and community impact)	**Middle school** students design a new and improved pyramid to be presented to the pharaoh, complete with a variety of antechambers. (Level 3 since it is simulating the real world)	**High school** students are creating a swimming pool that can meet the needs of all people who want to use it—high school swim team, children's swim lessons, or those who have special needs—and at the same time, it meets certain criteria in terms of community building codes, state safety guidelines, standard amounts of water and size, and so on. (Level 4 since it has a school or community impact)

Source: Adapted from Miller, 2011.

A word of caution: Just because the standard mentions "real world" does not mean that you or students are actually doing it. Just talking about a real-world topic does not make it relevant or real to students. Unless you are going deeper *in* the real world (such as level 4 or 5), it is not a high level of real-world learning for students. In other words, if student learning does not emphasize and have an impact on the classroom, school, or community, it is not a high level of real-world learning. The curriculum standards are primarily skills that are best learned while immersed in real-world problems. Because so many new curriculum standards now mention the real world, they give you permission to *do* the real world with your students. Some educators get so excited about the real-world connection that the project takes on a life of its own and the original content connection gets lost. You need to be sure that the content connections are carefully selected, planned, and monitored.

Connections of Real-World Learning With Other Components in the Create Excellence Framework

When the real world is the environment, setting, or background of student learning, it naturally merges with or encompasses cognitive complexity, student engagement, and technology integration. The Create Excellence Framework provides a new perspective for planning instruction to balance the needs of rigorous standards while creating engaging and meaningful instruction for student learning. Table 1.7 reveals the connections of the components of the Create Excellence Framework to real-world learning.

Table 1.7: Connection of Real-World Learning With Cognitive Complexity, Student Engagement, and Technology Integration

Real-World Learning
• Real-world learning is where the student learns from, interacts with, and has an impact on the real world.
• Learning is *in* the real world—students impact their class, school, community, nation, or world.
• Learning is integrated across subject areas.
• Students collaborate with field or discipline experts.
Cognitive Complexity
• Real-world problems are complex and messy, making critical thinking essential. They require student involvement and learning at the Analyze, Evaluate, and Create levels of the revised Bloom's taxonomy.
• At the top two levels of Create the *students*, instead of the teachers, are identifying the real-world questions, tasks, or projects. Students generate projects on the Create level of the framework while thinking like a real-world expert focused on an open-ended, global-learning issue.
Student Engagement
• Engagement is when students take responsibility for their own learning and they partner or collaborate with the teacher, other students, or outside, real-world experts to guide their own learning.
• Twenty-first century jobs or careers require collaboration; inquiry and solutions beyond the company; a voice and choice in projects; and differentiated assignments or projects according to skills, talents, interests, and individual responsibilities. These same requirements also apply to student learning in a real-world environment—need for collaboration, inquiry and solutions beyond the classroom, voice and choice, and differentiated assignments.
Technology Integration
• Technology is such an integral part of the real world in the 21st century that we cannot imagine not using technology for banking, communicating, researching, creating, and so on.
• Students can really *do* real-world work with the availability of information, resources, collaboration and communication tools, project-creation tools, and presentation tools.
• Effective technology integration not only enables 21st century, real-world learning but using technology tools is so natural that students are only focused on the content or project, not the technology.

Conclusion

Real-world learning is the cornerstone of the Create Excellence Framework. It is focused on connecting student learning to the real world as much as possible, real learning that is of concern to the student (not just relevant), having an impact on the real world, and working with outside experts. Unlike simply relevant learning, real-world learning doesn't just focus on topics that interest the students, it makes learning meaningful, and therefore more impactful, by also requiring students to collaborate with each other, their teacher, and outside experts. This is not the traditional formula where students work in isolation. Teachers and students can work together to integrate real-world learning across multiple subject areas while also mastering multiple standards in those subject areas. Yes, it does take planning and collaboration, but student learning is much deeper, richer, and longer lasting.

Learning goes deep when teachers and students delve into the complexities of real-world problems and at the same time interweave the appropriate student learning standards. An authentic-learning environment encourages real, substantive conversations with an open sharing of ideas. Teachers and students can begin real-world learning on a smaller scale and expand to more broad-scale, impactful projects as their comfort levels increase.

Discussion Questions

1. Why should we strive to situate student learning as close to the real world as possible?
2. How does real-world learning change the way we teach?
3. How might increasing real-world learning to the upper levels of the Create Excellence Framework help students beyond the classroom?

Take Action

1. Identify an assignment you gave last year that you consider to have had an authentic- (or real-world) learning connection. What level would it be on the Create Excellence Framework? Why do you think so? How could your assignment be modified to increase the level of real-world learning?
2. Complete the reproducible "Analyzing a Task or Project for Real-World Learning."
3. Explore any technology tool and tell how you and your students can use this tool at level 3 or higher on the real-world learning component of the Create Excellence Framework with your class.
4. Select one of the Create Excellence Framework projects in part II of this book. How could you modify one of the projects to use in your classroom? How could you improve one of the projects? Have a conversation with a colleague about implementing the project in your or the colleague's classroom.
5. Select another Create Excellence Framework project in part II of this book. Use the Create Excellence Framework to rate each component on the framework and justify your ratings. Compare your ratings to the Create Excellence Framework rating table that follows each project's sample student work. Were your ratings and justifications similar to those provided? Why or why not?
6. Develop a real-world task or project for your students. Discuss the challenges in creating this task or project. Do you have any concerns about your students' abilities?

Analyzing a Task or Project for Real-World Learning

Examine the scenario in the following table, and answer the questions. Then, compare your answers to the authors' responses.

Scenario: The school library media specialist is assisting seventh-grade students in researching local history and landmarks using print, nonprint, and digital sources at the school and regional public libraries. Students search the Internet for primary and secondary sources. Some students visit the local public library for some of these sources.	
Level of Real-World Learning	What is the level of real-world learning of this task? Use the following questions to guide your decisions. 1. How close to the real world does learning occur? ♦ If all learning is in the classroom and students are talking about the real world or pretending circumstances from the real world, then it can be classified as a simulation. This is level 3 (Investigating). ♦ If some or most of the learning occurs *in* the real world and interacting with the real world (outside of the classroom), then learning is more authentic. 2. Are students having any impact on or changing something in the classroom, the school, the community, the nation, or the world? Why do you think so?
Ways to Raise the Real-World Learning	What are some ways to increase the level of real-world learning for this task?
New Level of Real-World Learning	What is the new level of real-world learning?

Real-World Learning Framework for Secondary Schools © 2016 Solution Tree Press • solution-tree.com
Visit **go.solution-tree.com/instruction** to download this page.

Authors' Responses

1. What is the level of real-world learning of this task?

    This assignment is at level 2 in the real-world learning component because there is some application to real-world topics. The focus of this scenario is more about sources of information—print, nonprint, or digital and whether they are primary or secondary sources.

2. What are some ways to increase the level of real-world learning for this task?

    The focus of the assignment could be to design a new local landmark for an historical event for which there is no landmark already. Students should still research current landmarks using print, nonprint, or digital as well as primary and secondary sources.

    Students could interview community members knowledgeable of historical events and landmarks and locate individuals who can provide firsthand information about changes that have occurred in the community.

    Students could use CAD (computer-assisted drafting), SketchUp, or any drawing software to design the landmark and then prepare a multimedia presentation (student choice of project type) to the city planners to persuade them to create their landmark in real life.

    Depending on whether the city planners accepted and funded their proposal, the students could volunteer to help build the new landmark.

    Learning in this assignment would include language arts, mathematics, social studies, technology, and engineering.

3. What is the new level of real-world learning?

    This new level of real-world learning is 4 because student learning emphasizes and impacts the community. This assignment is interdisciplinary involving many subject areas.

Real-World Learning Framework for Secondary Schools © 2016 Solution Tree Press • solution-tree.com
Visit **go.solution-tree.com/instruction** to download this page.

CHAPTER 2

Cognitive Complexity

Students in Ms. James's class had been studying environmental science. As a culminating project, students were grouped in work teams to identify ways the school could be more environmentally conscious. The students toured the school and generated a list of possible ways to make the school more "green." The groups then debated which of those options would have the strongest environmental impact as well as be feasible to implement. After examining the options and debating the solution, the groups delivered a Prezi presentation to the school principal showcasing their ideas for a greener school. The principal selected the best solution to implement in the school.

There is a great emphasis in today's classrooms on problem solving and open-ended challenges. Ms. James's assignment represents the kind of instructional tasks that engage students in critical thinking while investigating the environmental impact on their school. Cognitive complexity in the Create Excellence Framework is the level of critical thinking required for an instructional task, project, or assessment based on Benjamin Bloom's (1956) original taxonomy and revised by Lorin W. Anderson and David R. Krathwohl (2001). With the revision of Bloom's original taxonomy, higher-level thinking has been clarified as applying knowledge in new ways and engaging in nonroutine problem solving. This chapter explains the levels in the taxonomy, describes the cognitive-complexity dimension in the Create Excellence Framework, and showcases instructional tasks and projects embedding critical thinking with real-world applications.

The Five Levels of Cognitive Complexity

Anderson and Krathwohl (2001) suggest revisions and redefine the levels of Bloom's (1956) original taxonomy as Remember, Understand, Apply, Analyze, Evaluate, and Create. Both the Create Excellence Framework and Bloom's taxonomy are hierarchical, requiring deepening levels of cognitive complexity and student engagement. At the first level of the framework—*Knowing*—teachers engage students in basic Bloom's Remember-level tasks. Advancing to the *Practicing* level of the framework, teachers plan what Bloom's taxonomy classifies as Understand- and Apply-level learning experiences. At *Investigating*, the third framework level, teacher instruction is at the Analyze, Evaluate, or Create level of Bloom's. The fourth level of the Create Excellence Framework, *Integrating*, embraces the top three cognitive levels from Bloom's taxonomy (Analyze, Evaluate, and Create). A key difference at this level is the students, instead of the teachers, are using the content standards to identify the questions, tasks, or projects. At the highest level, *Specializing*, on the Create Excellence Framework, students generate projects for Bloom's Create level while thinking as an expert or focused on an open-ended, global-learning emphasis. When objectives, activities, and assessments are properly aligned at higher levels of cognitive thinking, not only does instruction improve but student learning has a better chance of improving as well (Raths, 2002). Table 2.1 provides examples for each level of cognitive complexity in the Create Excellence Framework. At the highest three levels, projects and tasks often have a real-world focus. When real-world elements are interwoven into a task, it deepens the level of complexity as often there are more variables to consider and perhaps multiple correct solutions. As students simulate and perform tasks and projects like professionals in the field, it often naturally requires higher-order thinking skills as they analyze, evaluate, and solve problems just like skilled workers.

Table 2.1: Cognitive-Complexity Component of Create Excellence Framework

CREATE LEVEL	DESCRIPTION	SAMPLE TASK OR PROJECT
1: Knowing	• Teacher directs student interaction with the content at Bloom's Remember level (Recognizing, Recalling).	• To reinforce the unit vocabulary terms, play "Scatter, Space Race, Test" on Quizlet and then take the test on these vocabulary words.
2: Practicing	• Teacher directs student interaction with the content at Bloom's Understand level (Interpreting, Exemplifying, Classifying, Summarizing, Inferring, Comparing, Explaining) or Apply level (Executing, Implementing).	• Using Lino, post conjugations of five verbs in Spanish. • Create a newspaper headline on Fodey, a website that generates fictional newspaper headlines, to summarize a historical event. • Create a video presentation using Knovio explaining how to solve a quadratic equation.
3: Investigating	• Teacher directs student interaction with content and standard at Bloom's Analyze level (Differentiating, Organizing, Attributing), Evaluate level (Checking, Critiquing), or Create level (Generating, Planning, Producing).	• Identify which of the following is Edgar Allan Poe's best writing, "The Fall of the House of Usher," "The Raven," or "The Tell-Tale Heart" based on the development of a theme, voice, and thought-provoking or emotionally inspiring content. On DecideAlready, move the ratings meter to show which criteria are most important for your decision, and then indicate your choice. • Using MindMeister, a web-mapping tool, design a flowchart showing how critical events in a story changed a character's actions.

CREATE LEVEL	DESCRIPTION	SAMPLE TASK OR PROJECT
4: Integrating	• Students generate questions or projects with content at Bloom's Analyze level (Differentiating, Organizing, Attributing), Evaluate level (Checking, Critiquing), or Create level (Generating, Planning, Producing).	• All students in the school are required to write a research paper. The students discuss criteria for a good research paper and decide that some criteria are more important than others. Using *DebateGraph*, the students identify at least five criteria they would use to assess a research paper. Using the website, they rate the importance of each of the criteria.
5: Specializing	• Students generate questions or projects with content at Bloom's Create level (Generating, Planning, Producing). • Students engage in complex thinking like a content expert *or* with content that has an open-ended, global-learning emphasis.	• A class begins a unit on the water cycle. Students identify ways they would like to investigate the water cycle in their community. After researching, students identify scientific experiments they could conduct. They conduct the experiment and reflect on the results.

Revised Bloom's Taxonomy

While many educators know the revised Bloom's taxonomy levels (Remember, Understand, Apply, Analyze, Evaluate, and Create), many misunderstand the required level of thinking for each level. For example, a teacher might believe that when students *create* a poster that this task is on the Create level. The key is to examine how students are interacting with the content, not the technology. If students are copying facts about presidents on the poster, that would be a low-level task. To help teachers better understand the taxonomy, the revised version fortunately identifies cognitive processes under each level to clarify the level of thinking. The revised Bloom's taxonomy includes nineteen cognitive processes classified within the six levels (Anderson & Krathwohl, 2001). Table 2.2 illustrates where each cognitive process falls within Bloom's levels and how those processes align with the Create levels.

Table 2.2: Alignment of Levels and Cognitive Processes Between the Create Excellence Framework and Bloom's Taxonomy

CREATE EXCELLENCE FRAMEWORK LEVELS	BLOOM'S TAXONOMY LEVELS AND COGNITIVE PROCESSES
Knowing	Remember • Recognizing • Recalling

Continued →

CREATE EXCELLENCE FRAMEWORK LEVELS	BLOOM'S TAXONOMY LEVELS AND COGNITIVE PROCESSES
Practicing	Understand • Interpreting • Exemplifying • Classifying • Summarizing • Inferring • Comparing • Explaining Apply • Executing • Implementing
Investigating Integrating Specializing	Analyze • Differentiating • Organizing • Attributing Evaluate • Checking • Critiquing Create • Generating • Planning • Producing

In the following sections, we describe these levels and cognitive processes and provide examples of instructional tasks and projects that align to each cognitive process. To show ways to naturally integrate technology and real-world learning, these examples also showcase technology tools and real-world applications of knowledge used to support the critical thinking for each level.

Bloom's Level 1: Remember

The first level of the taxonomy is Remember. With Remember, learners must recover information previously memorized. While a low-level thinking process, memorizing information is important for higher-level thinking. For example, knowing the types of rocks can help students analyze problems with rock formations, a higher-level thinking skill. There are two cognitive processes within Bloom's Remember level: recognizing and recalling.

Recognizing and Recalling

Recognizing involves students selecting the correct memorized answer from answer choices provided, such as in a multiple-choice test. When recalling, students have to bring forth from their memory the correct memorized answer as required in a fill-in-the-blank question. Within the cognitive-complexity component, these tasks would be on level 1 of the Create Excellence Framework, the Knowing level. Following are examples of recognizing and recalling activities.

- Students use flashcards from Study Stack (www.studystack.com) to practice defining words and then checking the answers.
- Students create a set of word cards and definitions based on textbook information on Quizlet (www.quizlet.com) to study terminology.

Bloom's Level 2: Understand

While the Remember level is critical for establishing foundational concepts, information that is not processed at deeper levels can be forgotten. With the Understand level, students are establishing new connections with the content. Within the cognitive-complexity component, these tasks would be on level 2 (Practicing) of the Create Excellence Framework. There are seven cognitive processes associated with the Understand level: interpreting, exemplifying, classifying, summarizing, inferring, comparing, and explaining.

3 Interpreting

When interpreting, students convert information from one form to another, such as changing text into paraphrases, visuals, or music. Following are examples of interpreting activities.

- Text to paraphrase: Students paraphrase a reading passage in a Skype (www.skype.com) conversation with a student from another school.
- Text to visual: Using Scratch (http://scratch.mit.edu), an online drawing program, students create a picture that depicts what is happening in the novel they are reading.
- Text to music: Using GarageBand, a software designed to create music, students write a song describing one of the key terms they are learning in a curriculum unit.

4 Exemplifying

With exemplifying, students are asked to provide examples of a concept they are learning about. These examples may include connections to other content areas or to prior experiences. Following are examples of exemplifying activities.

- Using a search engine, find an example of a painting that shows texture.
- Find a picture showing Newton's first law in action, and use audioBoom (https://audioboom.com/about/education) to record your explanation of how it represents this concept.

5 Classifying

When students classify, they categorize information or items based on similar characteristics. Students can group information under headings based on their common attributes. Following are examples of classifying activities.

- In groups, students select ten quotes from a character in a book. Using Padlet (www.padlet.com), an online collaborative board, they create headings to reflect key attributes of the character and post the quotes under the appropriate headings.
- Using an interactive whiteboard, students group mathematics equations into categories based on the basic number properties (for example, associative property, distributive property, and so on).

6 Summarizing

When summarizing, students condense information in a succinct statement. The summary could be based on a reading, video clip, or observation of a natural event. Following are examples of summarizing activities.

- Students identify three websites that relate to chemical reactions. Using Delicious (http://delicious .com), a social-bookmarking site, they post links and a summary of each link.
- To summarize the group conversation, groups record key ideas on an online collaborative board using TitanPad (http://titanpad.com).
- To summarize the water cycle, students create a poster with pictures and text, called a glog, using Glogster (www.glogster.com).

7. Inferring

Inferring uses evidence and reasons to make a conclusion. Inferences drawn with limited evidence can be inaccurate. Following are examples of inferring activities.

- On Google Docs (http://docs.google.com), students review a passage and create comment boxes noting logical inferences that can be drawn from sections within the informational text.
- Groups use the online whiteboard Scriblink (www.scriblink.com) to post their results and findings. Then each group should post one new inference based on the overall results, making sure to post a new idea not listed by other groups.

8. Comparing

Comparing involves examining two different ideas or items to assess the similarities and differences. Students can use metaphors or analogies to make their comparisons. Following are examples of comparing activities.

- Using text and pictures with the online-presentation program Animoto (www.animoto.com), students create a metaphor of how the circulatory system is like another object (for example, a highway).
- Students complete a comparison diagram of two topics using a website with interactive graphic organizers such as ReadWriteThink (www.readwritethink.org) or Lucidchart (www.lucidchart.com).

9. Explaining

Explaining involves understanding cause-and-effect relationships. Following are examples of explaining activities.

- Students use the diagram-drawing website draw.io (www.draw.io) to show an independent variable and the anticipated results on the dependent variable for their science project.
- Students use the online time line generator Tiki-Toki (www.tiki-toki.com) to depict how the Brown v. Board of Education Supreme Court decision impacted U.S. education, culture, and government.

Bloom's Level 3: Apply

At the Apply level, students execute certain procedures or steps to address a new problem. Within the cognitive-complexity component, all of these tasks would be on level 2 (Practicing) of the Create Excellence Framework. There are two cognitive processes in the Apply level: (1) executing and (2) implementing.

10. Executing

In executing, students are presented with a new problem and must identify which procedure is needed to solve the problem, such as solving for a variable in an algebraic equation or editing a paper for punctuation. Following are examples of executing activities.

- Students create a Prezi (http://prezi.com) account showing how they solved an algebraic problem.

- Students record a video using Screencast (www.screencast.com) that shows how they edited a paper for correct subject-verb agreement.

11. *Implementing*

Implementing tasks often involve more variables or aspects than an executing task, and the procedure to complete the task or project is not immediately clear; thus, they are more challenging. Sometimes the problems might have more than one answer. Conceptual and procedural knowledge is needed to answer the problem. Following are examples of implementing activities.

- Students write several lines of music with varying tempos using GarageBand or Soundation (http://soundation.com), music-authoring tools.
- Groups identify the cheapest cereal available at the local store, and use Mindomo (www.mindomo.com) to show how they solved the problem.

Bloom's Level 4: Analyze

With the Analyze level, learners use knowledge and understandings to complete higher-level tasks or projects. If a student can search the Internet for the correct answer or provide the teacher an answer within a few minutes, the task or project is not at this level. When students complete Analyze-level tasks or projects, they need time to process, sort, examine, and recategorize the information. Analyze provides the basis for higher-level cognitive processes at levels 5 and 6 (Anderson & Krathwohl, 2001). Rebecca Stobaugh (2013) states, "A key component of critical thinking is the process of analyzing and assessing thinking with a view to improving it. Hence, many consider the Analyze level as the beginning of deep thinking processes" (p. 28). In the Analyze level, there are three cognitive processes: (1) differentiating, (2) organizing, and (3) attributing. Depending on whether they are teacher or student directed, these tasks could be at one of the top three levels of the Create Excellence Framework: Investigating, Integrating, and Specializing.

12. *Differentiating*

With this cognitive process, students must determine what information is relevant and irrelevant. What makes differentiating a higher-level cognitive process than the comparing cognitive process with the Understand level (Bloom's level 2) is that students must determine how parts fit into the overall structure of the concept. Following are examples of differentiating activities.

- Students read a science report in Microsoft Word and use different colors to highlight which information supports each hypothesis. With red highlights, they identify information that does not support the hypotheses. Students must justify how the information supports the primary hypothesis.
- Using Google Bookmarks, students create a database of statistics that provide support that climate change is or is not a compelling problem.
- Students search online for statements that back the idea that democracy is or is not the best type of government. Students will create a mind map demonstrating the connections and justifications for their stance.

13. *Organizing*

With organizing, students examine interactions and sequences of events. Students are able to identify connections among relevant information and then design a new arrangement or structure of the information to depict these relationships. To demonstrate their knowledge, students could construct charts, diagrams, outlines, flowcharts, or other graphic organizers to depict the interrelationships of items. Following are examples of organizing activities.

- Using Popplet (http://popplet.com), a mind-mapping application, students diagram the short- and long-term consequences of a president's action on the economy.
- Using the mapping tool Gliffy (www.gliffy.com), students create a flowchart showing how an invasive plant would impact our environment.
- Students create an infographic on Visual.ly (http://visual.ly) that depicts the interrelationships of four different habitats.

14. Attributing

The cognitive process of attributing involves students identifying biases, assumptions, or points of view in information. Assessing the credibility of sources helps students analyze information. Following are examples of attributing activities.

- Using ZooBurst (www.zooburst.com), students create a short story from the perspective of a literary or historical figure and include their point of view on current-day topics.
- Students examine an informational source in a word-processing program and add comments when biases, assumptions, or points of view are expressed.

Bloom's Level 5: Evaluate

Evaluate is the fifth level of the taxonomy. Typically, the Analyze level (4) and other lower-cognitive processes are employed to engage in the Evaluate level's cognitive processes. With the Evaluate level, informational sources are examined to assess their quality, and decisions are made based on the identified criteria. There are two cognitive processes in the Evaluate level: (1) checking and (2) critiquing.

15. Checking

Checking encompasses examining for fallacies or inconsistencies (Anderson & Krathwohl, 2001). Stobaugh (2013) explains, "Students possessing this cognitive ability pursue unsubstantiated claims, question ideas, and demand validation for arguments, interpretations, assumptions, beliefs, or theories" (p. 33). To check a source, the student can examine the author's qualifications, determine whether sufficient and valid evidence is provided, and assess whether reliable sources are used. Following are examples of checking activities.

- On the Edmodo (www.edmodo.com) class website, students address any questionable claims stated in an article posted on the class blog.
- Students complete a multistep-mathematics problem and record their explanation on Brainshark (www.brainshark.com). They then form pairs and watch their partners' Brainshark presentations and identify any mathematical errors.

16. Critiquing

Critiquing involves using set criteria to evaluate various options. Students use critiquing to identify reasons each option met or did not meet the criteria. Following is an example of a critiquing activity.

- Students identify a class field trip that would be interesting and help them learn about photosynthesis. They research four options and complete the graphic organizer showing how each option meets the criteria to be interesting and learn about photosynthesis. Finally, they vote on the best choice on Polldaddy (http://polldaddy.com), an online voting site.

- Using the IUCN (International Union for Conservation of Nature) standards for qualifying for an endangered animal, students will determine if a local animal qualifies for the endangered species list.

Bloom's Level 6: Create

Create is the highest level on Bloom's revised taxonomy. It involves organizing information in a new way to design a product. With this level, students utilize the cognitive processes of the Understand, Analyze, and Evaluate levels to *create* a new product with the content. Students designing a poster or website don't necessarily meet the Create level unless they are engaged in brainstorming new ideas, identifying the best idea, planning a solution, and then implementing an original solution. Authentic tasks and projects are great for planning a Create-level assignment. When students are placed in real-world roles such as journalists or investigators, they can engage in these higher-level processes. There are three Create-level cognitive processes, and they occur sequentially: (1) generating, (2) planning, and (3) producing.

Generating

When students engage in the generating cognitive process, they explore various ideas or solutions to solve an ill-defined problem through hypothesizing and exploring various relevant options. To begin this process, the topic must be researched and thoroughly understood so the ideas generated logically connect to the identified topic. The ideas should also be varied, unique, and detailed (Swartz & Parks, 1994). See table 2.3 for a creativity rubric to assess students' generating skills. Following are examples of generating activities.

- After discussing habitats, students select one habitat and brainstorm a new animal that could survive in that habitat. Groups generate a list of all the possible options and then select the best idea.
- After learning about the Day of the Dead, groups determine the best way to replicate the holiday in their school to promote Mexican culture. Students use DebateGraph (www.debategraph.org) to show their thinking processes as they brainstorm ideas. They present their brainstorming webs, and the class votes on the best plan to implement.
- In groups, students write a new school fight song using their knowledge of poetry.

Table 2.3: Creativity Rubric

	IMITATIVE	ORDINARY OR ROUTINE	CREATIVE	VERY CREATIVE
Variety of Ideas and Contexts	Ideas do not represent important concepts.	Ideas represent important concepts from the same or similar contexts or disciplines.	Ideas represent important concepts from different contexts or disciplines.	Ideas represent a startling variety of important concepts from different contexts or disciplines.
Variety of Sources	Created product draws on only one source or on sources that are not trustworthy or appropriate.	Created product draws on a limited set of sources and media.	Created product draws on a variety of sources, including different texts, media, resource persons, or personal experiences.	Created product draws on a wide variety of sources, including different texts, media, resource persons, or personal experiences.

Continued →

	IMITATIVE	ORDINARY OR ROUTINE	CREATIVE	VERY CREATIVE
Combining Ideas	Ideas are copied or restated from the sources consulted.	Ideas are combined in ways that are derived from the thinking of others (for example, of the authors in sources consulted).	Ideas are combined in original ways to solve a problem, address an issue, or make something new.	Ideas are combined in original and surprising ways to solve a problem, address an issue, or make something new.
Communicating Something New	Created product does not serve its intended purpose (for example, solving a problem or addressing an issue).	Created product serves its intended purpose (for example, solving a problem or addressing an issue), but is not original or does not effectively solve the problem.	Created product is interesting, new, or helpful, making an original contribution for its intended purpose (for example, solving a problem or addressing an issue).	Created product is interesting, new, or helpful, making an original contribution that includes identifying a previously unknown problem, issue, or purpose.

Source: Adapted from Brookhart, 2013.

18. Planning

Planning is the second step in the creation process. Students will take the best idea they generated and decide on a plan to carry out the project. Often there is more than one way to solve the problem. Also, in the planning process, students often realize they must revise their idea or consider a new idea. Following are examples of planning activities.

- Students take the new animal they developed in the generating process and create a story about the animal living in its habitat.
- Based on the goal from the generating process to educate students about the Day of the Dead, the class decides how to implement the ideas suggested. Groups are created to plan specific parts of the celebration. Each group creates a table listing actions to be accomplished, individual responsibilities, target dates for completion, and resources needed. The table is posted in Google Docs so all group members can access the file.
- Groups take their best idea for the school song from the generating process and develop a rough draft of their song, writing all the lyrics and deciding on the tune. They also decide how they will produce the song—with instruments or using GarageBand.

19. Producing

The final step is to follow through with the plan and produce the product. See table 2.3 (pages 41–42) for a creativity rubric to assess assignments on the Create level. Following are examples of producing activities.

- Using Microsoft Paint, students draw the animal created during the generating and planning processes and import it into Storybird (http://storybird.com) or another book-creation site. Students compose an original story about the new animal.
- Each group follows through with its plan to implement its school Day of the Dead celebration created during the generating and planning processes. One group polls the students before and after attending the celebration to measure students' learning about the holiday.

- Using GarageBand, the students develop the new school fight song they created during the generating and planning processes. Each group's song is video recorded and linked on the school's webpage. Students are encouraged to vote on the best song using the polling website Poll Everywhere (www.polleverywhere.com).

Standards and Cognitive Complexity

The concept of cognitive complexity is embedded in teaching standards as well as performance expectations for each of the content standards. Most teaching standards indicate that educators should challenge students to think at high levels. In addition, student content standards embrace the concept that students should be engaged in cognitively complex tasks and projects. Standards from the core areas of mathematics, science, social studies, and English language arts all pinpoint the focus on critical thinking while teaching content. Additionally, teaching standards note the importance of cognitively complex instruction. In the standards, words including *critique*, *generate*, and *evaluate*, represent the higher-level thinking required in the highest three levels of the Create Excellence Framework and Bloom's taxonomy. See table 2.4 for examples of standards aligned to the cognitive complexity component. We have italicized key high-level verbs in the standards to emphasize the level of thinking required.

Table 2.4: Alignment of Standards to Cognitive Complexity

SOURCE OF STANDARDS	STANDARD INDICATORS
STUDENT STANDARDS	
Social studies: College, Career, and Civic Life (C3) Framework	D2.Civ.6.9–12 "*Critique* relationships among governments, civil societies, and economic markets" (NCSS, 2013, p. 32). D2.Eco.6.9–12 "*Generate* possible explanations for a government role in markets when market inefficiencies exist" (NCSS, 2013, p. 37). D2.Geo.8.9–12 "*Evaluate* the impact of economic activities and political decisions on spatial patterns within and among urban, suburban, and rural regions" (NCSS, 2013, p. 43).
Science: Next Generation Science Standards	Science Practice 1: Asking Questions and Defining Problems • "*Define a design problem* that can be solved through the *development* of an object, tool, process or system and *includes multiple criteria and constraints*, including scientific knowledge that may limit possible solutions" (Achieve, 2013). Science Practice 4: Analyzing and Interpreting Data • "*Analyze and interpret data* to make sense of phenomena using *logical reasoning*" (Achieve, 2013). Science Practice 6: Constructing Explanations and Designing Solutions. • "*Construct and revise an explanation based on valid and reliable evidence obtained from a variety of sources* (including students' own investigations, models, theories, simulations, peer review) and the assumption that theories and laws that describe the natural world operate today as they did in the past and will continue to do so in the future" (Achieve, 2013).
Mathematics: Common Core mathematics standards	Mathematical Practice 2: "Reason *abstractly* and quantitatively" (NGA & CCSSO, 2010b). Mathematical Practice 3: "*Construct viable arguments and critique* the reasoning of others" (NGA & CCSSO, 2010b).

Continued →

SOURCE OF STANDARDS	STANDARD INDICATORS
English language arts: **Common Core English language arts standards**	W.9–10.4 *"Produce clear and coherent writing* in which the development, organization, and style are appropriate to task, purpose, and audience" (NGA & CCSSO, 2010a). RI.9–10.8 *"Delineate and evaluate* the argument and specific claims in a text, *assessing* whether the reasoning is valid and the evidence is relevant and sufficient; identify false statements and fallacious reasoning" (NGA & CCSSO, 2010a). W.9–10.1a *"Introduce precise claim(s), distinguish the claim(s) from alternate or opposing claims, and create an organization* that establishes clear relationships among claim(s), counterclaims, reasons, and evidence" (NGA & CCSSO, 2010a).
TEACHER STANDARDS	
Danielson Framework for Teaching	Domain 1: Planning and Preparation—1C Setting Instructional Outcomes • Distinguished Level: "All outcomes represent high-level learning in the discipline" (Danielson, 2014, p. 17). Domain 1: Planning and Preparation—1E Designing Coherent Instruction • Distinguished Level: "The sequence of learning activities follows a coherent sequence, is aligned to instructional goals, and is designed to engage students in high-level cognitive activity" (Danielson, 2014, p. 17).

Conclusion

Cognitive complexity is one of the dimensions in the Create Excellence Framework for real-world learning. Bloom's revised taxonomy identifies a hierarchy of six thinking levels and nineteen cognitive processes. The Create Excellence Framework builds on this taxonomy by defining five levels of integration of cognitive complexity. Teachers can draw from the examples of student activities found in this chapter to design critical-thinking tasks and projects to improve student learning in their classrooms.

Discussion Questions

1. Why do we need students to have critical-thinking skills?
2. How does embedding critical-thinking activities into your instruction change the way you teach?
3. How might increasing the level of cognitive complexity in your class help students beyond the classroom?
4. Identify a critical-thinking task you assigned, and determine where it fits into Bloom's taxonomy. Then, apply the Create Excellence Framework to raise the level of critical thinking.
5. Which instructional task or project listed in this chapter could you adapt to use in your classroom?

Take Action

1. Fill in the "Critical-Thinking Dispositions Evaluation Form" reproducible (page 46), and ask your students to complete the form as well. Use the results to engage in a discussion about critical thinking.
2. Complete the reproducible "Revised Bloom's Taxonomy Quiz" (page 47), and check your answers with the answer key. Alternatively, take the online quiz on Quizlet (http://quizlet.com/389701/test).

3. Examine the scenario in the reproducible "Analyzing a Task or Project for Cognitive Complexity" (page 49), and complete the questions. Review and compare your answers to the authors' responses provided in the reproducible.

4. Visit https://itunes.apple.com/us/book/designing-instruction-using/id536339837?mt=11 and explore the iBook *Designing Instruction Using Revised Bloom's Taxonomy* (Maxwell, 2012) about the cognitive-complexity dimension of the Create Excellence Framework.

5. Select one of the Create Excellence Framework projects in part II of this book. How could you modify the project to use in your classroom? How could you improve one of the projects? Have a conversation with a colleague about implementing the project.

6. Select another of the cognitive-complexity projects in part II. Rate each component of the project based on the framework levels. Compare your ratings to the Create Analysis rating table following the project description. How could you increase the ratings for each Create Excellence Framework component?

Critical-Thinking Dispositions Evaluation Form

Read each of the following statements. For each statement, mark if it is something you do seldom, occasionally, or frequently. Then, discuss your weaknesses and strengths. Have your students complete the checklist, and compare your strengths and weaknesses.

CRITICAL-THINKING DISPOSITIONS	SELDOM	OCCASIONALLY	FREQUENTLY
Seeks a clear statement of the thesis or question			
Seeks reasons			
Uses and mentions credible sources			
Takes into account the total situation			
Tries to remain relevant to the main point			
Keeps in mind the original or basic concern			
Looks for alternatives			
Is open minded			
Takes a position (and changes a position) when the evidence and reasons are sufficient to do so			
Seeks as much precision as the subject permits			
Deals in an orderly manner with the parts of a complex whole			

Source: Adapted from Ennis, 1987.

1. Which is the critical-thinking disposition that is the most challenging, and which is the easiest for you?

2. What do you need to do to improve on the area you struggle with?

Reference

Ennis, R. H. (1987). A taxonomy of critical thinking dispositions and abilities. In J. B. Baron & R. J. Sternberg (Eds.), *Teaching thinking skills: Theory and practice* (pp. 9–26). New York: Freeman.

Revised Bloom's Taxonomy Quiz

Directions: Identify the cognitive process under each revised Bloom's taxonomy level, and use the answer key that follows to check your answers.

Remember	
	1. Identify the components of a microcomputer system using the word bank provided.
	2. Define the meaning of an acronym as stated in class.
Understand	
	3. Design a symbol to represent the purpose of one of the technology tools.
	4. Contrast two characters in the story.
	5. Group objects into living or nonliving categories.
	6. What mathematical mistake was in each of the three problems?
	7. Compose a tweet that explains the point of today's lesson.
	8. In what ways is your family democratic?
	9. In your experiment, what caused the water to turn green?
Apply	
	10. Use the quadratic formula to solve a real-world problem.
	11. Use the formula to write a five-paragraph essay.
Analyze	
	12. Determine the essayist's point of view on the social implications of informational technology.
	13. Select three editorials, and, based on their sources, determine the differences between Democratic and Republican parties.
	14. Construct a flowchart showing how colonial rebellion led to the American Revolutionary War.
Evaluate	
	15. Read the scientific lab report, and examine if the conclusions are appropriate.
	16. Determine which of Edgar Allan Poe's poems represents his best work.
Create	
	17. Develop a list of the webpages and what content will be on each page.
	18. Design the webpage.
	19. Brainstorm all possible web layouts for our school webpage to best meet parent, teacher, and student needs.

Real-World Learning Framework for Secondary Schools © 2016 Solution Tree Press • solution-tree.com
Visit **go.solution-tree.com/instruction** to download this page.

Answer Key

Remember

1. Recognizing
2. Recalling

Understand

3. Interpreting
4. Comparing
5. Classifying
6. Inferring
7. Summarizing
8. Exemplifying
9. Explaining

Apply

10. Implementing
11. Executing

Analyze

12. Attributing
13. Differentiating
14. Organizing

Evaluate

15. Checking
16. Critiquing

Create

17. Planning
18. Producing
19. Generating

Real-World Learning Framework for Secondary Schools © 2016 Solution Tree Press • solution-tree.com
Visit **go.solution-tree.com/instruction** to download this page.

Analyzing a Task or Project for Cognitive Complexity

Examine the scenario in the following table, and answer the questions. Then, compare your answers to the authors' responses.

Scenario: Students will group pictures of prehistoric animals based on similar species.	
Level of Cognitive Complexity	What is the level of cognitive complexity of this task?
Ways to Raise the Cognitive Complexity	What are some ways to increase the level of thinking for this task?
New Level of Cognitive Complexity	What is the new level of cognitive complexity?

Authors' Responses

Level of Cognitive Complexity

This assignment is on the Understand level of the revised Bloom's taxonomy using the Classifying cognitive process.

Ways to Raise the Cognitive Complexity

To challenge students toward deeper learning:

- Students could brainstorm a new animal that could have survived along with the other prehistoric animals. They would need to consider the habitat and survival characteristics.
- Students could then use an online or software paint program to draw their animal and then import that picture into a presentation program like Prezi.
- Students then would record themselves explaining how their animal could best survive among the other animals making a PreziCast with the help of a screen-capturing program like Screenr.

New Level of Cognitive Complexity

This task or project would raise the assignment to the Create level on Bloom's revised taxonomy. Students would engage in the Generating cognitive process as they brainstormed possible animals that would be able to survive. They would be carefully rejecting many ideas that wouldn't work. Students would be thinking using the Planning and Producing cognitive dimensions as they drew their animal and justified in their presentation how it would best survive in that environment.

CHAPTER 3

Student Engagement

A seventh-grade student hops into class one day on crutches with one foot securely bandaged. She explains that she was walking with her mom on the road near their home when she slipped on loose gravel and tore a ligament in her ankle. The teacher capitalizes on the teachable moment. The class begins to discuss the absence of safe walking trails in their town and weighs their options for what they can do about it. The students study zoning regulations in their town, interview community members, and write letters to the mayor and council members. The students keep a blog journal as they partner with community members, the town council, and an architect (who designs walking trails) to create a proposal to build safe walking and running trails. The students give a video presentation at the town council meeting, and the town votes to accept their plan. Many of the students volunteer their time to help build the walking trail.

Student engagement happens when students, like the students described in this vignette, take responsibility for their own learning and partner or collaborate with the teacher, other students, or outside experts to guide their learning. The concept of engaged learning has a well-established history that has morphed since the 1990s into much more than simply attention to the learning task. Research demonstrates that engagement in learning involves student interest (Dewey, 1913), effort (Meece, Blumenfeld, and Hoyle, 1988), motivation (Skinner & Belmont, 1993), time on task (Berliner, 1990), and high levels of active learner participation (Bulger, Mayer, & Almeroth, 2006). Students in highly engaging classrooms perform an average of nearly 30 percentile points higher than other students on standardized tests (Marzano, 2007).

Create Levels of Student Engagement

The Create Excellence Framework's student-engagement component indicates the degree to which students take responsibility for their own learning; partner or collaborate with the teacher, other students, or outside experts; and use resources such as teachers, experts in the discipline, and tools and technology. The five levels of engagement are described in the following sections.

Create Level 1: Knowing

At level 1, very little engagement is required of students. The teacher may lecture or question while students take notes. Usually, this type of instruction or assessment expects one correct answer to questions.

Create Level 2: Practicing

Students at the Practicing level are working on a task or project designed and directed by the teacher. Unlike Knowing, where there is only one correct answer, multiple solutions are possible and accepted in the Practicing level. A task or project in which the teacher tells the class to write a paragraph on their iPad about the movement of hot and cold water in the ocean, using at least five of their ten science vocabulary words, is an example of a Practicing-level activity.

Create Level 3: Investigating

At level 3, Investigating, the teacher directs a task or project in which students have choice and that is differentiated by content, process, or product. An example of a level 3 task or project is a teacher directing students to select any endangered ocean animal, create an Animoto from the animal's point of view describing how it feels about why it is endangered, how it can be saved, and what a day is like in its life.

Create Level 4: Integrating

At level 4, Integrating, students partner with the teacher to define the content, process, or product; students use an inquiry-based approach; and students collaborate with other students. An example of an Integrating activity is a class that has been studying endangered ocean animals reading a news article about the United Nations considering stricter laws and regulations regarding practices that contribute to the endangerment of ocean animals. This article was not specific nor could students find any other information on the topic. In a class discussion, the teacher and students use Padlet to brainstorm ideas for UN laws. The class divides into four teams as students select the idea they want to work on. Each team decides to research its topic, which product to create, and each team member's role. Teams direct their own learning by creating a rubric (approved by the teacher) to assess their own learning and products. The teams' products illustrating their conclusions include a Prezi, a VoiceThread, a professional pamphlet using the desktop-publishing program Microsoft Publisher, and a video created in the editing program Movie Maker.

Create Level 5: Specializing

In the highest level, Specializing, students initiate their own inquiry-based learning projects. They are thoroughly immersed in the project, conduct full implementation from topic to solution, and initiate appropriate collaborations pertaining to their project. For example, students became upset after watching a documentary about children who were being poisoned in a third-world country. The students began communicating with world organizations that advocate for children in this country. The students began a campaign in their community to raise money to assist these children. Later, they even conducted a Skype session with some of the children the organizations have helped.

Table 3.1 provides the student-engagement component at the five levels as well as an example at each level.

Table 3.1: The Student-Engagement Component of the Create Excellence Framework

CREATE LEVEL	DESCRIPTION	SAMPLE TASK OR PROJECT
1: Knowing	*Teacher lecture* or questioning and students take notes *or* one correct answer expected	Match a list of sustainability terms to their definitions.

CREATE LEVEL	DESCRIPTION	SAMPLE TASK OR PROJECT
2: Practicing	Students are engaged in a task or project directed by the teacher and *multiple solutions* for one task or project are accepted.	Compare Green Cross's program for education of sustainable development with the UN's Decade of Education for Sustainable Development. How are they alike, and how do they differ?
3: Investigating	There is student choice for a task or project, and task or project is differentiated by content, process, product, or all of these (such as addressing learning preferences, interests, or ability levels).	Investigate at least five different fishing methods. Which methods are eco-friendly, and which are not? Create a presentation using Prezi to justify your answers.
4: Integrating	Students partner with the teacher to define the content, process, or product; student inquiry-based approach; and students collaborate with other students.	After studying about nutrition and food production, students were discussing whether a vegetarian-based or meat-based diet is better for health and for the industry. The students and the teacher decide to investigate the claims of both sides, identify any inconsistencies in their arguments, and create a public service announcement (PSA) video to promote better health with either a vegetarian diet, meat diet, or combination diet.
5: Specializing	*Students initiate their own inquiry-based learning projects; thorough immersion; full implementation from topic to solution, and students initiate appropriate collaborations pertaining to their project.*	Students from a local high school in the mountains are upset that so many trees are cut down leaving the land barren and unattractive. Student teams seek experts on deforestation and representatives from the forestry company that is stripping the land. The students hear both sides and debate the pros and cons of each. They decide to design and implement an advertising campaign against the deforestation in the mountains. The expert collaborates with the students by reviewing their work and giving pointers. The students get the local community involved by speaking and presenting their spreadsheet and video at local civic groups and other gatherings.

Elements of Engaged Learning

Student engagement has become an important quality in creating effective schools and advancing student achievement. Educators know now that students simply staring at the teacher or completing worksheets do not equal engaged learning, and that just because students are quiet and busy does *not* mean they are engaged in their learning. Activities that focus on procedures and rudimentary tasks as opposed to cognitively demanding learning opportunities have been found to actually impede student engagement (Blumenfeld & Meece, 1988). Engaged learning involves students solving problems or creating solutions to ill-structured, multidisciplinary, real-world problems. There are several facets of engaged learning, including the following.

- **Inquiry-based learning:** Students are engaged in solving problems or creating solutions to develop deep understandings.

- **Student-directed learning:** Students are active learners, take responsibility for their own learning, and have voice and choice.
- **Collaboration within and beyond the classroom:** Students collaborate or partner with other students, teachers, or outside experts.
- **Differentiated learning:** Students' interests, ability and readiness, and learning preferences are taken into consideration, and instruction is differentiated accordingly.

Inquiry-Based Learning

Student engagement is connected to a movement in education toward inquiry-based learning. With inquiry-based learning, students are engaging with real-world issues while solving problems or creating solutions to develop deep understandings. According to biology instructor Douglas Schamel and research associate Matthew P. Ayres (1992), students learn in a more effective manner when they generate their own questions based on their observations rather than developing a solution to a situation or problem with a predetermined answer. The National Science Education Standards (Achieve, 2013) state, "Inquiry is something that students do, not something that is done to them." Since inquiry-based learning is student directed, it would be placed at the Integrating level (4) of the Create Excellence Framework if students are collaborating with the teacher and other students. It would be considered level 5 (Specializing) if students are collaborating beyond the classroom.

The basis of inquiry-based learning is that students are key planners and designers in the learning process. Table 3.2 shows these comparisons between traditional and inquiry-based learning with students directing the learning, the teacher facilitating the learning, and students having input into the assessment.

Table 3.2: Comparison of Traditional and Inquiry-Based Learning

TRADITIONAL	INQUIRY BASED
Teacher directed	Student directed
Teacher as giver of knowledge	Teacher as facilitator of learning
Content mastery	Content mastery and beyond
Vertical and linear learning path	Learning is more web-like; concept development ranges from linear to spiral
Teacher-created assessment	Assessment requires student input

Source: Adapted from Crie, 2005.

With inquiry-based learning, students first explore the topic and identify a question. In collaboration with the teacher, students establish the learning target for the project and the assessment. An atmosphere of intellectual and emotional safety is essential so that students have the freedom to take risks without fear of embarrassment, punishment, or implications that they are inadequate. Students need the freedom to take unpopular risks and explain why their answer is plausible (Antonetti & Garver, 2015).

Second, students investigate through designing the plan, selecting information, and formulating the focus. Third, students analyze, evaluate, and organize the information to process it. Finally, students create a product or presentation to demonstrate their learning, an authentic-performance task. While this model moves away from the rote memorization of concepts, there is supporting evidence that students learn as many basic facts through this model as in a teacher-directed lecture. The benefit with this model is that students tend to be able to recall their learning for a longer time (Gabel, 1994). Inquiry-based learning is the umbrella term that encompasses the ideas of design thinking, problem-based learning, and project-based instruction.

Design Thinking

Design thinking is a student-driven, problem-solving model that requires high levels of student engagement. In design thinking, students identify a school or community issue and gather information about the problem. Next, they brainstorm solutions to the problem and research the best ideas. They then create a prototype for a select solution, gathering feedback from experts who review their work. Finally, they implement the solution and present their findings. Design thinking is perfect for the STEAM (science, technology, engineering, art, and mathematics) disciplines. It provides ways for students to structure their thinking to develop solutions.

Problem-Based Learning

Closely connected to design thinking is problem-based learning (PBL). The PBL model clearly connects to high levels of student engagement as it emphasizes the learning process, student choice, student-directed learning, inquiry-based approaches, student collaboration, and multidisciplinary, authentic problems that are not always well defined or clearly structured. The following is a summary of the PBL steps (Buck Institute for Education [BIE], 2014).

1. Explore the problem.
2. Record what you know that can help you solve the problem.
3. Develop a problem statement.
4. Identify possible solutions.
5. List actions to complete to solve the problem.
6. Research information to help solve the problem.
7. Record a solution that includes the data gathered, analysis of data, and support for the solution.
8. Present and defend your conclusion.

See figures 3.1 and 3.2 (pages 56–59) for tools to assess PBL projects. These rubrics apply to grades 6–12.

While many books, websites, and professional developers train teachers to completely design project-based learning units before rolling them out to students, the Create Excellence Framework encourages teachers to include their students in the planning. Students can help add novelty and variety to the project. Projects can have a variety of content, processes, or products; they can address diverse perspectives; and they can include competitions to instill excitement (Antonetti & Garver, 2015). Beyond novelty and variety, students can share perspectives that teachers may have overlooked or disregarded, which may be keys to engaging students.

The teacher can do some preliminary planning but should be willing to change the course of the project with some student suggestions. Some teachers who are not as comfortable with letting go of the reins may need to take smaller steps. Professor Gerald Grow (1991) outlines four stages of self-directed learning, as shown in table 3.3.

Table 3.3: Stages of Self-Directed Learning

STAGE	STUDENT	TEACHER	EXAMPLES
Stage 1	Dependent	Authority coach	Coaching with immediate feedback, drill, informational lecture, overcoming deficiencies and resistance
Stage 2	Interested	Motivator, guide	Inspiring lecture plus guided discussion, goal-setting and learning strategies
Stage 3	Involved	Facilitator	Discussion facilitated by teacher who participates as equal, seminar, group projects
Stage 4	Self-directed	Consultant, delegator	Internship, dissertation, individual work, or self-directed study group

Source: Grow, 1991.

INDIVIDUAL PERFORMANCE	BELOW STANDARD	APPROACHING STANDARD	AT STANDARD
Takes Responsibility for Oneself	• Is not prepared, informed, and ready to work with the team • Does not use technology tools as agreed upon by the team to communicate and manage project tasks • Does not do project tasks • Does not complete tasks on time • Does not use feedback from others to improve work	• Is usually prepared, informed, and ready to work with the team • Uses technology tools as agreed upon by the team to communicate and manage project tasks, but not consistently • Does some project tasks, but needs to be reminded • Completes most tasks on time • Sometimes uses feedback from others to improve work	• Is prepared and ready to work; is well informed on the project topic and cites evidence to probe and reflect on ideas with the team • Consistently uses technology tools as agreed upon by the team to communicate and manage project tasks • Does tasks without having to be reminded • Completes tasks on time • Uses feedback from others to improve work
Helps the Team	• Does not help the team solve problems; may cause problems • Does not ask probing questions, express ideas, or elaborate in response to questions in discussions • Does not give useful feedback to others • Does not offer to help others if they need it	• Cooperates with the team but may not actively help it solve problems • Sometimes expresses ideas clearly, asks probing questions, and elaborates in response to questions in discussions • Gives feedback to others, but it may not always be useful • Sometimes offers to help others if they need it	• Helps the team solve problems and manage conflicts • Makes discussions effective by clearly expressing ideas, asking probing questions, making sure everyone is heard, responding thoughtfully to new information and perspectives • Gives useful feedback (specific, feasible, supportive) to others so they can improve their work • Offers to help others do their work if needed
Respects Others	• Is impolite or unkind to teammates (may interrupt, ignore ideas, hurt feelings) • Does not acknowledge or respect other perspectives	• Is usually polite and kind to teammates • Usually acknowledges and respects other perspectives and disagrees diplomatically	• Is polite and kind to teammates • Acknowledges and respects other perspectives; disagrees diplomatically

TEAM PERFORMANCE	BELOW STANDARD	APPROACHING STANDARD	AT STANDARD
Makes and Follows Agreements	• Does not discuss how the team will work together • Does not follow rules for collegial discussions, decision making, and conflict resolution • Does not discuss how well agreements are being followed • Allows breakdowns in team work to happen; needs teacher to intervene	• Discusses how the team will work together, but not in detail; may just "go through the motions" when creating an agreement • Usually follows rules for collegial discussions, decision making, and conflict resolution • Discusses how well agreements are being followed, but not in depth; may ignore subtle issues • Notices when norms are not being followed but asks the teacher for help to resolve issues	• Makes detailed agreements about how the team will work together, including the use of technology tools • Follows rules for collegial discussions, decision making, and conflict resolution • Honestly and accurately discusses how well agreements are being followed • Takes appropriate action when norms are not being followed; attempts to resolve issues without asking the teacher for help
Organizes Work	• Does project work without creating a task or project list • Does not set a schedule and track progress toward goals and deadlines • Does not assign roles or share leadership; one person may do too much, or all members may do random tasks • Wastes time and does not run meetings well; materials, drafts, notes are not organized (may be misplaced or inaccessible)	• Creates a task or project list that divides project work among the team, but it may not be in detail or followed closely • Sets a schedule for doing tasks but does not follow it closely • Assigns roles but does not follow them, or selects only one "leader" who makes most decisions • Usually uses time and runs meetings well, but may occasionally waste time; keeps materials, drafts, notes, but not always organized	• Creates a detailed task or project list that divides project work reasonably among the team • Sets a schedule and tracks progress toward goals and deadlines • Assigns roles if and as needed, based on team members' strengths • Uses time and runs meetings efficiently; keeps materials, drafts, notes organized
Works as a Whole Team	• Does not recognize or use special talents of team members • Does project tasks separately and does not put them together; it is a collection of individual work	• Makes some attempt to use special talents of team members • Does most project tasks separately and puts them together at the end	• Recognizes and uses special talents of each team member • Develops ideas and creates products with involvement of all team members; tasks done separately are brought to the team for critique and revision

Source: Adapted from BIE, 2014. Used with permission.

Figure 3.1: Collaboration rubric for PBL.

CREATIVITY AND INNOVATION OPPORTUNITY AT PHASES OF A PROJECT	BELOW STANDARD	APPROACHING STANDARD	AT STANDARD
Launching the Project: Define the Creative Challenge	• May just follow directions without understanding the purpose for innovation or considering the needs and interests of the target audience	• Understands the basic purpose for innovation but does not thoroughly consider the needs and interests of the target audience	• Understands the purpose driving the process of innovation (Who needs this? Why?) • Develops insight about the particular needs and interests of the target audience
Building Knowledge, Understanding, and Skills: Identify Sources of Information	• Uses only typical sources of information (website, book, article) • Does not offer new ideas during discussions	• Finds one or two sources of information that are not typical • Offers new ideas during discussions, but stays within narrow perspectives	• In addition to typical sources, finds unusual ways or places to get information (adult expert, community member, business or organization, literature) • Promotes divergent and creative perspectives during discussions
Developing and Revising Ideas and Products: Generate and Select Ideas	• Stays within existing frameworks; does not use idea-generating techniques to develop new ideas for product(s) • Selects one idea without evaluating the quality of ideas • Does not ask new questions or elaborate on the selected idea • Reproduces existing ideas; does not imagine new ones • Does not consider or use feedback and critique to revise product	• Develops some original ideas for product(s), but could develop more with better use of idea-generating techniques • Evaluates ideas, but not thoroughly before selecting one • Asks a few new questions but may make only minor changes to the selected idea • Shows some imagination when shaping ideas into a product, but may stay within conventional boundaries • Considers and may use some feedback and critique to revise a product, but does not seek them out	• Uses idea-generating techniques to develop several original ideas for product(s) • Carefully evaluates the quality of ideas and selects the best one to shape into a product • Asks new questions; takes different perspectives to elaborate and improve on the selected idea • Uses ingenuity and imagination, going outside conventional boundaries, when shaping ideas into a product • Seeks out and uses feedback and critique to revise product to better meet the needs of the intended audience
Presenting Products and Answers to Driving Question: Present Work to Users or Target Audience	• Presents ideas and products in typical ways (text-heavy PowerPoint slides, recitation of notes, no interactive features)	• Adds some interesting touches to presentation media • Attempts to include elements in presentation that make it more lively and engaging	• Creates visually exciting presentation media • Includes elements in presentation that are especially fun, lively, engaging, or powerful to the particular audience

	BELOW STANDARD	APPROACHING STANDARD	AT STANDARD
Originality	• Relies on existing models, ideas, or directions; it is not new or unique • Follows rules and conventions; uses materials and ideas in typical ways	• Has some new ideas or improvements, but some ideas are predictable or conventional • May show a tentative attempt to step outside rules and conventions, or find new uses for common materials or ideas	• Is new, unique, surprising; shows a personal touch • May successfully break rules and conventions, or use common materials or ideas in new, clever, and surprising ways
Value	• Is not useful or valuable to the intended audience • Would not work in the real world; impractical or unfeasible	• Is useful and valuable to some extent; it may not solve certain aspects of the defined problem or exactly meet the identified need • Unclear if product would be practical or feasible	• Is seen as useful and valuable; it solves the defined problem or meets the identified need • Is practical, feasible
Style	• Is safe, ordinary, made in a conventional style • Has several elements that do not fit together; it is a mishmash	• Has some interesting touches, but lacks a distinct style • Has some elements that may be excessive or do not fit together well	• Is well-crafted, striking, designed with a distinct style but still appropriate for the purpose • Combines different elements into a coherent whole

Source: Adapted from BIE, 2013b.

Note: The term product is used in this rubric as an umbrella term for the result of the process of innovation during a project. A product may be a constructed object, proposal, presentation, solution to a problem, service, system, work of art or piece of writing, an invention, event, an improvement to an existing product, and so on.

Figure 3.2: Creativity and innovation rubric for PBL.

The teacher's purpose is to match the learner's stage of self-direction and prepare the learner to advance to higher stages. The process of inquiry-based learning involves a learning curve for the teacher and the students, but with practice, both teachers and students can become proficient at partnering for learning.

Project-Based Instruction

Project-based instruction (PBI) involves students designing a project or presentation as a demonstration of their understanding. Students gain knowledge and skills by working for an extended period of time to investigate and respond to a complex question, problem, or challenge. They are given some voice and choice in how the assignment is completed, and they plan a rigorous project through which key academic content is assessed and an authentic product or presentation conveys the knowledge they have gained (BIE, 2014). BIE further explains that essential elements of PBI include the following.

> Significant Content—At its core, the project is focused on teaching students important knowledge and skills, derived from standards and key concepts at the heart of academic subjects.
>
> 21st Century Competencies—Students build competencies valuable for today's world, such as problem solving, critical thinking, collaboration, communication, and creativity/innovation, which are explicitly taught and assessed.
>
> In-Depth Inquiry—Students are engaged in an extended, rigorous process of asking questions, using resources, and developing answers.
>
> Driving Question—Project work is focused by an open-ended question that students understand and find intriguing, which captures their task/project or frames their exploration.
>
> Need to Know—Students see the need to gain knowledge, understand concepts, and apply skills in order to answer the Driving Question and create project products, beginning with an Entry Event that generates interest and curiosity.
>
> Voice and Choice—Students are allowed to make some choices about the products to be created, how they work, and how they use their time, guided by the teacher and depending on age level and PBL experience.
>
> Critique and Revision—The project includes processes for students to give and receive feedback on the quality of their work, leading them to make revisions or conduct further inquiry.
>
> Public Audience—Students present their work to other people, beyond their classmates and teacher. (BIE, n.d.)

Student-Directed Learning

Student-directed learning is another key component of student engagement. Student-directed learning places the learning focus directly on the students and less heavily on the teacher's actions. As incorporated in all elements of inquiry-based learning, students are active learners, take responsibility for their own learning, and constantly formulate new ideas and refine them through their collaboration with others (Hung, Tan, &

Koh, 2006). In project-based learning, students have voice and choice. Students help teachers set clear expectations so that they know what success looks like. Students articulate the targets or goals and examine targets in their own work (Antonetti & Garver, 2015).

Finding the spark—a real-world subject, idea, or project that makes a student light up—is the key to customizing learning experiences and engaging individual students. In order to tailor learning to meet students' educational needs and aspirations, teachers seek and develop knowledge of each student's unique tendencies, circumstances, and interests through both formal processes (surveys, advisories) and informal processes (including casual conversations and insight from partner or cooperating organizations, community members, or other teachers) (Martinez, 2014). For example, on a level 4 project, students might partner with the teacher to decide which tasks they need to complete or determine what type of products they might produce.

Student-directed learning in comparison to teacher-directed approaches has been shown to increase students' depth of understanding, increase critical-thinking skills, improve long-term retention, and increase students' positive feelings toward the subject studied (Crie, 2005). At the highest levels of student-directed learning, students establish the learning goals based on their interests or questions they pose. At this level of self-directed learning, students may also co-construct knowledge, assume varied roles and tasks, and participate in self-monitoring and assessment. Several levels have been identified in the inquiry process based on the level of student input. In figure 3.3, open inquiry involves this top level of student engagement in the learning process with *no predetermined questions since students propose and pursue their own questions.* This level could correlate with Create framework levels 4 or 5 in the student engagement component depending upon the amount of student initiation of inquiry and collaboration. In the second level, guided inquiry, the teacher decides on the topic, but the students can decide how they will approach the topic and investigate the problem. This level could connect with Create framework level 3 or 4 depending upon the amount of teacher input or student collaboration. At the third level, structured inquiry, the teacher determines the topic and method for investigation and students explore various solutions. This level could correlate with Create framework level 2 or 3 depending upon task choices and differentiation. In the lowest level, limited inquiry, students follow the directions and make sure their results match those given in the text. This level would be Create framework level 2 since students are engaged in a teacher-directed task.

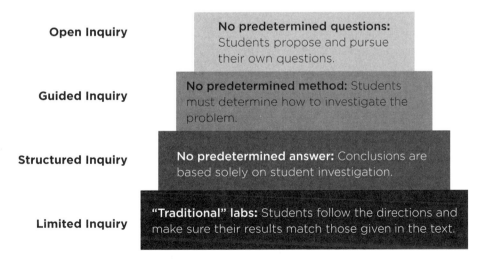

Source: Stewart & Rivera, 2010.

Figure 3.3: Levels of student input in student-directed learning.

Collaborating Within and Beyond the Classroom

Collaboration is the third key to student engagement. In engaging tasks, students should collaborate within the classroom with other students and teachers or beyond the classroom with outside experts. Teachers and experts provide real-world tools, techniques, and support that allow for open communicating and sharing (Hung et al., 2006).

Extending learning beyond the traditional classroom provides students with real-world learning experiences that allow them to communicate with experts, take ownership of their learning, and extend their support networks. Educators, including principals, act as consummate networkers throughout the process—searching for meaningful resources that meet school's learning goals and student interests in places like museums, colleges, and community organizations. For many educators, tapping these resources has been done to arrange internships or mentorships, but the Create Excellence Framework encourages teachers and principals to use their networking skills for deeper learning (Martinez, 2014).

Student-Student Collaboration

Within the classroom, students can work in teams on problems through cooperative-learning tasks. When structured effectively, cooperative-learning tasks can teach students collaborative social interaction and team-building skills. Student collaboration works best when shared and flexible roles are defined, and accountability for the task or project is determined (Abrami, Lou, Chambers, Poulsen, & Spence, 2000). See figures 3.1 and 3.2 (pages 56–59) for rubrics to assess individual performance and collaboration with a team.

Student-Teacher Collaboration

Prensky (2010) promotes a partnering pedagogy where teachers and students collaborate on what to learn, how to learn, and how to assess. Each party in the collaboration draws on its own strengths to improve student learning. Student roles include researcher, technology user and expert, thinker, world changer, and self-teacher. The teacher roles include coach and guide, goal setter and questioner, learning designer, context provider, rigor and quality assurer, and assessor. There must be mutual trust and respect among students and teachers for true partnering to prosper. The teacher can guide students in locating resources to support their work.

Student-Expert Collaboration

Finally, collaboration can occur with outside experts, as is the case with projects at level 5 of the Create Excellence Framework. Communicating with experts through email, Skype, and other technologies can bridge the divide and provide up-to-date, real-world information to students. Education researchers Monica Bulger, Richard E. Mayer, and Kevin C. Almeroth (2006) assert that an engaged learning design should include a real-world task or project presented via directed interactive activities, collaborative group work, teacher facilitation, or role modeling, and a requirement to reference and integrate resources from beyond the boundaries of the classroom. This process allows students to benefit from the most up-to-date information as well as reconcile any misconceptions or inconsistent information from other sources as they collaborate with experts.

Students are more careful in their work if they know others are going to read it, especially if it is someone outside the school. An outside audience also instills a sense of responsibility to group work (Antonetti & Garver, 2015).

Differentiated Learning

Opportunities for choice combined with a broad variety of instructional strategies result in the highest levels of engagement (Raphael, Pressley, & Mohan, 2008). When students are given choices, they have a sense of ownership of their personal learning. A diverse collection of instructional strategies should be paired with students' prior knowledge and readiness to learn in order to promote student engagement. However, the level and complexity of the varied instructional strategies and activities must also be challenging (Gregory & Chapman, 2007). Table 3.4 presents three types of differentiation with examples of how they may be applied in a statistics project.

Table 3.4: Three Types of Differentiation

TYPE OF DIFFERENTIATION	EXAMPLES OF A STATISTICS PROJECT
Differentiation of Content via Interests: Appealing to students' interests is one of the easiest and quickest ways to differentiate content. However, one must keep the content in mind to ensure that students' interests do not take them down rabbit trails too far away from learning the content. The teacher must make expectations and learning criteria clear to the students.	Every student is interested in eating. When studying the effects of nutrition on the human body, student teams choose foods that they like, research the nutritional value, and devise original ideas and projects to increase nutrition. Examples could include devising a method to increase the nutritional value of their food, designing a new food, growing their own food in the school garden, or any other original plan or project the students want to do. (Level 4)
Differentiation of Process via Ability and Readiness: Another differentiation tactic is through addressing students' ability and readiness level. This method can provide focused instruction, and it aligns well with response to intervention (RTI). Students' educational needs differ in regard to pace and complexity; therefore, this method gives students an opportunity to achieve at their own cognitive level (Gavin, Casa, Adelson, Carroll, & Sheffield, 2009). All students can be studying the same content topic at the same time, yet some will experience and learn on different levels than others. Preassessment of the content is necessary to plan and focus on meeting students' needs.	Students are in different groups based on ability or readiness level. Continuing the example of the effects of nutrition on the human body, the teacher may give information to one group at a lower readiness level and assign it a project such as recording the foods members eat for two days. Use the information provided by the teacher to determine the nutrition they ingested in that period. (Level 2)

The second group of average ability or readiness may choose foods that its members like, research the nutritional value, and devise original ideas or projects to increase nutrition with teacher guidance. Examples could include designing a new food, growing their own food in the school garden, or any other original plan or project the students want to do. (Level 3 or 4, depending on the amount of teacher direction versus student direction in project decision)

The third group with higher ability may choose foods that it likes, research the nutritional value, and devise original ideas or projects to increase nutrition with minimal teacher supervision. Examples could include devising a method to increase the nutritional value of members' food, designing a new food, growing their own food in the school garden, or any other original plan or project the students want to do. (Level 4) |
| **Differentiation of Product via Learning Preferences:** Differentiation based on learning preferences can be realized through choice in product. Student products may be technological (blogs, webpages, and PowerPoints), visual (posters, pamphlets, and drawings), written (essays, vignettes, and articles), oral (speeches, interviews, and monologues), or kinesthetic (models, dioramas, and role play) (Roberts & Inman, 2009). | Students have choice in their product for their nutrition project based on learning preferences where they will create an original product. Groups may be formed based on learning styles. Project choices can be based on learning styles (determined by a learning styles inventory). For example, a group of kinesthetic learners may grow organic food in the school garden. Students who prefer writing may select to write a congressperson in favor of GMO labeling. Visual learners may create graphs or infographics depicting their food or nutrition consumption over a week. (Level depends on the amount of teacher direction and student voice in product selection and creation: if the teacher tells them what to create, it is level 3; if students are allowed to decide and create an original product, it could be level 4.) |

Differentiation begins at level 3 with the teacher differentiating content, process, or product. At level 4, students partner with the teacher to define their own content, process, or product. At level 5, students initiate their own inquiry-based projects from topic to full implementation to solution. Students initiate their own outside collaborations with field experts. With both of these top levels, instruction is differentiated as students choose what content to examine, what processes they will use to find the solution, and how they will demonstrate their learning (product).

Standards and Student Engagement

Content standards and new teaching standards emphasize student engagement. In each of the content areas, the standards indicate that students should be actively involved in learning. The content standards direct student engagement in discussions, writing, solving problems, assessing options, and evaluating solutions. For example, the National Governors Association Center for Best Practices (NGA) and Council of Chief State School Officers' (CCSSO) literacy standards state that students should "Engage effectively in a range of collaborative discussions" (SL.8.1, NGA & CCSSO, 2010a). In social studies, the College, Career, and Civic Life (C3) Framework states that students should "Assess options for individual and collective action to address local, regional, and global problems by engaging in self-reflection, strategy identification, and complex causal reasoning" (D4.7.9–12, National Council for the Social Studies [NCSS], 2013). These content standards are heavily focused on ways students can engage in and demonstrate their learning.

The emphasis on student engagement is also mirrored in the teaching standards. In the Danielson Framework for Teaching (Danielson, 2014), for a teacher to be scored exemplary for the indicator "Using Questioning and Discussion Techniques Within Domain 3: Instruction," students must initiate higher-order thinking questions, extend the discussion, and invite comments from their classmates. In this domain, an indicator is also dedicated to measure student engagement in the learning. To score exemplary on this indicator, students must be intellectually engaged in the lesson and take initiative to improve the lesson by modifying a learning task or project to make it more meaningful or relevant to their needs, suggesting modifications to the grouping patterns used, or suggesting modifications or additions to the materials being used (Danielson, 2014).

These indicators focus on student voice as a key component in leading the instruction, instead of in the past where the teacher planned the complete lesson without student input. See table 3.5 for examples of additional standards in the Danielson framework that focus on student engagement.

Table 3.5: Alignment of Standards to Student Engagement

SOURCE OF STANDARDS	STANDARD INDICATORS
STUDENT STANDARDS	
English language arts: Common Core English language arts standards	• SL.8.1 *"Engage effectively in a range of collaborative discussions* (one-on-one, in groups, and teacher-led) with diverse partners on grade 8 topics, texts, and issues, building on others' ideas and expressing their own clearly" (NGA & CCSSO, 2010a).
Mathematics: Common Core mathematics standards	• HSS-ID.B.6a "Fit a function to the data; use functions fitted to data to *solve problems in the context of the data.* Use given functions or choose a function suggested by the context. Emphasize linear, quadratic, and exponential models" (NGA & CCSSO, 2010b). • 7.SP.A.2 *"Use data from a random sample to draw inferences about a population* with an unknown characteristic of interest. Generate multiple samples (or simulated samples) of the same size to gauge the variation in estimates or predictions" (NGA & CCSSO, 2010b).

Social studies: College, Career, and Civic Life (C3) Framework	• D4.7.9–12 "Assess options for individual and collective action to address local, regional, and global problems by engaging in self-reflection, strategy identification, and complex causal reasoning" (NCSS, 2013, p. 62). • D4.3.9–12 "Present adaptations of arguments and explanations that feature evocative ideas and perspectives on issues and topics to reach a range of audiences and venues outside the classroom using print and oral technologies (e.g., posters, essays, letters, debates, speeches, reports, and maps) and digital technologies (e.g., Internet, social media, and digital documentary)" (NCSS, 2013, p. 60).
Science: Next Generation Science Standards	• HS-ETS1–3 *"Evaluate a solution to a complex real-world problem* based on prioritized criteria and trade-offs that account for a range of constraints, including cost, safety, reliability, and aesthetics as well as possible social, cultural, and environmental impacts" (Achieve, 2013). • HS-ESS3–4 "Evaluate or refine a technological solution that reduces impacts of human activities on natural systems" (Achieve, 2013).
TEACHER STANDARDS	
Danielson Framework for Teaching	Domain 3: Instruction—Using Questioning and Discussion Techniques (3b) Critical Attributes • "Students initiate higher-order questions. Students extend the discussion, enriching it. *Students invite comments from their classmates* during a discussion and challenge one another's thinking. All students are engaged in the discussion" (Danielson, 2014, p. 63). Domain 3: Instruction—*Engaging Students in Learning* (3c) Critical Attributes • "Virtually *all students are intellectually engaged* in the lesson. *Students take initiative to adapt the lesson* by (1) modifying a learning task to make it more meaningful or relevant to their needs, (2) suggesting modifications to the grouping patterns used, and/or (3) suggesting modifications or additions to the materials being used" (Danielson, 2014, p. 69).

Planning for Student Engagement

It is ultimately the teacher's responsibility to select curriculum standards that will be incorporated into the unit. However, the goal is for teachers and students to partner together to select curriculum. Real-world learning projects provide numerous options for standards students can learn. For example, in the vignette at the beginning of this chapter, as students pursue their walking trail project, there are opportunities to learn several social studies standards (laws about zoning, volunteer service, collaboration), health standards (health and safety of the community, communication to promote health, positive effect of physical activity on health), language arts standards (many writing, speaking and listening, and language standards), mathematics standards (ratios and proportions, probability and statistics), critical thinking, and career-readiness standards.

When planning instruction to maximize student engagement, consider the following questions.

1. Are students given choices in tasks? Are tasks differentiated by content, process, and product? (Level 3)
2. Are students partnering with the teacher to define the content, process, and product? Are students using an inquiry-based approach to learning? Are students collaborating with each other? (Level 4)
3. Are students initiating their own inquiry-based projects? Are they thoroughly immersed in the problem? Are students engaged in full implementation from topic development to solution? Do students initiate appropriate collaborations pertaining to their project? (Level 5)

Curriculum mapping is key to achieving the necessary curriculum standards within lessons and units throughout the year. If a teacher partners with and guides students on four to five authentic projects during a school year, interspersed among required topics and standards, students will reap amazing benefits of real engagement in their own learning on authentic projects that are of interest to them.

Conclusion

Student engagement is probably the Create Excellence Framework's most misunderstood component. Teacher flexibility in controlling (or allowing students to responsibly take more control of) the learning environment is a key to successful student engagement. As with all of the Create components, student engagement to achieve at the higher levels of the Create Excellence Framework takes planning and collaboration, resulting in student learning that is much deeper, richer, and longer lasting.

Discussion Questions

1. Why should we channel students toward more self-directed learning?
2. How does students' self-directed learning change the way we teach?
3. How might increasing student engagement to the upper levels of the Create Excellence Framework help students beyond the classroom?
4. As a teacher, which of the attributes of student engagement do you think you are the strongest in implementing? Why? Give examples.
5. As a teacher, which of the attributes of student engagement do you think you implement the least? What are some changes you could make to implement this attribute of engagement with your students?

Take Action

1. Develop an idea for a highly engaging task or project for your students. How will you incorporate the four characteristics of engaged learning?
2. Identify an assignment or project your class was involved in last year that you thought involved a high level of student engagement. What level would it be on the Create Excellence Framework's student-engagement component? Why do you think so? How could your assignment be modified to increase the level of engagement?
3. Which instructional task or project idea in the student-engagement component of the Create Excellence Framework (table 3.1, page 52) could you adjust to use in your classroom? Describe how your students would react and what changes you would make.
4. Review the reproducible "Analyzing a Task or Project for Student Engagement" (page 68). Answer the questions to analyze the task. Then compare your analysis to the sample analysis provided at the end of the reproducible.
5. Review figures 3.1 and 3.2 (pages 56–59). What would you modify to apply one of these rubrics to your students' projects? To your subject area? Is there anything in either rubric that is in violation of your school's policies or ways of operating? Explain and tell how you could still use a similar rubric to encourage high levels of student engagement.

6. Review three online web 2.0 collaboration tools such as VoiceThread, Wiggio, Skype, Scribblar, or Google Drive. Describe how you can use these tools to increase student engagement for your students.

7. Select one of the Create Excellence Framework projects in part II of this book. How could you modify the project to use in your classroom? How could you improve one of the projects to increase engagement? Have a conversation with a colleague about implementing the project in either of your classrooms.

8. Select another of the sample student-engagement projects in part II. Rate the level of each component on the Create Excellence Framework. Compare your ratings to the Create Analysis rating table following the sample student work. How do they compare?

Analyzing a Task or Project for Student Engagement

Examine the scenario in the following table, and answer the questions. Then, compare your answers to the authors' responses.

Scenario: The teacher asks students to collect information about menu items from a fast-food restaurant. Students will develop two meal plans and spreadsheets with graphs about the data (such as nutrition, calories, and ingredients) and compare their two meals.	
Level of Student Engagement	What is the level of engagement of this task? Why do you think so?
Ways to Raise the Level of Student Engagement	What are some ways to increase the student-engagement level for this task?
New Level of Student Engagement	What is the new level of engagement?

Authors' Responses

Following is an example of an improved project based on the scenario in the preceding table.

Level of Student Engagement

This task is at level 2. It is teacher directed, and multiple solutions are accepted. It is not a higher level because there is no differentiation, no student choice, and no collaboration, and no student inquiry is required.

Ways to Raise the Level of Student Engagement

This activity could be more student directed if the teacher and the class had a discussion about ways they could study nutrition at fast-food restaurants. Students may suggest that they research nutrition facts at various fast-food restaurants, perhaps mix and match to create more healthy meals, study inconsistencies in advertising and real nutrition facts, collaborate to create a PSA about why people should or should not eat at fast-food restaurants, and critique other groups' work and give suggestions for improvement. Finally, the teacher and students would collaboratively create an assessment rubric for the student-designed projects.

New Level of Student Engagement

This level of engagement could be level 4 depending upon activities the students chose to complete.

CHAPTER 4

Technology Integration

Racism has been an issue at John Gray Middle School for years. Ms. Bowen asked her students to use their writing skills to help address the problem in the school. Students formed groups and discussed the causes of racism. They researched to identify another school that had addressed racism in its classrooms. Groups of students contacted officials from the school and prepared interview questions. The class used Skype to dialogue with the administrators and students at the identified school. After synthesizing the information from the interview and their own research, each class group identified ways to use their professional writing skills to address the problem. One group created an online survey for students, teachers, and parents to determine the perceptions of others about the problem and used the data to develop a school newscast centering on the topic. One group created an educational video to be used in classrooms with a target audience of students in their school, highlighting the negative effects of racism. Another group prepared a Prezi presentation showcasing a way they believed the school-based council could help address the problem.

With advances in technology doubling every eighteen months (McGinnis, 2006), there is a plethora of technologies available to schools. In order to maximize the impact of these technologies to enhance student learning, schools must have a planned approach (Pence & McIntosh, 2010). Educators, however, struggle to integrate technology in meaningful ways that involve higher-order thinking, collaborative tasks, and authentic problem solving (UNESCO, 2004). Optimally, technology integration should be a seamless component of instruction to engage students in authentic, creative-thinking tasks, as demonstrated in this chapter's opening scenario.

Our research shows high correlation of technology integration with the other three components of the framework (Maxwell, Stobaugh, & Tassell, 2011). The technology-integration component is intertwined with real-world learning. Technology should be used not simply as an add-on but to meaningfully support the work to more efficiently and effectively accomplish the task, just as it is in the professional world. In the sections that follow, we explore traditional technology use and research-based technology integration and demonstrate the supportive relationship between technology integration and real-world learning, cognitive complexity, and student engagement. In addition, we discuss the alignment of technology integration in the Create Excellence Framework to national technology standards and provide examples of instructional tasks.

Because we look at how students interact with the content using higher-level thinking before we look at technology use, we also examine how technology integration relates to the levels of Bloom's taxonomy. Authors

Ian Jukes, Ted McCain, and Lee Crockett (2010) state that the revised Bloom's taxonomy reflects the "new era of creativity that has been facilitated by the emergence of the online digital world" (p. 69). Technology paired with critical thinking, student engagement, and real-world learning provides opportunities for students to produce novel products to address authentic problems.

Create Levels of Technology Integration

When classifying a task or project on the technology-integration dimension, an assignment could be anywhere from level 0 to level 5. If no technology is used in the lesson or instructional plan, for this dimension they would be considered a level 0 for technology integration. Following are descriptions of levels 1–5. The hope is that teachers are teaching a majority of the lessons at the Investigating and Integrating levels of the Create Excellence Framework with a few lessons each year at the Specializing level (level 5).

Create Level 1: Knowing

At the Knowing level, a teacher may use technology for demonstration or lecture. This could include showing a video, presenting a PowerPoint presentation, or demonstrating how to dissect an animal using web technology. Students may use technology for low-level thinking tasks at the Remember level such as taking an online quiz of vocabulary terms. At the Knowing level using technology may be merely optional for students. Use of technology may be limited to simple keyboarding tasks. In these examples, technology is not meaningfully contributing to real-world learning.

Create Level 2: Practicing

At the Practicing level, students use technology for Understand- or Apply-level thinking tasks or for gathering information. The instruction is still teacher-directed but at a higher level of cognitive complexity than level 1. Examples of Practicing-level tasks are students searching the Internet for information on a topic, using technologies to summarize information, or using websites to practice mathematics skills.

Create Level 3: Investigating

At level 3, students are using technology for higher-level thinking assignments at the Analyze, Evaluate, and Create levels. However, the technology appears to be an add-on and not essential for completing the task. For example, students may make an audio recording explaining a mathematical mistake in a complex mathematics problem. While adding the technology may pique students' interest in completing the assignment, students could have written their explanation on paper. The technology might be an afterthought, added after planning the lesson, to meet state teaching standards that require inclusion of technology in the lesson.

Create Level 4: Integrating

At the Integrating level, teachers are adept at infusing technology into their classroom, and student technology use includes content standards essential to project completion, promotes collaboration among students and partnership with the teacher, and helps them solve authentic problems at Bloom's Analyze, Evaluate, or Create levels. This level engages all four Create Excellence Framework components with (1) real-world applications of knowledge, (2) critical thinking at the highest cognitively complex levels, (3) student engagement through collaboration and partnerships, and (4) technology infused in a meaningful way. Technology at this level is not an add-on but is infused into the design of the assignment. Students partner with the teacher to design the assignment and rubric, and the teacher is more of a coach than a leader of direct instruction. For example, students in a mathematics class could discuss a recent futuristic movie and how mathematics was used to create the movie. Students might then ask the teacher if their project could be to create a video showing how the Pythagorean Theorem could be used to solve a real-world problem in the year 2030.

Create Level 5: Specializing

At the highest level on the Create Excellence Framework, students continue to direct their technology use. The Specializing level involves students designing projects that (1) are integrated seamlessly in content at the Create level, (2) include several technologies, and (3) incorporate collaboration with field experts or global organizations to find solutions to real, complex problems. As with level 4, all four of the Create Excellence Framework components are engaged in this level. Students complete projects at the highest level on Bloom's taxonomy: Create. Students must consider the constraints of the problem, situation, or task and use their knowledge to produce a high-quality solution or product, employing several appropriate technologies to accomplish the task. In addition, students collaborate with experts to develop solutions to authentic problems. This level requires classrooms to be structured as collaborative-learning environments in which students' interests and passions are nurtured to engage in rich, deep thinking tasks. For example, students in one class decided to help earthquake victims in Nepal. They used their smartphones and tablets to look up organizations providing relief. One team of students Skyped with Samaritan's Purse, an international relief organization, and discovered the organization's needs, which included a flashy announcement for its website. That team created a public service announcement in Adobe Flash for the website. Samaritan's Purse's webmaster worked with this group in training, consultation, and evaluation of its work. Another team created a survey in SurveyMonkey to determine student interest in helping the earthquake victims and the best type of fundraiser to hold. Members ultimately held a running event and raised money to send to Samaritan's Purse. A third team used Prezi to design a snazzy presentation that it presented to three local civic groups who donated to the cause. A fourth team designed a spreadsheet and charts to keep up with the funds raised by the other groups.

Table 4.1 (page 72) showcases each of the technology integration levels within the Create Excellence Framework along with task and project examples aligned to each level.

Applying Technology in a Meaningful Way

Most students are well-versed in technology. Prensky (2001) coins the term *digital natives* to describe those students who, throughout their lives, have always had exposure to using digital technology, Internet connectivity, and social networking. These students favor technology-based learning tasks that provide for collaboration on real-life application of concepts (Oblinger, 2003). In a survey of student engagement, 55 percent of the high school students indicated they believe the projects or lessons involving technology are exciting or engaging (Yazzie-Mintz, 2010). However, while students desire a rich, media-based learning environment, many of the instructional tasks in classrooms do not include opportunities for students to use technology. In fact, a 2007 joint report from ISTE, the Partnership for 21st Century Skills, and State Educational Technology Directors Association (SETDA) indicates that of all industries in the United States, the education sector is the least infused with technology. Additionally, the National Center for Education Statistics reports that 97 percent of teachers had access to a computer in 2009, but only 72 percent of all teachers used the computers for instruction (Gray, Thomas, & Lewis, 2010).

Table 4.1: Technology-Integration Component of the Create Excellence Framework

CREATE LEVEL	DESCRIPTION	SAMPLE TASK OR PROJECT
1: Knowing	Teacher uses technology for demonstration or lecture, student technology use is at the Remember-level thinking task, or technology is a student option but not required or used for keyboarding.	• Students complete a teacher quiz on Google Forms, a polling technology, on vocabulary terms for the unit. • The teacher plays a Hello Slide presentation to summarize the author's background prior to studying a book.
2: Practicing	Students use technology for Understand or Apply thinking tasks, or students use technology for gathering information.	• Students go to the AAA Math website to practice multiplying decimals. • Students search the web for information on 20th century authors. • Students take digital pictures of architectural features in their community that show ancient Greece's influence on current architecture. • Using an interactive web–diagram graphic organizer, students identify five ways their day would be different if U.S. colonists lost the war to Britain.
3: Investigating	Technology use appears to be an add-on or alternative—not essential for task or project completion—and students use technology for Analyze, Evaluate, or Create thinking tasks.	• After reading *Julius Caesar,* students use an online newspaper generator to write an article taking a stance on whether Caesar deserved to die. • Ask students to describe three changes they would make and the positive long-term effects they would have if they could go back in time and positively change the world by affecting Christopher Columbus's actions. They should create a Prezi account and use Screenr to record their presentation. • Students create a music video expertly integrating five poetic devices. • Using the Historical Thinking Matters website, students engage in the online tasks requiring them to meticulously evaluate historical sources. • Determine if the New Deal represented a revolution or a reform in U.S. history by using the DocsTeach website to view historical documents. • Using the Picturing Modern America 1880–1920 website, students analyze historical photographs and artifacts.

CREATE LEVEL	DESCRIPTION	SAMPLE TASK OR PROJECT
4: Integrating	Student-directed technology use is embedded in content and essential to project completion, student-directed technology use promotes collaboration among students and partnerships with the teacher, and student-directed technology use helps students solve authentic problems at the Analyze, Evaluate, or Create thinking tasks.	• In U.S. history class, students have studied the significant impact of books and news articles on public thinking. Students want to use WeVideo to create a persuasive video convincing their pen pals in England to read a book that is at least fifty years old that had an impact on U.S. history. • When studying about other countries, students decide to plan a holiday celebration from another country, such as the Mexican Day of the Dead, for the school. Create a collaborative document on Google Docs to plan the preparations and inform school officials and students of the activities. • In English class, students and the teacher hatch the idea of writing a poem and create a video using Animoto (https://animoto.com) with music and pictures celebrating either a family member, community leader, or someone important to them, to be shown at the school's heroes celebration.
5: Specializing	Student-directed technology use is seamlessly integrated in content at the Create thinking skill, student-directed technology use has several technologies, and student-directed technology use includes collaboration with field experts or global organizations to find solutions to an in-depth, real problem.	• After a Skype session with their pen-pal class in Nairobi, Kenya, students began questioning why the students were so poor. The teacher led them into a discussion about the economy, politics, and education of Kenya and challenged them to investigate the effects of these issues using Gapminder (www.gapminder.org). The students were so moved by the data and pictures on other websites that they wanted to do something to help their sister class. In their Skype session, they noticed that not all students had chairs to sit in, many did not have shoes, and some had torn clothes. Each student team took a different issue to examine and propose a solution. One team contacted UNICEF and discovered a project to donate shoes for children in Africa. After emailing the person directing this project, the students learned they could donate shoes to UNICEF, and it could deliver them to a designated school in Kenya. The students were so excited that they consulted with the city planner to plan their project, and a local graphic artist advised them on creating advertising posters around the school and community for shoe donations. They collected enough shoes for almost every child in the school, not just their sister class! They visited businesses for donations to cover the shipping costs of the shoes. Both classes could not wait until the next Skype session, and the Kenyan class showed off its new shoes! (In this example, students are partnering with the teacher and outside experts. Thinking is at the Create level of Bloom's since they are designing and implementing a solution, and they had a global impact on an issue.)

Traditional Technology Integration

Traditionally, technology has been used in classrooms as a gadget to obtain students' attention or inserted as an add-on to instruction to meet curriculum or teaching standards, but it fails to meaningfully impact instruction. Technology used to deliver teacher-directed content (as a glorified blackboard) and digital worksheets has not delivered the rate of return expected for the millions of dollars spent on technology (Schwartzbeck, 2012). Without sound application of technology integration, money spent on technology is wasted. Authors Thomas W. Greaves, Jeanne Hayes, Leslie Wilson, Michael Gielniak, and Eric L. Peterson (2010) state, "Educational technology best practices have a significant positive impact on improvements in student achievement, and must be widely and consistently practiced" (p. 10). Technology should be a tool to reach an educational goal; technology is not the goal itself. Educator Will Richardson (2013) comments, "It's not about the tools. It's not about layering expensive technology on top of the traditional curriculum. Instead, it's about addressing the new needs of modern learners in entirely new ways" (p. 12).

Effective Technology Integration

Effective technology integration involves using technology tools in a new way. It involves transforming the classroom into an environment where students engage in real-world, critical-thinking tasks that involve students and teachers collaborating together. Through these tasks, students are inspired to innovate. Technology provides tools that enable users to process their thinking and be effective and efficient. The Create Excellence Framework's technology-integration component advocates for this new approach, incorporating real-world tasks that are naturally infused with critical thinking and student engagement. Effective technology integration seamlessly embeds technology tools as part of the instructional design in order to engage students with significant content at high levels of thinking, whereby students use varied technologies to collaborate with others, explore solutions to real-life problems, and share their results in an authentic manner.

The web provides an unlimited source of information and opportunities to connect with others that is changing the way we view what is important in education. When there were limited sources of information, knowledge and remembering were critical. Now, with more readily accessible information, education can focus on new areas: real-world interactions, cognitive complexity, student engagement, and technology integration. Unfortunately, many of these foci are not present in classrooms. Psychology professor Daniel T. Willingham (2009) finds a lack of student engagement in many schools due to teacher-directed instruction, often at lower thinking levels, without authentic applications. However, when critical thinking, real-world applications, and student engagement are combined with technology integration, powerful learning can occur. While some may view technology as helpful in building basic foundations of knowledge through online games that reinforce basic applications of content, technology is more effectively used by students to design solutions and create new products, which are high-level thinking activities. Technology tools have the potential to enhance student learning, but they must be implemented in a research-based framework to ensure sound implementation. See table 4.2 for a comparison of traditional ways of using technology to supplement curriculum and research-based ways to infuse technology as a part of high-level learning.

Table 4.2: Traditional Technology Versus Research-Based Technology Approaches

TRADITIONAL TECHNOLOGY APPROACH	RESEARCH-BASED TECHNOLOGY APPROACH
Technology is used to search for information or practice skills.	Technology is used to expand students' learning as it is embedded with high-quality instruction requiring students to critically think, solve complex real-world problems, and create products. Students engage in deep project-based learning tasks.
Teacher plans instruction that meets the needs of students with average ability.	Technology is used to customize and individualize instruction, making learning personalized or learner centered.

TRADITIONAL TECHNOLOGY APPROACH	RESEARCH-BASED TECHNOLOGY APPROACH
Teacher uses textbook to guide instruction.	Students use technology to address relevant and authentic tasks aligned to content standards.
Teacher leads instruction.	Teachers are coaches or facilitators of the learning process.
Teacher uses technology to plan lessons or present information.	Students use multiple technology tools to address real-world problems.

Source: Adapted from Wolf, 2012.

The Create Excellence Framework embraces the view that technology integration can bolster real-world learning through the areas of cognitive complexity and student engagement. Technology is not merely an add-on but is the vehicle through which the other Create Excellence Framework components can be accomplished. Effective digital learning engages students in high-level thinking tasks with real-world applications to improve student achievement.

Standards and Technology Integration

Before the abundance of technology, a knowledge-based society depended on people memorizing information, but we can now quickly search for facts on the Internet. Digital learning resources challenge students to engage in deeper learning as they analyze and evaluate information to employ complex, authentic problem solving that promotes the transfer of learning to other contexts. As students engage in digitally rich environments, they can become self-driven, independent thinkers prepared for the real world. Technology affords students opportunities to collaborate beyond the classroom with peers or experts in a digital environment to develop original products. Students can share their work to a wider global audience to impact change (Richardson, 2013).

Groups such as ISTE (2007) and Partnership for 21st Century Skills (2011) have identified best practices to establish a framework for effective technology integration. The ISTE standards embrace a holistic view of technology integration, focusing on creativity and innovation; communication and collaboration; research and information fluency; critical thinking, problem solving, and decision making; digital citizenship; and technology operation and concepts.

P21 (2011) identifies information, media, and technology skills as supporting arches for 21st century learning in the core subjects. The Create Excellence Framework similarly asserts that technology resources can support critical thinking, communication, collaboration, and creativity as students master the core subjects. Further, key points for the Common Core State Standards (CCSS) for English language arts state, "Just as media and technology are integrated in school and life in the twenty-first century, skills related to media use (both critical analysis and production of media) are integrated throughout the standards" (NGA & CCSSO, 2010a). The integration of technology in the standards is also included in the revised science standards. The Next Generation Science Standards conceptual framework states, "New insights from science often catalyze the emergence of new technologies and their applications, which are developed using engineering design. In turn, new technologies open opportunities for new scientific investigations" (National Research Council, 2012, p. 210). In science, teachers are naturally expected to use the technologies that support the learning whether they be probes, microscopes, or other technologies. Of course use of technology varies greatly in each discipline, as we'll see in the following text and supporting examples.

Real-World Learning

When students engage in real-world problems focused on research and inquiry, teachers can guide them to select and utilize appropriate technologies to address the problem (Jones, Valdez, Nowakowksi, & Rasmussen, 1995). Project-based learning experiences can combine multimedia projects with authentic audiences and purposes.

ISTE developed technology standards for students in 2007. Within the standards there are several indicators that link technology and authentic learning. The critical-thinking, problem-solving, and decision-making standard states that "students use critical-thinking skills to plan and conduct research, manage projects, solve problems, and make informed decisions using appropriate digital tools and resources" (ISTE, 2007). It also specifies that students should be able to "identify and define authentic problems and significant questions for investigation" (ISTE, 2007). These technology standards clearly reflect that technology must be appropriately integrated with real-world issues.

Students can use technology to solve problem-based learning challenges surrounding real community or world issues. Technology can be used to research, collaborate, and present each group's findings. The following list highlights examples of how technology integration can be paired with real-world learning.

- Working in groups, students can start for-profit or nonprofit enterprises using financial tools such as Excel worksheets and graphs to track expenses and profits. In this student-directed task at level 4 on the Create Excellence Framework, the technology is appropriately supporting the project. Students are designing their own company, thus working at the Create level while collaborating with others.
- After consulting with experts on the best way to communicate with the public about their cause, students can lobby for school policies or social causes in their community by creating presentations, websites, and blogs. This project is on the fifth level of the Create Excellence Framework as students are impacting a real community problem and utilizing several technologies to accomplish the purpose. To gain valuable information, students are collaborating with experts.
- Students can develop ideas for redesigning a playground by designing a layout in SketchUp, using online tools iBrainstorm or MindMeister to brainstorm ideas, and using Excel to develop a budget and fundraise. The group could then present a proposal using Animoto for the school council to consider. On the fourth level of the Create Excellence Framework, students in the project are developing their own ideas, hence it is a student-directed task. The groups are collaborating through utilizing technologies for brainstorming and budgeting which appropriately supports the purpose of the task.
- In science, students can use technology to improve a current product and prepare a sales presentation using Haiku Deck to pitch their ideas. This project would be on the fourth level of the Create Excellence Framework as students are designing a solution to a current problem and then utilizing technologies to present their ideas.
- Students identify a problem in their school and, in groups, discuss ways of using their writing skills and digital abilities to solve the problem. This project is at the fourth level of the Create Excellence Framework as students are defining the problem and identifying appropriate technologies to support their work. As they solve an authentic school problem they could utilize technologies like Bubbl.us to brainstorm solutions or create digital presentations and use SlideShare to showcase their solution.

Critical Thinking

Critical thinking and technology are emphasized in the most recent technology standards ISTE created. The ISTE standards include students using technology to create and innovate, solve problems, and make decisions

(ISTE, 2007). The ISTE technology standards for students were revised again in 2012 to portray expectations of 21st century learning, which include principles of effective technology integration embedded with critical thinking. The ISTE standards reinforce the effective integration of technology with high-level thinking that the Create Excellence Framework and the revised Bloom's taxonomy embrace. The following lists highlight ISTE standards that promote the use of technology along with cognitive complexity.

- **Creativity and innovation:** Students demonstrate creative thinking, construct knowledge, and develop innovative products and processes using technology. Students—

    a. Apply existing knowledge to generate new ideas, products, or processes

    b. Create original works as a means of personal or group expression

    c. Use models and simulations to explore complex systems and issues

    d. Identify trends and forecast possibilities

- **Research and information fluency:** Students apply digital tools to gather, evaluate, and use information. Students—

    a. Plan strategies to guide inquiry

    b. Locate, organize, analyze, evaluate, synthesize, and ethically use information from a variety of sources and media

    c. Evaluate and select information sources and digital tools based on the appropriateness to specific tasks

    d. Process data and report results

- **Critical thinking, problem solving, and decision making:** Students use critical-thinking skills to plan and conduct research, manage projects, solve problems, and make informed decisions using appropriate digital tools and resources. Students—

    a. Identify and define authentic problems and significant questions for investigation

    b. Plan and manage activities to develop a solution or complete a project

    c. Collect and analyze data to identify solutions, make informed decisions, or both

    d. Use multiple processes and diverse perspectives to explore alternative solutions (ISTE, 2007)

Ian Jukes et al. (2010) also developed a list of 21st century competencies including students thinking creatively to address real-world issues, critically assessing the quality of digital content, and creating their own digital projects.

This need for the integration of cognitive complexity and technology is supported by many other organizations beyond those focused solely on education. The U.S. 21st Century Workforce Commission's (2000) National Alliance of Business maintains that, "The current and future health of America's 21st century economy depends directly on how broadly and deeply Americans reach a new level of literacy—21st Century Literacy" (p. 4). Their alliance identifies 21st century literacy as including digital literacy, inventive thinking, and results-based thinking. As routine jobs transition to high-skill positions, students must possess 21st century skills to meet workforce demands (Chao, 2001). Employers comment that, despite young employees' knowledge of technology, they are unable to use their thinking skills and technology on the job. Gordon (2011) notes:

> Work readiness is no longer just about the three Rs; now it's also about turning infor-
> mation into knowledge through web searching and vetting . . . developing effective
> multimedia presentations . . . [and] . . . seamlessly using digital tools to collaborate
> and problem-solve. (p. 32)

The Council on Competitiveness reports that over 75 percent of all jobs in the service industry in the United States require high-level skills including problem solving, communication, entrepreneurship, computational analysis, and collaboration (van Opstal, 2008).

Teachers can partner with students to design open-ended assignments that have no single right answer and require students to design solutions to problems that require higher-level thinking and naturally embed technology. Students can provide feedback on other students' work through peer editing as they add comments to a digital document on Google Docs or using Microsoft Word. Students can also engage in inquiry learning focused around answering a question. Following are some examples that exemplify the natural connection between cognitive complexity and technology integration.

- Students design a proposal for a school club. They collect and analyze survey data and then prepare a persuasive presentation using statistics showing why the club will be successful. (Level 4)
- Students want to propose a new way to do scheduling at their school. They use their writing skills to construct logical arguments to support their ideas. Students use Wix (www.wix.com), an online presentation tool, to create a persuasive presentation to show their principal. (Level 4)
- Students are frustrated with poorly designed parking at school and decide to design a more functional parking lot for students and staff using their mathematics skills. Students use SketchUp to create a map depicting their proposed plan. (Level 4)

Student Engagement

When there are real-world classroom tasks and projects, there are often high levels of technology integration and student engagement. Digital tasks can invite students to emotionally invest in learning as they learn in their "native" [digital] language. Students' passion and purpose can be ignited as students define their own problems and create content with technology. It involves shifting the ownership of the learning to make instruction self-directed and self-paced. The teacher's role then becomes a partner and co-learner with the students as they are immersed into the content. Students are able to approach learning in a differentiated way by investigating their interests and passions. This individualized approach to learning enhances students' intrinsic motivation as they select and examine areas of concentration instead of the teacher directing the learning. This type of self-directed learning is often expected in the workplace.

ISTE standards endorse the view that technology should be connected to student engagement in learning. Its communication and collaboration standard states that students will "contribute to project teams to produce original works or solve problems" (ISTE, 2007). Also related to engagement, the digital citizenship standard asserts that students should "exhibit a positive attitude toward using technology that supports collaboration, learning and productivity" (ISTE, 2007). The following list features a sampling of additional ISTE standards of technology and student engagement.

- **Communication and collaboration:** Students use digital media and environments to communicate and work collaboratively, including at a distance, to support individual learning and contribute to the learning of others. Students—
    a. Interact, collaborate, and publish with peers, experts, or others employing a variety of digital environments and media

    b. Communicate information and ideas effectively to multiple audiences using a variety of media and formats

    c. Develop cultural understanding and global awareness by engaging with learners of other cultures

    d. Contribute to project teams to produce original works or solve problems

- **Digital citizenship:** Students understand human, cultural, and societal issues related to technology and practice legal and ethical behavior. Students—

    a. Advocate and practice safe, legal, and responsible use of information and technology

    b. Exhibit a positive attitude toward using technology that supports collaboration, learning, and productivity

    c. Demonstrate personal responsibility for lifelong learning

    d. Exhibit leadership for digital citizenship (ISTE, 2007)

Beyond ISTE recommendations, other researchers and authors have supported using technology to increase student engagement. Research has shown that when teachers integrate technology into classrooms, such as with interactive whiteboards, students remain passive learners unless teachers purposefully plan higher-level thinking and student-directed instructional tasks (Lemke, Coughlin, & Reifsneider, 2009). Thus, simply integrating technology without purposely planning for rich student engagement can produce little impact on student achievement. Online partnerships are one method teachers can use in planning student engagement through technology. There are many examples of successful online partnerships, including classrooms from different parts of the world Skyping or having pen pals that digitally communicate. In these experiences students can discover different perspectives as they pose questions and seek understanding. Students' curiosity is piqued as they have a real-world audience engage in higher-level thinking as they formulate questions and consider different viewpoints. The partnership is student centered as students' interests and questions drive the conversation and communication. In research on the benefits of online partnerships, schools using online collaboration find reduced disciplinary actions and dropout rates (Greaves, Hayes, Wilson, Gielniak, & Peterson, 2012). Therefore, technology enhances student collaboration in a meaningful way while positively impacting student achievement and other measures of school success.

As teachers infuse technology into their daily teaching, researchers find that the roles of the teacher and student have morphed into adaptable and enhanced roles, with both parties introducing additional content. Through the use of technology, traditional issues of space and time are minimized, thus increasing student engagement (Forkosh-Baruch, Mioduser, Nachmias, & Tubin, 2005). In short, the focus on student engagement reflects the needs of contemporary learners to use digital tools to locate information, assimilate meaning, create products, and collaborate during the learning process (Maxwell, Constant et al., 2011). Technology-infused classrooms can transform students' role from passive consumers to active producers of products as they engage in hands-on, collaborative work that replicates the workplace. This student-centered learning meets students' individual learning needs. Following are a few examples of technology integration fused with high levels of student engagement.

- Students plan a webinar to discuss ways to improve water conservation in their community. Students research the issue and invite community members to attend. Students present local water conservation data and plan questions for the participants. Students use Piktochart (http://piktochart.com) to prepare an informational graphic to depict the water-conservation challenges. (Level 4)

- The school has a flooding issue near the school's entrance. Via Skype, students interview several city-planning officials and school-district leaders. Students use the interview information and research to design an effective way to address the problem. In groups, students use a web presentation tool, Projeqt (https://projeqt.com), to design their presentation. (Level 5)

See table 4.3 for examples of additional teaching and content standards that align to technology.

Table 4.3: Alignment of Standards to Technology Integration

SOURCE OF STANDARDS	STANDARD INDICATORS
STUDENT STANDARDS	
Social Studies: College, Career, and Civic Life (C3) Framework	D2.Geo.1.9–12 "Use *geospatial and related technologies* to create maps to display and explain the spatial patterns of cultural and environmental characteristics" (NCSS, 2013, p. 41). D4.3.6–8 "Present adaptations of arguments and explanations that feature evocative ideas and perspectives on issues and topics to reach a range of audiences and venues outside the classroom using print and oral technologies (e.g., posters, essays, letters, debates, speeches, reports, maps) and *digital technologies (e.g., Internet, social media, digital documentary)*" (NCSS, 2013, p. 60).
Science: Next Generation Science Standards	Science Practice 5: Using Mathematics and Computational Thinking • "*Use digital tools* (e.g., computers) to analyze very large data sets for patterns and trends. • *Use digital tools* and/or mathematical concepts and arguments to test and compare proposed solutions to an engineering design problem" (Achieve, 2013). Science Practice 4: Analyzing and Interpreting Data • "*Analyze data using tools, technologies*, and/or models (e.g., computational, mathematical) in order to make valid and reliable scientific claims or determine an optimal design solution" (Achieve, 2013).
Mathematics: Common Core mathematics standards	Mathematical Practice 5 • "Use *appropriate tools* strategically" (NGA & CCSSO, 2010b). • "Mathematically proficient students consider the available tools when solving a mathematical problem. These tools might include pencil and paper, concrete models, a ruler, a protractor, a calculator, a spreadsheet, a computer algebra system, a *statistical package, or dynamic geometry software*" (NGA & CCSSO, 2010b). • "When making mathematical models, they know that *technology* can enable them to visualize the results of varying assumptions, explore consequences, and compare predictions with data. Mathematically proficient students at various grade levels are able to identify relevant external mathematical resources, such as *digital content located on a website*, and use them to pose or solve problems" (NGA & CCSSO, 2010b). • "Mathematically proficient students at various grade levels are able to identify relevant external mathematical resources, such as *digital content located on a website*, and use them to pose or solve problems. They are able to use *technological tools* to explore and deepen their understanding of concepts" (NGA & CCSSO, 2010b).

SOURCE OF STANDARDS	STANDARD INDICATORS
English language arts: Common Core English language arts	SL.11–12.5 "Make strategic use of digital media (e.g., textual, graphical, audio, visual, and interactive elements) in presentations to enhance understanding of findings, reasoning, and evidence and to add interest" (NGA & CCSSO, 2010a).
	W.11–12.6 "Use technology, including the Internet, to produce, publish, and update individual or shared writing products in response to ongoing feedback, including new arguments or information" (NGA & CCSSO, 2010a).
	SL.11–12.2 "Integrate multiple sources of information presented in diverse formats and media (e.g., visually, quantitatively, orally) in order to make informed decisions and solve problems, evaluating the credibility and accuracy of each source and noting any discrepancies among the data" (NGA & CCSSO, 2010a).
TEACHER STANDARDS	
Danielson Framework for Teaching	Domain 2: Classroom Environment—2E Organizing Physical Space "The classroom environment is safe, and learning is accessible to all students, including those with special needs. The teacher makes effective use of physical resources, including computer technology. The teacher ensures that the physical arrangement is appropriate to the learning activities. Students contribute to the use or adaptation of the physical environment to advance learning. (Distinguished rating description)" (Danielson, 2014, p. 51).

Conclusion

While students increasingly desire to learn with technology, some classrooms still resist integrating student use of technology to increase student achievement. Others see technology integration as superficial as teachers check off that they have integrated it into instruction. It is critical that educators integrate technology in a purposeful, research-based way to avoid wasting instructional time. The ISTE standards and other documents support the use of technology seamlessly integrated in content to challenge students to think at high levels while collaborating with others to solve authentic tasks. This holistic view of technology integration is also embraced in the Create Excellence Framework. The technology-integration component focuses on students using technology to cooperatively solve real-world problems while challenging students to think critically. This view of technology integration can truly make strides toward advancing student learning. The Create Excellence Framework is different than the ISTE standards in that it provides a system for educators to analyze lesson plans and instructional tasks and projects to determine the levels of cognitive complexity, engagement, and technology integration into real-world learning.

Discussion Questions

1. How do you define technology integration? How might this chapter's definition of technology cause schools to change how they allocate money for technology?
2. What instructional projects or tasks in this chapter could you adapt for your classroom?
3. Read *Standards Crosswalk—Common Core & Educational Technology* (www.k12.wa.us/EdTech /Standards/edtechcoresubjects.aspx) to examine the state of Washington's standards crosswalk between the Common Core English language arts standards and technology indicators. What ideas in the crosswalk for integrating technology to support instruction could you use in your classroom?

4. Are you better at integrating technology with cognitive complexity, real-world learning, or student engagement? Why so?

5. Review one of your lessons and identify the level of technology integration in the Create Excellence Framework. How could you move it to a higher level?

Take Action

1. Visit the Create Excellence Framework webpage at http://create-excellence.com/resources and examine the technology links to media projects. What idea can you adapt to improve student learning in your classroom?

2. Examine the reproducible "Analyzing a Task or Project for Technology Integration," and answer the questions in the blank form. Then, examine the sample scenario provided in the reproducible, and compare your responses to the authors'.

3. Explore the technology tools listed in the reproducible "Websites With Lessons Embedding Technologies" (page 85) and on the Create website (http://create-excellence.com/resources). Which tool(s) could help you better meet your students' learning needs as well as more effectively address your learning targets?

4. Select one of the Create Excellence Framework projects in part II of this book. How could you modify the project to use in your classroom? How could you improve one of the projects? Have a conversation with a colleague about implementing the project in your or the colleague's classroom.

5. Select one of the Create Excellence Framework projects for technology integration in part II. Rate the level of each component on the Create Excellence Framework. Compare your ratings to the Create Analysis rating table following the project's sample student work. How could you increase the ratings for each framework component?

Analyzing a Task or Project for Technology Integration

Examine the scenario in the following table, and answer the questions. Then, compare your answers to the authors' responses.

Scenario: After studying causes of teen bullying and violence, students create a blog about a time they were bullied.	
Level of Technology Integration	What would be the level of technology integration on the Create Excellence Framework?
Ways to Raise the Technology Integration	What would be some ways to raise the level of technology integration?
New Level of Technology Integration	What would be the new level of technology integration on the Create Excellence Framework?

Real-World Learning Framework for Secondary Schools © 2016 Solution Tree Press • solution-tree.com
Visit **go.solution-tree.com/instruction** to download this page.

Authors' Responses

Compare your answers to the authors' responses to the scenario questions.

Level of Technology Integration

What would be the level of technology integration on the Create Excellence Framework?

This assignment is on level 2 (Practicing) of the Create Excellence Framework. Students are using technology for a reflection activity. There is no collaboration required for this task or attempt to solve a real-world problem.

Ways to Raise the Technology Integration

What would be some ways to raise the level of technology integration?

After studying causes of teen bullying and violence, collaborative teams of ninth-grade students will propose a plan (cognitive complexity) to address teen bullying in their school or community (real-world learning). Students must collaborate with community resources (student engagement) and use two or more appropriate technologies (technology integration).

New Level of Technology Integration

What would be the new level of technology integration on the Create Excellence Framework?

Cognitive complexity: Students use complex thinking in analyzing the type and frequency of bullying that affects middle- and high-grades students and decision-making skills regarding what to include in the character education skit (the team created multiple versions of a skit appropriate for each grade level and acted out the skits for middle school classes).

Student engagement: Students designed their message, presentation format, and sought out counselors from the teen violence center for advice and assistance in mentoring the elementary students on the *Safe Zone* blog.

Real-world learning: Bullying is a real issue for teens and preteens; students presented to a group outside of their own school, creating an impact beyond their own school through interactions with middle school students.

Technology integration: The electronic blog format was chosen as a more inviting anonymous method for posting bullying concerns; the team also created a screencast for training purposes for students in grades 6–12, demonstrating how to use the blog.

Real-World Learning Framework for Secondary Schools © 2016 Solution Tree Press • solution-tree.com
Visit **go.solution-tree.com/instruction** to download this page.

Websites With Lessons Embedding Technologies

LearnZillion is a free learning site that provides Common Core–aligned lessons with video explanations, assessments, and progress reporting. The site offers more than two thousand teacher-created lessons. Visit http://learnzillion.com to access the site.
Open Tapestry is a website that helps teachers select, organize, and share resources. Users can alter the content to meet their students' needs and add information to the site. Visit www.opentapestry.com to access the site.
PowerMyLearning is a web platform with more than one thousand digital learning activities. This free teacher resource provides an opportunity for educators to design their own playlist of activities and contribute information to the site. Visit http://powermylearning.org to access the site.
Share My Lesson is an online portal of over 250,000 digital learning resources reviewed and created by two hundred teachers. Visit www.sharemylesson.com to access the site.
EdTech Teacher offers a variety of assignments under their "Tools for Teachers" tab that include digital projects. Visit www.edtechteacher.org/index.php/teaching-technology/presentation-multimedia/lesson-plans to access the site.
University of South Florida shows examples of digital projects with varying levels of technology integration. Visit http://fcit.usf.edu/matrix/gradelevel.php to access the site.
appoLearning is a website that ranks education apps by experts. Visit www.appolearning.com/?cg=4 to access the site.

CHAPTER 5

Implementation of the Create Excellence Framework

At a professional learning community (PLC) meeting, teachers are discussing their difficulties with planning meaningful projects. Frances shares how she had a realization about her beliefs recently. She had always thought that if students were doing a "project" that at least they were involved in work that was an enhancement to their curriculum at that time. However, she confides in her colleagues that with many of these projects she often felt that something was missing—some projects seemed shallow or felt like an add-on to the curriculum, without any meaningful connection to the real world. Her PLC colleagues agree and add to the conversation. Larry shares that he always strived for the engagement aspect of the project, but sometimes the project did not connect seamlessly to the curriculum. Glen shares how he was frustrated with how to incorporate student use of technology. He knows that he, himself, is excellent at teaching and modeling with technology, but he cannot figure out how to take the time out of the instruction and curriculum to give the students the opportunity to stretch and grow personally with the content. The teachers agree that they want to find an instructional planning tool for real-world projects that could help them move forward together.

Planning is paramount when implementing the Create Excellence Framework in a classroom, school, or district. Once educators understand the rationale behind the framework, they need tools to implement the instructional changes successfully. Through this chapter, you will learn about instruction design and logistics and gain tips and critical questions to consider for designing Create Excellence Framework projects. You will also learn how professional development could look at a school or district level, and interact with the sample meeting agendas, tables, and helpful implementation instruments throughout this chapter and in the Take Action section. Through this chapter you will find many discussion tools and templates to help with this journey.

Instructional Design and Logistics

The Create Excellence Framework can help teachers adjust or even overhaul instructional planning. Although Create Excellence Framework projects do and will take more time than a typical lesson or task, we recommend that you still use them because they facilitate meaningful and deep learning. When you ask students to tell you what the most memorable learning experience they have had as a student is, or even if you consider this question in regard to your own learning, most often, the answer will involve the Create Excellence Framework elements.

Frequency

When trying to determine how often to interweave a high-level Create Excellence Framework project into your instruction, we recommend once per grading or every six to nine weeks at the beginning of implementation, and then adding more each year. This is manageable and works well to maintain your students' excitement throughout the year rather than giving them the feeling that you will never do this again. You will also find that as students have more experience with Create Excellence Framework projects, they will not take as much time. As students learn and practice these skills, they can apply them to other projects, as well.

Introductions

It is important to consider the climate of the classroom. How are you going to get your students on board and involved in the task planning? How are you going to gather ideas that meet their interests? How are you going to communicate to parents about this way of connecting with your students? Remember to involve the students—they are your target audience! An example personal learning survey is provided as a reproducible in the introduction (page 13).

When introducing the Create Excellence Framework to students, teachers have shared the components with the students by having a discussion about an actual task or project itself. This is the key behind a successful implementation of a Create Excellence Framework design. Begin by generating ideas from the class for the activity. You may decide to begin with the content standards in mind, or you may choose to begin with a classroom, school, or community issue. Then continue the conversation by discussing the targeted level of framework components. Focus the conversation with the students on developing an understanding of the rubric for assessing the task or project, as this will address the four components of the Create Excellence Framework. The discussion should involve how the task or project always focuses on the entire Create Excellence Framework comprehensively—involving all of the components. Especially emphasize with the students opportunities for the project to be student driven.

Collaboration With Colleagues

A great way to thoroughly think through the task or project planning is to utilize the list of critical questions in the Create Task or Project Planning Chart (see table 5.1). The tool can also be used as a checklist as teachers are developing their instruction or after the development. This is helpful to use in a peer-discussion format as well.

While real-world learning is the goal, sometimes it is challenging to make the real-world connection to the required curriculum. In that case, consider beginning with Cognitive Complexity or Student Engagement in planning tasks or projects. For example, an approach that teachers may choose is to focus on cognitive complexity or student engagement first for a more targeted task or project. Notice that technology integration is not the initial focus in planning a Create Excellence Framework project but should be considered as flowing from the natural development of the instruction. For example, if you know that you would like your task or project to focus on a particular content standard and at a certain level of Bloom's revised taxonomy, this may be a case where you would like to design your task or project with cognitive complexity. If you are interested in a particular topic at your school or in your community that you believe your students would want to study, you may want to plan from the real-world learning focus. If you are focusing on how you differentiate for content, process, or product, and collaboration techniques, you would probably want to begin by thinking

Table 5.1: Create Task or Project Planning Chart

DESIGN ANGLE	CRITICAL QUESTIONS
INITIAL TASK OR PROJECT PLANNING	
• Identify the standard, or determine the real-world problem that connects to students' lives. • Develop the objectives. • Determine the task or project.	• Is the task or project teacher or student directed? (Note that, to make a stronger impact, student-directed instruction is the goal.) • Does the task or project involve all four components at level 3 or higher?
PLANNING FOR STUDENT LEARNING	
Real-World Learning • Examine the level of authentic learning required in the standard. Remember that standards are a minimum expectation; learning can go beyond the standard. For example, suppose a sixth-grade class is working on the standard, "Write arguments to support claims with clear reasons and relevant evidence" (W.6.1). While this standard does not mention real-world learning, it is perfect for authentic applications (for example, persuasive letters to the city council).	• Did you begin with ideas from your students or from something you know they are concerned about or passionate about? • What is the authentic-learning connection? • Does the learning provide a solution to an open-ended problem? • Does the content connect to the students' lives? • How can the students have an emotional connection to the project? • Does learning *investigate* and *simulate* the real world (level 3), or does learning really affect the real world? • Are students really having an influence on the classroom, school, or community (level 4)? • Are students really having an impact on a national or global issue or problem (level 5)? • Are students really collaborating (not just cooperating) with field experts (level 5)?
Cognitive Complexity • Examine the level of thinking required in the standard. What verb is stated in the standard? If students are supposed to infer, then develop a task or project that aligns to this cognitive skill. • Identify which cognitive-complexity level on the Create Excellence Framework you will be working on. ♦ The revised Bloom's thinking skills build on each other. If the standard calls for a student to infer (a cognitive process within the Understand level), the teacher can design an assignment at the Analyze level or higher. The student will learn the inferring standard *and* go beyond that level to learn at the Analyze level. • Determine if the project aligns to curriculum or standards.	• What is the Bloom's level of student thinking in the task? • Will the student work produce this level of thinking? • Is the project standards based and part of the curriculum? • Is the project teacher directed (level 3) or student directed (level 4)? • Do students have opportunities to generate open-ended, high-level thinking questions (level 5)?

Continued →

DESIGN ANGLE	CRITICAL QUESTIONS
Student Engagement • Focus on significant content. ▴ Define the problem with the students. ▴ What do they need to know about the problem? Use digital tools to research the problem. • Examine the level of student engagement required in the problem and in the standards. Remember that standards are a minimum expectation—learning and student engagement can go beyond the standard. ▴ For example, suppose a middle-grades class is working on the social studies standard, "Assess options for individual and collective action to address local, regional, and global problems by engaging in self-reflection, strategy identification, and complex causal reasoning" (D4.7.6–8, 9–12). ▴ Students are engaged in self-directed learning when they "assess options for individual and collective action to address problems" and when they identify strategies to solve a problem.	• Are students given choices in tasks or projects? • Are tasks or projects differentiated by content, process, or product (level 3)? • Are students using an inquiry-based approach to learning? Are students collaborating with each other (level 4)? • Are students initiating their own inquiry-based projects? Are they thoroughly immersed in the problem? Are students engaged in full implementation from topic development to solution? Do students initiate appropriate collaborations pertaining to their project (level 5)?
Technology Integration • It is best to consider the other components first and then select technology to support the task or project. ▴ Focus on student use of technology, rather than teacher use, when solving the problem. ▴ Students should be having a choice as to what technology to use, but the use of technology should be seamless in solving the problem. • The technology needs to be a necessary and integral method of accomplishing the task or project. • Objectives need to support the task or project requirements.	• Is student use of technology planned? • If the technology is an add-on (level 3), what could be done to make it more integrated (levels 4–5)? • Does technology promote collaboration among students and teacher (level 4)? • Are several technology tools used (level 5)?
ASSESSMENT DEVELOPMENT • Develop the appropriate type of assessment to match the task or project. Incorporate the key components of the framework for the level targeted for the task or project. • Develop assessment criteria. Rubrics are needed to help in assessing open-ended portions of the project, such as the solution to an open-ended mathematics problem, a presentation, or a written project. • Implement the Student Work Management Chart (table 5.2, page 92) that outlines steps to complete the project and the time line for the project, and identifies students' responsibilities.	• What is the student product, and how is it going to be assessed? • Does the assessment of the project align to the objectives and the intended Create Excellence Framework levels? • Were students involved in developing the assessment criteria?

about the student-engagement angle. Regardless, it is best to avoid starting your plan by considering which technology you want students to use. Because technology is the vehicle through which the other elements can be delivered, starting with technology inherently and unnecessarily limits the level of student learning, student engagement, and student decision making.

Communication With Parents

Parents will be both excited and possibly nervous about this opportunity for their child. It is important to remember to emphasize that you are trying to give the students an opportunity for a student-driven task or project versus a teacher-driven task or project. Consider communicating with parents via a letter to explain the Create Excellence Framework and how it will be used to improve learning (see a sample parent letter in figure 5.1; a reproducible version of the letter is also available on page 106) and help students develop skills so they can become college and career ready. It is also important to be sure that you monitor the work that the student does as an individual versus in a group. Oftentimes, group projects are perceived negatively by parents due to certain students always ending up doing all of the work. It is important to ensure individual accountability and learning for all.

Dear Parent,

During this school year, your student will experience a new way of learning. We will be having lots of conversations and taking many ideas from the students' interests to drive the learning when possible.

The Create Excellence Framework for real-world learning will guide how we strive to complete the projects and tasks and push our learning.

- Your student will be striving to learn at levels beyond rote memorization and instead creating new connections and evaluating her or his learning.

- Your student will be experiencing and incorporating meaning from his or her own life and world into the tasks and projects.

- Your student will be working with the teacher as a partner in learning, consulting with experts, interacting with students in teams, and having choice in products, process, and content.

- Your student will be using technology to complete tasks and projects in a seamless fashion while enhancing learning.

The goal is that throughout the course of the year your students will be able to experience student-directed tasks and projects in addition to the typical teacher-directed tasks and projects.

The exciting part of using a lesson-planning tool of this kind for this class is that I can make sure all of the vital learning components are included and that your student is experiencing challenging and well-rounded tasks and projects.

I appreciate your support in this endeavor of my instruction and of your student's inevitable growth! Feel free to ask any questions that you may have.

Sincerely,

Teacher

Figure 5.1: Sample parent letter.

Teacher's Role in Facilitating Tasks and Projects

When you implement the task or project, the students will need facilitation and partnering from you. What this role looks like varies depending on the type of class and age, independence, and capability level of the students. One example is a teacher meeting with the students to brainstorm ideas for how to narrow their interests for their topic of study. Another partnering example is a teacher meeting with a pair or group of students to help the students organize how they are going to design their study. This help may be in different forms, such as helping students consider ways to engage with peers and topic experts or providing students with genuine yet reasonable product options. Another way to partner with students is to work with them to develop a rubric that outlines criteria for success. Groups should outline the tasks that need to be completed with due dates and the person responsible. As groups check off items completed, teachers can formatively identify if the groups are on target.

To help students manage the magnitude of tasks, projects, and scenarios, tools can be used to organize their group work. Great organizational tools can be found in *Students Taking Charge* (Sulla, 2011). We suggest utilizing a student work management chart (table 5.2) adapted from that resource. With this tool, students can define their tasks and organize the work to be done in the responsibilities and design time lines for the completion of the learning. Not all tasks and projects will necessarily be the one-week length on this chart, but some will. The example in table 5.2 provides an idea of how a small group notes members' jobs and the work is completed.

Table 5.2: Student Work Management Chart

	NOTE CARDS	GRAPHIC ORGANIZER	DESIGN PROTOTYPE	SKYPE WITH OUTSIDE EXPERT	PEER EDITING WITH TWO STUDENTS	FINAL COPY
Ainsley	X—Oct. 1			X—Oct. 4		X—Oct. 8
Noel		X—Oct. 3		X—Oct. 4		X—Oct. 8
Parker			X—Oct. 4-7		X—Oct. 6	X—Oct. 8
Darby			X—Oct. 4-7		X—Oct. 6	X—Oct. 8

Source: Adapted from Sulla, 2011.

Professional Development Support

As seen in this chapter's opening scenario, teachers are seeking opportunities for collaboration and professional growth. If you are a principal or teacher who wants to have your school or professional learning community (PLC) implement the Create Excellence Framework at the grade level, program level, or school level, some considerations need to be incorporated in the planning. The following is an outline of a professional development plan that could be used to train teachers on the Create Excellence Framework and implementation.

1. Train all of the targeted teachers on the Create Excellence Framework—make sure all of those who will be using the Create Excellence Framework in the classroom understand the different components in the same way.

   Day 1 learning targets:

   - Identify the Create Excellence Framework components.
   - Describe the revised Bloom's taxonomy skills.
   - Classify assignments at various Bloom's levels.
   - Create assignments and assessments at the highest three levels of Bloom's revised taxonomy.
   - Describe the levels of real-world applications.
   - Analyze the level of real-world applications in sample assignments.
   - Design assignments and assessments at the highest three levels of the Create Excellence Framework's real-world learning component.

   Day 2 learning targets:

   - Identify the different student-engagement levels.
   - Classify assignments based on their student-engagement level.
   - Create assignments and assessments at the highest three levels of the Create Excellence Framework's student-engagement component.
   - Describe the technology-integration levels.
   - Determine the technology-integration level in featured sample projects.
   - Describe assignments and assessments at the highest three levels of the Create Excellence Framework's technology-integration component.

   Follow-up sessions:

   - Share assignments implemented in classes.
   - Identify ways to address implementation challenges.
   - Leave with ideas of additional Create Excellence Framework projects.

2. Provide sample lessons for the teachers to score together and discuss. Emphasize the difference between the teacher-driven task or project and the student-driven task or project levels.

3. Incorporate study-group discussions throughout the school year about:
   - Tasks and projects that the teachers have designed (see Create Task or Project Planning Chart, table 5.1, pages 89–90).
   - Student work when the framework tasks and projects have been completed (see Discussion Tool for Student Work, table 5.3, page 94).

Table 5.3 (page 94) is a tool for teachers to use in study groups to discuss whether their task or project was designed in such a way that it produced the desired and targeted student outcomes as planned. This tool is essential to use, and it is critical to review student work because although teachers can do all kinds of planning, until they look critically at their level of work on the assessment, they do not truly know the student's level of achievement. A reproducible version of the tool can be found on page 107. Also see the "Create Excellence Framework Task or Project Template" reproducible on page 104 for an additional tool to plan a lesson or project using the Create Excellence Framework.

Table 5.3: Discussion Tool for Student Work

Student Product	• Did the students in the class work through the task or project as teacher or student directed? • Was the task or project low- or high-level learning? • Did the product designed to assess student learning align with the task or project? • Did your scoring instruments align learning targets of the task or project? • What needs to be revised? • Does the student product align with each planned level of each component in the Create Excellence Framework?
Real-World Learning	• Did students connect to the task or project? • In what ways did students make the task or project more authentic as they worked through the solution? • Did you find them adding in their own ideas? • What would you strengthen or do differently?
Cognitive Complexity	• Did the students perform at the level designed for the task or project? • What revisions are needed? • What revised Bloom's taxonomy level do you believe the task or project ended up being at? Do you believe the student work met the thinking level intended? • Did students have opportunities to raise questions?
Student Engagement	• What choices did students have? • How did partnering with the teacher work out? • In what ways did students work with others in and out of the classroom?
Technology Integration	• What variety of technology was used? • Did students use multiple technologies within a single task or project? • Did the technology feel seamless, or was it an add-on? • If the technology is an add-on, what could be done to make it more integrated?

District-Level Implementation

For a district to implement the Create Excellence Framework in schools, it is first and foremost important to have buy-in from all administrators and building leaders. Then, we also recommend having a districtwide philosophy-building session about why you would choose this initiative. Suggested inspiration for this would be to show a presentation that explains the rationale and inspiration behind choosing the Create Excellence Framework as a district initiative. See http://create-excellence.com for additional resources.

A couple of the districts that have implemented the framework host competitions for using this framework with their teachers. They ask all of their K–12 teachers to participate in designing and implementing a lesson (see the reproducible "Create Lesson Plan Template," page 102, for an example of one district's lesson plan template). After designing and submitting a lesson plan, teachers participated in rating the lessons with the framework and gave suggestions for improvement. The objective was to increase real-world learning in the classroom, while enhancing the other components of cognitive complexity, student engagement, and technology integration.

Tools for Designing and Managing Create Excellence Framework Tasks and Projects

It will probably take more time to develop a Create Excellence Framework task or project than a typical assignment. However, when implementing the task or project, the students will take charge of learning and the classroom will be more student led. Elizabeth A. City, Richard F. Elmore, Sarah E. Fiarman, and Lee Teitel (2009), authors of *Instructional Rounds in Education*, state that the "task predicts performance" (p. 30). Thus, if assignments are of low quality and not aligned to standards, then learning also will be negatively impacted. However, if teachers take the time to design high-quality tasks and projects, there can potentially be better learning results.

When students are working in groups, it can be challenging for the teacher to determine a grade or score for the work and hold each of the individual students accountable. First and foremost, it is important to remember that the learning is the most critical part of the task or project—more so than the grading of it! Do not let the scoring get in the way of the learning! The Group Collaboration Feedback Instrument (figure 5.2) is a tool that students can use to help give informal feedback on how the group performed and on how members are contributing (see page 108 for a reproducible version of this figure). However, this is something that needs to be used with critical consideration of the classroom environment and awareness of a positive culture. Students need to understand that this is a way to provide feedback to classmates to help them improve and to point out their strengths. The teacher needs to consider this as part of how the overall task or project is assessed and should emphasize that the students need to work together and support each other's growth.

Each group member should rate the following statements on a scale of 1 to 4, with 1 being the lowest score and 4 being the highest. Rate independently. Be honest in your ratings!

	1 BEGINNING	2 DEVELOPING	3 ACCOMPLISHED	4 EXEMPLARY
The group actively began working on the task or project without prompting from the teacher.				
The group interacted to organize, plan, and generate ideas and plans for the task or project solution.				
The group used the Student Work Management Chart (table 5.2, page 92) to plan its work and divide responsibilities and keep track of its time line.				

Figure 5.2: Group collaboration feedback instrument.

Continued →

Each group member should rate the following statements on a scale of 1 to 4, with 1 being the lowest score and 4 being the highest. Rate independently. Be honest in your ratings!

	1 BEGINNING	2 DEVELOPING	3 ACCOMPLISHED	4 EXEMPLARY
Each group member contributed and participated for the duration of the task or project planning and work.				
Each member was encouraged to voice his or her opinions for how to achieve each component of the task or project.				
The group worked through conflicts by discussing options and reaching consensus.				
Group members used their time efficiently.				
Each group member collaborated well with the others.				
The group learned, initiated, and used the inquiry-based approach for finding its solution.				

Teachers may also need a tool to help them determine if their task or project is a well-rounded, project-based scenario that will lend itself well to the underlying base of the Create Excellence Framework components. Figure 5.3 provides a tool to preassess a project for these features. A reproducible version of this tool is available on page 109.

The teacher may find it helpful for the students to use a clarification questionnaire to help them determine what roles they want to assume during the project and to help the teacher meet students' individual learning needs (see figure 5.4). A reproducible version of this questionnaire is available on page 110.

Case Study of a Project in Action

In this section, we present a case study to show how the ideas originated from the teacher and students in the classroom, blossomed into a project, and played out into the instruction. We encourage you to take time to interact with the case study and consider the Take Action activities (page 99).

After a classmate tore a ligament in her ankle when she slipped on loose gravel, her class began discussing how they could convince the town to build safe walking and running trails. As they orally brainstormed ideas and information they needed, each student added ideas to Etherpad (http://etherpad.com) so they would be

THE TASK OR PROJECT IS . . .	YES	NO
1. Stemming from an idea important to the students		
2. Designed within the student's level of success		
3. Content related and relevant to the learner's needs		
4. Designed to stretch the student's achievement level		
5. Devised to engage the student in researching and processing information		
6. Designed to fit the time frame		
7. Providing the student experience with new learning		
8. Filled with opportunities to self-guide students' learning		
9. Includes accessible resources and materials		
10. Designed with a framework for students to add progress checkpoints		
11. Designed with an assessment tool that is included		

Figure 5.3: Checklist for preassessing a task or project.

For help with project planning, have students complete this questionnaire, and review the responses to determine your students' interests.

Questions to get ideas for a project from students:

- What are the most interesting topics of this study for me?
- Consider the content being studied in class currently. Which part would make a good project?
- If I could design any project, what would I want to do? What do I want to learn? What would be the time line?
- How do I typically like to work on a project—alone, in partners, in groups?
- Do I like to collaborate or work with people beyond the classroom?

Questions to refine the project designed by the teacher:

- Which part of the project am I most excited about?
- What do I want to learn most from this project?
- What will be my time line?
- How will I meet the requirements of the progress checkpoints?
- Where can I find the material and resources?
- What are my greatest concerns or needs related to the assignment?
- What do I need to do before I begin the project?
- How will I collaborate with my peers? Will I want to work alone, with a partner, or in a group?
- How will I partner with my teacher? Others?
- How will the product look when it is finished?
- How will technology be involved in my project?
- How will I present the project?
- How will my work be assessed?

Figure 5.4: Sample student clarification questionnaire for an engaging, real-world project.

visible to all students on the projector from the teacher's computer. Information they knew they would need included: pictures of roads and streets around the town, pictures of safe walking areas (from another town), material outlining the impact of walking and low-impact exercise, cost, location, fitness habits of citizens, how much support they would have, citizens' thoughts about the county building walking trails, who to talk to at the town or county level for advice in zoning, what the zoning laws and regulations are, how they can convince the officials, and whether local businesses would donate to the cause.

It was quickly evident that different students had interests in different aspects of the problem. The students split themselves into teams according to task. One team worked on the legal aspects, one on health and fitness benefits, one surveyed the community, one designed the walking trail, one worked on fundraising aspects, and one created a multimedia presentation. The whole class discussed tasks, projects, and assessment. Everyone had input into the self-monitoring (each student would keep a personal blog that only the teacher had access to) and assessment rubrics for the project as a whole. The teacher coached each group, facilitated the creation of a tasks and responsibilities list that the recorder entered into List After List (http://listafterlist.com) during the discussion, and a group contract was designed and signed by all. The teams used either Tracky (http://tracky.com) or Timetonote (http://timetonote.com) to manage their project. Most teams used Creately (http://creately.com) or Mind42 (http://mind42.com) to map out their network of ideas and Google Docs to write up their documents so different team members could contribute to the writing. The survey team decided to use Google Forms for its survey, and members obtained emails from the chamber of commerce in their town.

The teacher consulted with the teams on designing appropriate interview or survey questions. The team designing the walking trail contacted and visited a local architect whose specialty was exercise trail design in a large city nearby. The architect led the team in using the PadCAD (http://padCAD.com) tool to design the walking trail. He was most helpful in pointing out which legal aspects to look for, what types of streets to look for, the importance of lighting, and maintenance tips. Later he remotely reviewed and critiqued the team's design when the team was finished. One of the students on the architect team emailed the legal team from class while in the architect's office to keep in communication with the rest of the class.

Once the survey and interview data were collected, compiled, and analyzed in an Excel spreadsheet, the teacher took this opportunity for a whole-class mathematics lesson on probability and statistics with this authentic student-collected data. The communication team then used Google Drive to compose a letter of proposal to community businesses and civic organizations. Some students visited businesses and civic groups in person to promote their cause. The multimedia team began teaching itself how to use ReviewStudio (www.reviewstudio.com), a collaborative video site, and scouring the Internet for royalty-free photos it may use. After school, team members took pictures of local streets and potential sites with their smartphones.

The fundraising team met with a mentor from a local university to learn how to raise funds for a not-for-profit project. The team then designed its plan and began contacting donors and local businesses with a campaign for collecting funds. Team members researched and developed a multifaceted plan for gathering donations and also met with businesses, conducted a phone campaign, and wrote emails and letters.

The legal team researched any legal issues related to a walking trail, interviewed the county judge, the mayor, a banker, a physical therapist, a fitness trainer, and a local doctor. After all data, pictures, video, and so on were gathered, the walking-trail team submitted its design, and the health benefits team submitted its information and interview data, the whole class discussed the message that it really wanted to portray in the multimedia presentation they would give to the town council. The multimedia team completed its video, the class critiqued it, and the multimedia team revised again in ReviewStudio. The walking trail was put on the agenda for the next town council meeting. Each team elected one student to be on the presentation team while the rest of the students were in the audience. Having practiced the presentation with the principal, other teachers, and students, the presentation team was ready and gave the presentation perfectly.

Since the fundraising team had secured financial commitment for half of the cost of the walking trail, the town council approved its plan. Many of the students volunteered on Saturdays to help to build the walking trail.

Conclusion

Thoughtful planning of the Create Excellence Framework implementation is important because our task of reaching students and ensuring what they learn is important. We provide the steps and tools suggested in this book for implementing the framework at the classroom, school, or district level to help facilitate a smoother path to your instructional success.

Discussion Questions

1. What are some ways students can generate ideas for a Create Excellence Framework project based on a topic they are studying?
2. What is your style as a teacher? Would you tend to begin with the standards or the real-world topic to generate your task?
3. How comfortable are you in involving your students with developing a rubric and targets for a task or project?
4. What concerns might you have about communicating with parents about the Create Excellence Framework?

Take Action

1. Consider an idea for a Create task or project. Use table 5.1 (pages 89–90) to jot down your idea. Share your idea with a colleague.
2. Use table 5.3, Discussion Tool for Student Work (page 94), to discuss completed student work from a Create Excellence Framework project to see if the work correlates to the targets of the project.
3. Choose a group of students to pilot the Group Collaboration Feedback Instrument (see figure 5.2, page 95). What kind of feedback do you get from your students working in groups? Do your students prefer this format?
4. Another angle that can help you discern whether your task or project is ready for use with your class is the "Checklist for Preassessing a Task or Project" reproducible (page 109). Pair with a colleague and apply this checklist to your tasks or projects. Discuss the checklists, and note the Framework elements. In what areas are you strong, and in what areas are you lacking?
5. Using Sample Student Clarification Questionnaire for an Engaging, Real-World Project (figure 5.4, page 97), have students give you feedback in general about what kind of project they would like to do. Then have students give specific feedback about a preliminary project idea. How can you incorporate their feedback?
6. Using the Create Excellence Framework, rate the level of the case study in this chapter (page 96) for each of the Framework components, and justify the rating. What suggestions would you give to bump it even higher?

7. Analyze the case study (page 96), and answer the following questions.
   ◆ How would you describe the real-world learning scenario and connection to the students?
   ◆ What standards are addressed?
   ◆ How are each of the Create Excellence Framework components addressed?
   ◆ How could you convert this scenario to a lesson plan?
   ◆ What assessment would you design for this scenario?
   ◆ What formative assessments would you use with this scenario?

Final Thoughts

So why change instructional practices? This book was designed out of passion and a need to share great changes that are happening in education. With the Create Excellence Framework, teachers are transforming their ways of thinking—focusing on how to connect with students through real-world learning. Even though this kind of real-world instruction does not necessarily happen every day in each classroom, educators have an appreciation for each component and how the pieces combine to form a comprehensive lesson. Amid a world of constant change, the Create Excellence Framework can provide a foundation to manage this change and ensure high-level, real-world, standards-based instruction that remains at the forefront for our students.

The Create Excellence Framework is a lesson-planning framework that guides students, teachers, and parents in thinking about learning in a different yet comprehensive way. Teachers can aspire for the upper levels of the framework, levels 4 and 5, which are student directed. Teachers can use the framework to plan lessons that will deeply engage students in self-directed learning experiences, resulting in students being eager to come to school, intrinsically motivated to learn more, and prepared for the rigor of higher education or high-skill workplaces.

When knowledge and skills are embedded in real-world learning, students will see the connections in content knowledge and skills in the standards. While many teachers and principals are highly concerned with the acquisition of this knowledge and these skills, we believe that intentionally designing learning experiences to be unified around real-world concepts and ideas is the key. By using real-world themes and essential questions to integrate their learning objectives and align content standards, students have an authentic context for the projects and tasks they undertake. Students will also achieve a deeper level of understanding because of the integration of the standards in real-world themes and experiences. Students will begin to see that everything is related (Martinez, 2014).

National content standards and teacher standards emphasize students leading their own learning while engaging in critical-thinking tasks and projects and applying their knowledge in real-world contexts using 21st century tools. Therefore, educators must plan instructional experiences that involve real-world learning, high levels of cognitive complexity, student engagement, and technology integration. If teachers embed these components into their teaching, students and teachers can be confident that learning targets will be met.

If teachers are going to demonstrate being highly effective, and if our students are going to take responsibility for their own learning, then teachers need a planning framework to help organize instruction for student learning of these new standards. We suggest addressing these challenges with quality instructional planning through the Create Excellence Framework. To design a comprehensive project that truly encompasses real-world learning and all components for student learning and growth in the 21st century classroom, we assert that the Create Excellence Framework is an integral design framework that complements any set of curriculum standards. Our research, framework, and sample projects demonstrate a design for student learning with more depth and breadth than simply teaching the standards in isolation. With the real-world learning component tying it all together, we believe that this comprehensive student learning will have far-reaching results such as higher test scores, increased student excitement about learning, and increased student responsibility for their own learning.

Change needs to happen. For decades, many leading educators have been admired for innovation and educational initiatives for change. Now is the time to press onward with highly effective instructional experiences that incorporate authentic-learning experiences connected to the real world. This is an exciting time in education. We have the opportunity to partner with students to encourage them to take responsibility for their own learning, generate their own questions, design projects, facilitate discussions, assess peers, and meet with outside experts. Embrace the challenge. Let the Create Excellence Framework transform your classroom!

Create Lesson Plan Template

Teacher: _____ Grade Level: _____ Create Level: _____

School: _____ Course/Class: _____ Date of Lesson: _____

Content Connection (Standards section):
Overall Unit Goal:
Learning Targets/Objectives:
Lesson Description (Brief overview of this specific lesson as it relates to overall unit and general description of how the lesson is to be implemented):

Create Excellence Framework Rating

CREATE COMPONENT	LEVEL	JUSTIFICATION
Real-World Learning		
Cognitive Complexity		
Student Engagement		
Technology Integration		

page 1 of 2

Sequence of Strategies and Activities

STRATEGY OR ACTIVITY	TIME REQUIRED	SPECIFIC SKILL OR CONTENT CONNECTION	STUDENT ASSESSMENT (DESCRIBE AND SPECIFY FORMATIVE OR SUMMATIVE)	PLANNED DIFFERENTIATION

Attachments

- Please attach three student work samples associated with this lesson (required).
- Please attach any supporting files or resources (PowerPoint files, graphic organizers, and so on; encouraged but not required).

Questions for Reflection

1. What went especially well with this lesson, and why?

2. What lesson components would you refine when or if you deliver the lesson again?

3. How did (or could) the use of technology impact student engagement, delivery of content, or student performance associated with this lesson?

Source: Adapted from Hart County School District. (2011). Create task/project template. Hart County, KY: Author. Used with permission.

Create Excellence Framework Task or Project Template

On the first page of the lesson plan, include the following information.

Project title: Create a fun and interesting, catchy title.

Grade level or course: List grade level for K–8 assignment, but list the course for high school.

Learning objectives: Start each objective with "Students will . . ." followed by a verb and the learning goal. You can have more than one objective.

Standards: List the standards being addressed, such as the Common Core State Standards, Next Generation Science Standards, and so on.

Project options: Give students multiple choices for completing the assignment. Consider offering several technology options.

Resources needed: List items, including software and web tools, needed for the assignment.

On the second page of the template, include the project title again and the following.

Scenario: Create a real-world learning scenario that establishes the context of the project. This could be where students simulate real-world roles or actually do something like writing a public service announcement that will be shared with the school.

Project tasks: Insert student directions for the assignment. This is what will be copied and given to students. Add extensions to the project (not required).

Scoring rubric: For younger students you may want to use a checklist; for older students, a four-point rubric. On the four-point rubric, put the objective in the first column, and then identify rubric headings.

Scoring Rubric

	1 SIGNIFICANT REVISION NEEDED	2 SOME REVISION NEEDED	3 PROFICIENT	4 EXCEEDS EXPECTATIONS
Write the first learning objective in this space.				
If applicable, write the second learning objective in this space.				
If applicable, write the third learning objective in this space.				

Sample student work: Include a sample project with the lesson plan illustrating what the finished product should look like.

Create Excellence Framework rating: Use the following table to evaluate the project for each component of the framework. At what level does each component rate: 1 (Knowing), 2 (Practicing), 3 (Investigating), 4 (Integrating), or 5 (Specializing)?

Create Excellence Framework Rating

CREATE ANALYSIS		
CREATE COMPONENT	**LEVEL**	**JUSTIFICATION**
Real-World Learning		
Cognitive Complexity		
Student Engagement		
Technology Integration		

page 2 of 2

Sample Parent Letter

Dear Parent,

During this school year, your student will experience a new way of learning. We will be having lots of conversations and taking many ideas from the students' interests to drive the learning when possible.

The Create Excellence Framework for real-world learning will guide how we strive to complete the projects and tasks and push our learning.

- Your student will be striving to learn at levels beyond rote memorization and instead creating new connections and evaluating her or his learning.
- Your student will be experiencing and incorporating meaning from his or her own life and world into the tasks and projects.
- Your student will be working with the teacher as a partner in learning, consulting with experts, interacting with students in teams, and having choice in products, process, and content.
- Your student will be using technology to complete tasks and projects in a seamless fashion while enhancing learning.

The goal is that throughout the course of the year your students will be able to experience student-directed tasks and projects in addition to the typical teacher-directed tasks and projects.

The exciting part of using a lesson-planning tool of this kind for this class is that I can make sure all of the vital learning components are included and that your student is experiencing challenging and well-rounded tasks and projects.

I appreciate your support in this endeavor of my instruction and of your student's inevitable growth! Feel free to ask any questions that you may have.

Sincerely,

Teacher

Discussion Tool for Student Work

Student Product	• Did the students in the class work through the task or project as teacher or student directed?
	• Was the task or project low- or high-level learning?
	• Did the product designed to assess student learning align with the task or project?
	• Did your scoring instruments align learning targets of the task or project?
	• What needs to be revised?
	• Does the student product align with each planned level of each component in the Create Excellence Framework?
Real-World Learning	• Did students connect to the task or project?
	• In what ways did students make the task or project more authentic as they worked through the solution?
	• Did you find them adding in their own ideas?
	• What would you strengthen or do differently?
Cognitive Complexity	• Did the students perform at the level designed for the task or project?
	• What revisions are needed?
	• At what revised Bloom's taxonomy level do you believe the task or project ended up being? Do you believe the student work met the thinking level intended?
	• Did students have opportunities to raise questions?
Student Engagement	• What choices did students have?
	• How did partnering with the teacher work out?
	• In what ways did students work with others in and out of the classroom?
Technology Integration	• What variety of technology was used?
	• Did students use multiple technologies within a single task or project?
	• Did the technology feel seamless, or was it an add-on?
	• If the technology is an add-on, what could be done to make it more integrated?

Group Collaboration Feedback Instrument

Each group member should rate the following statements on a scale of 1 to 4, with 1 being the lowest score and 4 being the highest. Rate independently. Be honest in your ratings!

	1 BEGINNING	2 DEVELOPING	3 ACCOMPLISHED	4 EXEMPLARY
The group actively began working on the task or project without prompting from the teacher.				
The group interacted to organize, plan, and generate ideas and plans for the task or project solution.				
The group used the Student Work Management Chart (table 5.2, page 92) to plan their work and divide responsibilities and keep track of its time line.				
Each group member contributed and participated for the duration of the task or project planning and work.				
Each member was encouraged to voice his or her opinions for how to achieve each component of the task or project.				
The group worked through conflicts by discussing options and reaching consensus.				
Group members used their time efficiently.				
Each group member collaborated well with the others.				
The group learned, initiated, and used the inquiry-based approach for finding its solution.				

Checklist for Preassessing a Task or Project

THE TASK OR PROJECT IS . . .	YES	NO
1. Stemming from an idea important to the students		
2. Designed within the student's level of success		
3. Content related and relevant to the learner's needs		
4. Designed to stretch the student's achievement level		
5. Devised to engage the student in researching and processing information		
6. Designed to fit the time frame		
7. Providing the student experience with new learning		
8. Filled with opportunities to self-guide students' learning		
9. Includes accessible resources and materials		
10. Designed with a framework for students to add progress checkpoints		
11. Designed with an assessment tool that is included		

Sample Student Clarification Questionnaire
for an Engaging, Real-World Project

For help with project planning, have students complete this questionnaire, and review the responses to determine your students' interests.

Questions to get ideas for a project from students:

- What are the most interesting topics of this study for me?
- Consider the content being studied in class currently. Which part would make a good project?
- If I could design any project, what would I want to do? What do I want to learn? What would be the time line?
- How do I typically like to work on a project—alone, in partners, in groups?
- Do I like to collaborate or work with people beyond the classroom?

Questions to refine the project designed by the teacher:

- Which part of the project am I most excited about?
- What do I want to learn most from this project?
- What will be my time line?
- How will I meet the requirements of the progress checkpoints?
- Where can I find the material and resources?
- What are my greatest concerns or needs related to the assignment?
- What do I need to do before I begin the project?
- How will I collaborate with my peers? Will I want to work alone, with a partner, or in a group?
- How will I partner with my teacher? Others?
- How will the product look when it is finished?
- How will technology be involved in my project?
- How will I present the project?
- How will my work be assessed?

PART II

While the following projects are divided into the subject areas of English language arts (pages 113–145), mathematics (pages 147–172), social studies (pages 173–188), and science (pages 189–210), all projects are interdisciplinary, and readers should consider perusing projects from other subject areas for ideas.

The structure for projects is as follows.

- The first segment of each project lists content standards, learning objectives, and resources needed. This segment explains the background of the lesson for the teacher.
- The second segment of each project contains a short introduction, project tasks, and a scoring rubric. (This segment is reproducible for students because it provides project directions and a rubric.)
- The third segment contains sample student work to show a final product. To help readers critically examine each project, an analysis table explains how the project aligns to each of the four framework components.

WHAT IT MEANS TO BE GREEN

Source: Samantha McMahan. Used with permission.

Content: English language arts

Learning Objectives:

1. Students will create a plan of action to solve an environmental issue.
2. Students will design a blog about their environmental solution.

Standards:

Common Core English Language Arts—

- W.9–10.6 Use technology, including the Internet, to produce, publish, and update individual or shared writing products, taking advantage of technology's capacity to link to other information and to display information flexibly and dynamically (NGA & CCSSO, 2010a).
- W.9–10.7 Conduct short as well as more sustained research projects to answer a question (including a self-generated question) or solve a problem; narrow or broaden the inquiry when appropriate; synthesize multiple sources on the subject, demonstrating understanding of the subject under investigation (NGA & CCSSO, 2010a).

Next Generation Science Standards—

- HS-ESS3–4 Evaluate or refine a technological solution that reduces impacts of human activities on natural systems (Achieve, 2013).

Project Options: Students can choose any environmental topic and any medium of publication that is accessible around the world.

Resources Needed: Computer with Internet access; Google Drive; "We the People" webpage

What It Means to Be Green

Can you imagine the world without the beautiful variety of plants and animals that are familiar to us, with cars that can't run because there is no fuel source, or with water sources that are so full of chemicals that we can no longer filter and drink from them? Humans have many habits that are destructive to the world as we know it, even if we are unable to see those problems right now. What can you do to save our planet?

Project Tasks

1. In groups of three, choose an environmental issue that is relevant to your lives. It could be: alternative forms of energy, alternative fuel for cars, drilling for oil offshore or onshore, global warming, pesticides, genetically engineered crops, mountain-top removal, littering, water pollution, air pollution, endangered species of animals, or any other issue relating to the environment.

2. Create a plan of action to address the issue. This includes (1) defining the issue and (2) choosing a stance, even if it means that you believe the action is detrimental to the environment but helpful to a certain group of people. Use Google Drive for all of your writing so that all members of your group can contribute to the collaborative document.

3. Divide responsibilities among your group members, and research the issue until you feel that you are experts on the topic. This includes speaking to experts on the topic (professors in the agriculture or environmental departments at a local university would be good sources of information). Contact global organizations that take interest in your topic and consider the solutions that they suggest.

4. Create awareness of the issue. Document the impact of your effort. Complete the following activities:

   ◆ Create a blog. Thoroughly inform people about the issue on the page, including a solution or plan of action for people to take. Spread the news about the page and encourage people to read it. You need at least ten other students to log into your blog and make comments about your plan.

   ◆ Create a petition about your issue on the "We the People" webpage (http://petitions .whitehouse.gov). If there is already one created, then add your support to it.

Scoring Rubric

	1 SIGNIFICANT REVISION NEEDED	2 SOME REVISION NEEDED	3 PROFICIENT	4 EXCEEDS EXPECTATIONS
Objective 1: Students will create a plan of action to solve an environmental issue.	• Group members failed to contact both an expert and a global organization and did not conduct any paper or electronic research. • The finished product is not appropriate for the task, purpose, and audience. Students did not collaborate to design a plan of action to solve their selected environmental issue, or plan is not logical and much work is needed. • Students did not post petitions concerning their environmental issue on "We the People" website.	• Group members failed to contact either an expert or a global organization, and the paper or electronic research is somewhat unreliable or incomplete. • The finished product is not entirely appropriate for the task, purpose, and audience. Students did not collaborate to design a plan of action to solve their selected environmental issue, or plan is incomplete. The solution needs more work. • Students post poorly-written petitions concerning their environmental issue on "We the People" website.	• Group members contacted experts on their topic and global organizations and conducted paper or electronic research by using reliable sources, but more information is needed for expertise. • The finished product is appropriate for the task, purpose, and audience. Students collaborated together to design a plan of action to solve their selected environmental issue. Good solution proposal. • Students post well-developed petitions concerning their environmental issue on "We the People" website.	• Group members contacted experts on their topic and global organizations and conducted paper or electronic research by using reliable sources. • The finished product is appropriate for the task, purpose, and audience. Students collaborated with field experts to design a realistic plan of action to solve their selected environmental issue. Excellent, well thought-out solution with evidence of expert thought. • Students post well-developed petitions concerning their environmental issue on "We the People" website and monitor their petition for responses from others.
Objective 2: Students will design a blog about their environmental solution.	• The solution plan was published on a poorly designed blog. The blog makes no attempt to reach people globally. The message is poor or unconvincing. Fewer than six other students commented on their proposal, and most comments were incomplete or did not relate to the solution.	• The solution plan was published on a blog that should have better design. The blog does not reach people globally. The message is not realistic or convincing. Fewer than ten other students commented on their proposal, and some comments were incomplete or did not relate to the solution.	• The solution plan was published on a blog or other form of technology that can reach people globally. The message is not completely convincing. Ten other students commented on their proposal with related responses.	• The solution plan was published on an attractive, well-designed blog or other form of technology that can reach people globally. The message is compelling and convincing. More than ten other students commented on their proposal with logical, excellent responses.

page 2 of 2

Sample Student Work

Visit *Going Green With Radon Resistance* (http://fightradon.blogspot.com) to view a sample project. The blog presents the issue and problem, an original solution and its benefits, and (fictitious) success stories. This sample project exceeds expectations of the two objectives.

Create Excellence Framework Rating

CREATE ANALYSIS		
CREATE COMPONENT	**LEVEL**	**JUSTIFICATION**
Real-World Learning	5: Specializing	The students' solutions and petitions could impact national issues, while their blog pages have the potential to impact the world. While researching, students are required to collaborate with experts in the field.
Cognitive Complexity	5: Specializing	This project is at Bloom's Create level; students are in charge of generating a topic, planning their research and rationale, and generating an organized and persuasive webpage. They must become experts on a project that impacts our world at a global level (any environmental problem is a global problem due to the connected nature of all ecosystems).
Student Engagement	5: Specializing	This is a student inquiry-based project that leaves nearly all of the decision making up to the students, including determining a topic, conducting research, and initiating their own collaborations.
Technology Integration	4: Integrating	Students are using Google Docs, creating a blog, and posting petitions on "We the People." Part of the research requires that students use technology to communicate with global organizations that deal with the issue to obtain information and propose solutions.

SCHOOL SOLUTIONS

Source: Samantha McMahan and Sam Northern. Used with permission.

Content: English language arts

Learning Objectives:

1.   Students will defend a position using a variety of sources.
2.   Students will propose one specific way to improve the public school system.

Standards:

Common Core English Language Arts—

- RI.9–10.1 Cite strong and thorough textual evidence to support analysis of what the text says explicitly as well as inferences drawn from the text (NGA & CCSSO, 2010a).

- W.9–10.8 Gather relevant information from multiple authoritative print and digital sources, using advanced searches effectively; assess the usefulness of each source in answering the research question; integrate information into the text selectively to maintain the flow of ideas, avoiding plagiarism and following a standard format for citation (NGA & CCSSO, 2010a).

- W.9–10.7 Conduct short as well as more sustained research projects to answer a question (including a self-generated question) or solve a problem; narrow or broaden the inquiry when appropriate; synthesize multiple sources on the subject, demonstrating understanding of the subject under investigation (NGA & CCSSO, 2010a).

Project Options: The students will choose the problem that they believe still exists in the public school system and decide upon their own solution to the problem. The students will choose the forms of research that they conduct (interviewing professionals, looking at journals, and so on). The students can choose the electronic presentation format that they use, including the possibilities of a multimedia presentation, video, or documentary.

Resources Needed: Resources vary for this project, but in general students may need a computer and Internet access.

School Solutions

Problems in the public school system are not a recent development. In *To Kill a Mockingbird*, author Harper Lee is fairly critical of Alabama's public education system in the 1930s. Many of these problems still exist in our public schools today. As the determiners of our future, it is your job to take action and advocate for improvements in this system for future generations!

Project Tasks

1. First, work with a partner to locate and write down quotes from the novel that show Lee's frustration with her educational experience. For example:

    " . . . as I inched sluggishly along the treadmill of the Maycomb County school system, I could not help receiving the impression that I was being cheated out of something. Out of what I knew not, yet I did not believe that twelve years of unrelieved boredom was exactly what the state had in mind for me. (p. 33)

2. From these quotes, you and your partner create a list of *specific* problems the 1930s public school system had as illustrated by Lee's complaints. For example, the quote in question one suggests her problem is a lack of challenging and mentally stimulating activities.

3. With your partner, come up with the criteria to determine which problem is the most relevant to the current public school system and which presents the greatest obstacle to student progress.

4. Choose the problem from your compiled list that best fits the criteria.

5a. One partner must research what professionals say about the topic. They may contact educators, researchers, administrators, and so on. Find facts and statistics that illustrate why the problem exists, as well as the detrimental effects of the problem (if there are any). Compare the traits of a successful school that does not have the problem. Gather any and all information that you can find regarding the problem that you selected.

5b. The other partner will research solutions to the problem. These should be specific, reasonable solutions that can be executed in a step-by-step fashion. Find as many different solutions as possible, and then decide on the one that you believe would be most successful if implemented at your school.

6. Together, create a digital presentation. You might use SlideRocket, Prezi, or another presentation technology. It can be a multimedia presentation, video, or documentary. Partner 1's information should introduce the problem, explain why it exists, and cite professionals' opinions about the issue. Partner 2's information will outline the different potential solutions and then narrow the focus to the most effective solution. You should provide a step-by-step process to reach an intended goal for your high school; it should be reasonable, specific, and achievable over a time span of five years.

7. Present your information to the school council meeting.

Scoring Rubric

	1 SIGNIFICANT REVISION NEEDED	2 SOME REVISION NEEDED	3 PROFICIENT	4 EXCEEDS EXPECTATIONS
Objective 1: Students will defend a position using a variety of sources.	• The reliability of the sources is questionable, and there is no variety to defend their position.	• The information has been primarily obtained through reliable sources, but they are lacking variety to defend their position.	• The information has been obtained through a variety of reliable sources to persuade the audience.	• The information has been obtained through a variety of reliable sources, including professionals in the field to thoroughly persuade the audience.
Objective 2: Students will propose one specific way to improve the public school system.	• The problem does not seem to be significant; the solution is not clearly explained. The plan of action is not realistic, and the step-by-step process is not entirely clear. • The student uses a stale form of technology; it is not appropriate to task, purpose, or audience. • The students' presentation is not professional and contains many errors. • Their demeanor and speech are not formal or persuasive.	• The problem and solution are somewhat explained. The plan of action is not realistic, and the step-by-step process is not entirely clear. • The students use a somewhat new form of technology; it is not entirely appropriate to task, purpose, or audience. • The students' presentation does not have a professional appearance due to instances of informal speech, images, or mechanical errors. Their demeanor and speech are not entirely formal or persuasive.	• The problem and solution are clearly explained, but the plan of action is not realistic or the step-by-step process is not entirely clear. • The students use a new form of technology in an effective manner to present their findings. • The students' presentation is professional in appearance but contains one to two spelling or grammatical errors. Their demeanor and speech are formal and persuasive.	• The problem and the proposed solution are clearly explained with a realistic plan of action that includes a step-by-step process. • The students use a new form of technology in a creative and effective manner to present their findings. • The students' presentation is professional in appearance; there are no spelling or grammatical errors. Their demeanor and speech are formal and persuasive.

Real-World Learning Framework for Secondary Schools © 2016 Solution Tree Press • solution-tree.com
Visit **go.solution-tree.com/instruction** to download this page.

Sample Student Work

Visit www.youtube.com/watch?v=VHze4iNli3M to access a sample project. In this student work sample, the student explains the key themes of the book while utilizing several sources. The work connects the story to the current challenge of bullying and provides several solutions to the problem by using appropriate technology.

Create Excellence Framework Rating

CREATE ANALYSIS		
CREATE COMPONENT	**LEVEL**	**JUSTIFICATION**
Real-World Learning	4: Integrating	This project could impact the school, and it is shared at the school council meeting.
Cognitive Complexity	4: Integrating	The student-generated project is at the Create level—the students are generating ideas, planning a way to address a problem, and producing an original presentation.
Student Engagement	4: Integrating	Students work with a partner to determine the topic of their research and to develop ideas over the course of the project. The teacher approves their ideas and offers insight, serving as a facilitator for the student inquiry-based project.
Technology Integration	3: Investigating	Students use technology both by researching their topic and by using an unfamiliar medium to create a professional presentation that showcases their ideas. In this way, the students use several technologies to solve authentic problems with the help of another student and the teacher.

GEN-NO-CIDE

Source: Erica Cassady and Sam Northern. Used with permission.

Content: English language arts

Learning Objectives:

1. Students will conduct reliable research concerning a current act of genocide.
2. Students will compare and contrast the Holocaust to another act of genocide.
3. Students will design a project that will provide help to people being affected by acts of genocide.
4. Students will create a webpage concerning an act of genocide and promoting ways to provide relief.

Standards:

Common Core English Language Arts—

- W.8.6 Use technology, including the Internet, to produce and publish writing and present the relationships between information and ideas efficiently as well as to interact and collaborate with others (NGA & CCSSO, 2010a).
- W.8.7 Conduct short research projects to answer a question (including a self-generated question), drawing on several sources and generating additional related, focused questions that allow for multiple avenues of exploration (NGA & CCSSO, 2010a).

Project Options: Students will use various forms of technology to research and create informational webpages. Students can choose from various blogging sites or webpage builders including: Edublogs, Edmodo, Yola, Webs, SnapPages, Webnode, Weebly, Hipero, or various others. Each of these sites is free and easily accessible.

Resources Needed: Computers with Internet access; research databases; various blogging sites or webpage builders

Gen-NO-cide

Anne Frank used a diary to document her experiences during the Holocaust—an example of genocide. Genocide is still a prevalent problem in today's world.

Project Tasks

1. After reading *Anne Frank: The Diary of a Young Girl*, work in groups to search for one example of genocide that is still occurring.

2. Compare and contrast the genocide you researched to the Holocaust. You may want to consider comparing motive, impact, and groups of people affected.

3. Next, your group should research ways that your school can help the people being affected by the genocide, and create a project proposal. Seek information from an outside expert. Email or conference via Skype an expert or organization for more information. Create a table to identify several possible solutions to the problem. Identify pros and cons to each idea. Then, meet with the teacher to discuss which option is the best solution and your plan of action.

4. Finally, create an advocacy blog or website! You may use blogging websites such as Edublogs or Edmodo, or you may use webpage builders such as Yola, SnapPages, Weebly, Webnode, or Google sites.

5. Your website should be a summation of all your research. Include general information about the conflict and the comparison between the current genocide and the Holocaust.

6. The main purpose of your webpage will be to advocate for your plan in action in a different and more effective way than previous advocacy efforts. Be sure you give all the essential information, including important contact information and dates, necessary supplies, what kinds of donations you are requesting, and your project proposal.

7. Each group's webpage will be evaluated by *at least* two other groups in the class to be sure the webpage is top-notch! Provide a one-page description of how your website is different from others and more effectively advocates for your cause.

8. As a class, we will choose which proposed project we would like to carry out in our efforts to say *no* to genocide!

GENOCIDE SOLUTION	PROS	CONS

page 1 of 2

Scoring Rubric

	1 SIGNIFICANT REVISION NEEDED	2 SOME REVISION NEEDED	3 PROFICIENT	4 EXCEEDS EXPECTATIONS
Objective 1: Students will conduct reliable research concerning a current act of genocide.	• Information is inaccurate or taken from an unreliable source. • Information is not properly cited.	• Information is fairly accurate, but not taken from a reliable source. • Information is not properly cited.	• Information is accurate and taken from a reliable source. • Information is properly cited, with a few errors in citation.	• Information is accurate and taken from a highly reputable source. • Information is properly cited, with no errors.
Objective 2: Students will compare and contrast the Holocaust to another act of genocide.	• Student was not able to provide a comparison between a recent genocide and the Holocaust.	• Student listed one comparison between a recent genocide and the Holocaust, but did not contrast.	• Student listed at least two points of compare and contrast between a recent genocide and the Holocaust.	• Students listed three or more points of compare and contrast between a recent genocide and the Holocaust.
Objective 3: Students will design a project that will provide help to people being affected by acts of genocide.	• Students do not design a project that is functional. • Idea for project does not align with research.	• Two or more components of the project are missing. • Idea for project does not align with research.	• Each component of the project is logical. • Idea for project aligns with research.	• Each component of the project is excellent, logical, and detailed. • Ideas for project align perfectly with research.
Objective 4: Students will create a webpage concerning an act of genocide and promoting ways to provide relief.	• Webpage does not contain any of the required components. • Webpage is sloppy in design.	• Webpage is missing several components. • Webpage is sloppy in design.	• Webpage has all the components. • Webpage is neat in design.	• Webpage presents all the components in appealing, logical design. • Webpage is exceptional in design.

Real-World Learning Framework for Secondary Schools © 2016 Solution Tree Press • solution-tree.com
Visit **go.solution-tree.com/instruction** to download this page.

Sample Student Work

Visit https://sites.google.com/site/flavorsforfreedom/home to view a sample project. On this website the student profiles the problem of genocide in Darfur and makes comparisons with the Holocaust. It suggests solutions to the problem and ways to spread awareness.

Create Excellence Framework Rating

CREATE ANALYSIS		
CREATE COMPONENT	**LEVEL**	**JUSTIFICATION**
Real-World Learning	5: Specializing	Students work together to tackle a global issue by collaborating and seeking guidance from outside resources, such as relief organizations.
Cognitive Complexity	4: Integrating	Students generate questions and use research to develop a solution to a global issue. They design a website that uniquely advocates for the issue. In addition, students analyze two situations to determine how they are related. If students design a novel solution to a real-world problem, then it would be at Bloom's Create level.
Student Engagement	3: Investigating	Each initiative is entirely student led. Students choose what to research, what strategy to implement, and what project to choose. Students must collaborate with their group members, but also have the opportunity to collaborate with other global organizations.
Technology Integration	3: Investigating	Technology is the key component to this activity. Students use technology to research and create their advocacy websites. Students also have several different technological options available to them.

SNEAKY SNEAKER SALESMAN

Source: Erica Cassady. Used with permission.

Content: English language arts

Learning Objectives:

1. Students will create an advertisement for a new style of tennis shoe utilizing persuasive techniques.
2. Students will present the product to their peers in the form of a sales pitch.

Standards:

Common Core English Language Arts—

- RI.8.8 Delineate and evaluate the argument and specific claims in a text, assessing whether the reasoning is sound and the evidence is relevant and sufficient; recognize when irrelevant evidence is introduced (NGA & CCSSO, 2010a).
- SL.8.2 Analyze the purpose of information presented in diverse media and formats (e.g., visually, quantitatively, orally) and evaluate the motives (e.g., social, commercial, political) behind its presentation (NGA & CCSSO, 2010a).

Project Options: Students will use technology to research their products and to create an advertisement. The advertisement can take many forms or utilize various technologies. Students may choose flyers or infographics using websites such as Piktochart (http://piktochart.com) or Glogster EDU (http://edu.glogster .com/?ref=com). Students may also choose to create a commercial with technologies such as GoAnimate, Toondoo, or Xtranormal. In addition, they could make a webpage using resources such as Edublogs, Edmodo, Yola, Webs, SnapPages, Webnode, Weebly, Hipero, or various others. Finally, students may use custom shoe design tools online through companies like Nike, Adidas, or Vans.

Resources Needed: Computer with Internet access; spreadsheet or other software to track research findings; drawing paper and writing utensils; video cameras or other video software

Sneaky Sneaker Salesman

Welcome aboard! Are your tennis shoes worn or uncomfortable? Here is your chance to design new shoes. Your group is going to be responsible for launching the next big thing in tennis shoe design!

Project Tasks

Use your creativity and the power of persuasion to promote a new tennis shoe design that sells well.

1. In your group, brainstorm ideas for a new tennis shoe. Consider the design, what features the shoes will have, and what they will help the consumer to do.

2. Use your computer or tablet to look up blogs of famous runners. Email some of them to find out what they like in running shoes, what features they wish were available, and what marketing techniques they like or dislike.

3. Once you have a basic idea, interview your classmates, family, and friends to find out what they want in tennis shoes. Remember, your peers (preteens and teenagers) are your target audience. You may ask them about which color, shape, or other features they would most like in a tennis shoe. Be sure to record your answers, so that you can utilize as much of this information in your advertisement as you can.

4. Next, research advertisements for products similar to yours. Evaluate at least three advertisements for sports shoes. Which persuasive techniques are used? Use a graphic organizer to keep track of each of the persuasive techniques that you find and evaluate their purpose and motives. You may choose to replicate some of these techniques in your own advertisement.

5. You may choose to use custom shoe designs online through companies like Nike, Adidas, or Vans to design your shoe. You could also sketch a prototype.

6. Use the persuasive techniques you have learned in class, as well as techniques you found in your research, to create your own advertisement for your new product. You may use any form of technology to generate your advertisement. Sites such as Piktochart or Glogster EDU will help you create flyers or poster advertisements. However, you may also animate your advertisement, create commercials, or design a webpage.

7. Be sure to utilize *at least* three different persuasive devices in your advertisement. You should also incorporate pictures, graphics, or statistical data (of course this could be made up) to sell your product. Include *at least* two graphics.

8. Once this step is complete, it is time to pitch your product. In *Shark Tank* TV-show fashion, each group will give a two-minute sales pitch (using their technology presentation) to present to a panel of high school students convincing them to buy your product. Remember you should use good speaking skills, enthusiasm, posture, and eye contact.

9. Once all groups have presented, the judges will give their evaluations of each advertisement and select the winner.

ADVERTISEMENT	PERSUASIVE TECHNIQUES	PURPOSE OR MOTIVE	EFFECTIVENESS 1 = NOT EFFECTIVE 2 = SOMEWHAT EFFECTIVE 3 = MOSTLY EFFECTIVE 4 = EXTREMELY EFFECTIVE	NOTES AND EXAMPLES
Advertisement 1				
Advertisement 2				
Advertisement 3				

Scoring Rubric

	1 SIGNIFICANT REVISION NEEDED	2 SOME REVISION NEEDED	3 PROFICIENT	4 EXCEEDS EXPECTATIONS
Objective 1: Students will create an advertisement for a new style of tennis shoe utilizing persuasive techniques.	• Shoe design is not original. • Shoe design is not based on research or consumer needs. • The product advertised is not original. • One or fewer persuasive techniques are utilized. • One or fewer graphics are included, or graphics are irrelevant.	• Shoe design is slightly unoriginal. • Shoe design is loosely based on research and consumer needs. • The product is original, but shows very little creativity, or is much like a product already available. • Only two persuasive devices are used. • Only one graphic is used, or one graphic is irrelevant.	• Shoe design is original, but uncreative. • Shoe design is based on research and consumer needs. • The product is original and unique. • Student uses three appropriate persuasive devices. • Two appropriate graphics are included in the advertisement.	• Shoe design is original and creative. • Shoe design is highly based on research and consumer needs. • The product is exemplary in terms of creativity. • Student uses three or more effective persuasive devices. • Graphics are extremely appropriate and contribute to the effectiveness of the advertisement.
Objective 2: Students will present the product to their peers in the form of a sales pitch.	• Students make little to no attempt to incorporate persuasive techniques in their presentation. • The students use ineffective speech, posture, and eye contact during the presentation. • Little to no enthusiasm is exhibited during the presentation.	• Students make a minimal attempt to incorporate persuasive techniques. • Students exhibit beginning qualities of effective speech, posture, and eye contact. • Students' enthusiasm is minimal, but some attempt is made.	• Students use somewhat effective persuasive techniques during the presentation. • Students exhibit satisfactory qualities of effective speech, posture, and eye contact. • Students exhibit satisfactory enthusiasm during the presentation.	• Students use highly effective persuasive techniques during the presentation. • Students exhibit exemplary speech, posture, and eye contact. • Students are highly enthusiastic during the presentation.

Sample Student Work

The following student work is a sample custom sneaker design and advertising poster.

Power of Persuasion

ADVERTISEMENT	PERSUASIVE TECHNIQUES	PURPOSE OR MOTIVE	EFFECTIVENESS 1= NOT EFFECTIVE 2=SOMEWHAT EFFECTIVE 3= MOSTLY EFFECTIVE 4=EXTREMELY EFFECTIVE	NOTES AND EXAMPLES
Advertisement 1	Weasel Words, Bandwagon, Ethos	Uses faulty logic in order to convince consumers that "everyone" is buying that product.	2	"Feel like you're running on air." *Everyone at the track is wearing them. "Podiatrist-approved design"
Advertisement 2	Pathos	Appeals to the viewers' emotions. The purpose of this is to make consumer feel emotional attachment.	4	Shows a boy in his first pair of shoes. He wears the brand his whole life, then gives a pair to his son.

Continued →

ADVERTISEMENT	PERSUASIVE TECHNIQUES	PURPOSE OR MOTIVE	EFFECTIVENESS 1= NOT EFFECTIVE 2=SOMEWHAT EFFECTIVE 3= MOSTLY EFFECTIVE 4=EXTREMELY EFFECTIVE	NOTES AND EXAMPLES
Advertisement 3	Unfinished Claim, Ethos	Uses celebrities to appeal to ethos. This is to increase interest in product. Claims the product is "better," but does not finish claim.	3	Celebrities make consumers want to buy products. Especially popular figures. Says the product "gives you more" but doesn't say more of what.
Advertisement 4	Simplicity, Catchwords	Uses only a few key words so that the consumer will remember the important features of the product and want to find out more.	4	Choose a word that makes the consumer want more. Use popular words that make the consumers feel like they need the product.

Create Excellence Framework Rating

CREATE ANALYSIS		
CREATE COMPONENT	**LEVEL**	**JUSTIFICATION**
Real-World Learning	3: Investigating	While students are working on a real-world topic and have talked to real consumers, they are not having an impact on their school or community. They are really simulating a design for sports shoes.
Cognitive Complexity	4: Integrating	Students must collect data and choose the persuasive strategies that will most appeal to their audience. This will require them to analyze, evaluate, and eventually, create a design that fits the consumer needs. This meets the Create level of the revised Bloom's taxonomy.
Student Engagement	4: Integrating	Students collaborate with other students to complete the project. They must also engage with various other sources as they collect data as well as talk to real consumers of sports shoes. This lesson differentiates instruction based on process and product.
Technology Integration	4: Integrating	Students use technology in each step of this process. The activity requires collaboration across groups, with teachers, and technology will be used to share the product with other students.

STANDING UP FOR WHAT YOU BELIEVE IN

Source: Sam Northern. Used with permission.

Content: English language arts

Learning Objectives:

1. Students will propose a plan of action for a social movement targeting key decision makers that illustrates the important aspect(s) of the movement's campaign.
2. Students will create a multimedia presentation to present their campaign to key decision makers.

Standards:

Common Core English Language Arts—

* W.7.1 Write arguments to support claims with clear reasons and relevant evidence (NGA & CCSSO, 2010a).
    * W.7.1.a Introduce claim(s), acknowledge alternate or opposing claims, and organize the reasons and evidence logically.
    * W.7.1.b Support claim(s) with logical reasoning and relevant evidence, using accurate, credible sources and demonstrating an understanding of the topic or text.
    * W.7.1.c Use words, phrases, and clauses to create cohesion and clarify the relationships among claim(s), reasons, and evidence.
    * W.7.1.d Establish and maintain a formal style.
    * W.7.1.e Provide a concluding statement or section that follows from and supports the argument presented.
* W.7.5 With some guidance and support from peers and adults, develop and strengthen writing as needed by planning, revising, editing, rewriting, or trying a new approach, focusing on how well purpose and audience have been addressed. (Editing for conventions should demonstrate command of language standards one to three up to and including grade 7 [NGA & CCSSO, 2010a].)
* W.7.6 Use technology, including the Internet, to produce and publish writing and link to and cite sources as well as to interact and collaborate with others, including linking to and citing sources (NGA & CCSSO, 2010a).

Project Options:

* Each student committee is to prepare a technology presentation (of its choice from a list of options) to illustrate the important aspect(s) of its social movement to key decision makers who can advance its goals. The following are the options for the group's multimedia presentations.
    * **Website:** Pupils create a website with at least two to three webpages; include one to three pictures or graphics on each page and one to two embedded web 2.0 additions.
    * **Digital story:** Pupils create a (minimum) ten to fifteen-slide digital story with clear images, text on slides, narration, and title and credits slide (Microsoft Movie Maker for PC).
    * **Desktop publishing:** Pupils create an eight-page booklet signature or two-page newsletter using Microsoft Publisher.
* Each group is to watch a video tutorial for how to use the technology it selected while taking notes. Students will learn to add transitions, title and credits slide, and music and narration.

Resources Needed: eInstruction Classroom Performance System (CPS)-Student Responders and related software; eInstruction CPS Quiz; KPREP Assessment Short Answer Space; brainstorming graphic organizer multimedia software; Wikispaces tutorial video; digital story using Movie Maker tutorial video; newsletter in Microsoft Publisher tutorial video; Inspiration Software; scoring rubric for preassessment; scoring rubric for eInstruction CPS Quiz; scoring rubric for learning objectives

Standing Up for What You Believe In

You can have an impact on your school by proposing your own social-movement campaign. You will target students at your school to gather support for your cause by creating and presenting a multimedia presentation to the class.

Project Tasks

What society often sees as normal is oppressive to specific groups of people. For centuries, ordinary people have challenged these norms by organizing and implementing various social movements. Even in our world today, certain issues constitute oppression, and it is up to every-day people to stand up for what they believe in for a change to be made. This lesson gives you the opportunity to examine your own classroom and school for issues that negatively affect the student body or a group of students. You will synthesize the information you have learned to create a campaign for a social movement for their school. You will create and present a multimedia presentation to persuade key decision makers to support a specific cause.

1. You and the teacher review the scoring rubric so that you know the project criteria.

2. Break into small groups to discuss an important issue facing the United States, such as growing economic inequality, homelessness, and so on. Discuss the issue using the key ideas associated with the framework of social movements.

3. Find a news article within the past five years that deals with oppression. Discuss the following questions.

   * What events are happening that constitute oppression?
   * What kinds of discrimination appear to be present?
   * What kinds of social movements have addressed this problem or could address this problem?

4. This activity helps you develop an in-depth awareness of at least one current social move-ment in the local community, state, country, or world. Working in small groups, identify a classroom or school issue that a group of students could mobilize around and retain a distinct collective identity. Either through the media, or online, or through personal contact or experience, group members research the issue to develop a central purpose and nature of their social movement. Students are to answer the following questions.

   * Is this an offensive or defensive social movement?
   * What are the political opportunities, and who are the elite groups associated with this social movement?
   * What, if any, are community implications in regard to the social movement?
   * What is the structure on which the movement is built?
   * To what extent is technology being used to further the aims of the social movement?
   * How does your social movement's framework address an existence of the problem, the window of opportunity, setting goals, and deciding on courses of action?
   * How attractive is this social movement for other students; would this be a movement that students would join? Why or why not?

page 1 of 4

5. After group members research the issue and develop a central purpose and the nature of their social movement, communicate your message to your targeted audience using a variety of tools and artifacts.

6. Next, research and discuss persuasion techniques.

7. Use the information gathered throughout the project to develop your social-movement campaign and an outline of arguments to accompany your multimedia presentation.

8. Then, choose three artifacts that you will actually create. You can create a poster, music, poem, political cartoon, banner, website, or something similar.

9. Use appropriate persuasive techniques to convince the principal to adopt your group's plan.

10. Plan and create arguments for your multimedia presentation to influence key decision makers to support the campaign's main aspects.

Note to teachers about presentations to the class and decision makers: Each group presents its campaign to the class. Each student from the group is to present an argument regarding his or her movement's main goals and objectives. Students will present their three artifacts during their campaign as well as the technology presentation (of their choice from a list of options) to illustrate the important aspect(s) of their social movement. Other groups will ask questions and make comments about the campaign, which the group presenting will use to make necessary revisions before their final campaign. The final campaign will be given by each group during the school's morning assembly. By presenting the campaign during morning assembly, each social movement has the opportunity to not only engage potential individual supporters, but voice the importance aspect of its campaign to targeted decision makers.

Scoring Rubric

	1 SIGNIFICANT REVISION NEEDED	2 SOME REVISION NEEDED	3 PROFICIENT	4 EXCEEDS EXPECTATIONS
Objective 1: Students will propose a plan of action for a social movement targeting key decision makers that illustrates the important aspect(s) of the movement's campaign.	• Outline does not identify a real issue of concern in the classroom or school qualified for a social movement. • Outline does not propose a plan of action for an issue in the classroom or school. • Outline does not offer arguments for key decision makers to support the movement's cause. • Justification of each argument is less than thirty-five words (making more than 105 words total). • There are five or more grammar mistakes.	• Outline provides a poor critique of a real issue of concern in the classroom or school. • Outline proposes one possible solution for the campaign's issue. • Outline offers at least one valid argument for key decision makers to support the movement's cause. • Justification of each argument is thirty to fifty words (making 105–150 words total). • There are three to four grammar mistakes.	• Outline provides a logical critique of a real issue of concern in the classroom or school. • Outline proposes one or two possible solutions for the campaign's issue. • Outline offers at least two sound arguments for key decision makers to support the movement's cause. • Justification of each argument is fifty words (making 150 words total). • There are one to two grammar mistakes.	• Outline provides a correct, logical, detailed critique of a real issue of concern in the classroom or school. • Outline proposes two or more excellent possible solutions for the campaign's issue. • Outline offers at least three sound, comprehensive, valid arguments for key decision makers to support the movement's cause. • Justification of each argument is at least fifty words (making at least 150 words total). • There are no grammar mistakes.

Continued →

Real-World Learning Framework for Secondary Schools © 2016 Solution Tree Press • solution-tree.com
Visit **go.solution-tree.com/instruction** to download this page.

	1 SIGNIFICANT REVISION NEEDED	2 SOME REVISION NEEDED	3 PROFICIENT	4 EXCEEDS EXPECTATIONS
Objective 2: Students will create a multimedia presentation to present their campaign to key decision makers.	• Product: art or photos, color, and space not original and do not carry theme, tone, or concept • Unprofessional look; overall graphical theme does not appeal to the audience, compliment the information, and not based upon logical conclusions and sound research • Product is inaccurate, missing components, or unorganized; many grammar or spelling errors • Many technical problems; inconsistent navigation and formatting; no graphics from outside sources; no use of advanced features or enhancements such as video, transitions, sounds, animations (appropriate to software or project), or all of the above • Includes little essential information and one or two facts • No attempt at persuasive technique to convince key decision makers	• Some original, unique features in product; art or photos, color, and space not original and do not carry theme, tone, or concept • Unprofessional look; overall graphical theme does not appeal to the audience, compliment the information, and not based upon logical conclusions and sound research • Product is not accurate, in-depth, neat, or organized; many grammar or spelling errors • Some technical problems; inconsistent navigation and formatting; two or less graphics from outside sources • Use of one advanced feature or enhancement such as video, transitions, sounds, animations (appropriate to software or project), or all of the above • Includes some essential information with few citations and few facts • Poor attempt at persuasive technique to convince key decision makers	• Original, unique product; art or photos, color, and space used in original ways that mostly carry theme, tone, or concept • Professional look with an overall graphical theme that mostly appeals to the audience, compliments the information, and based upon logical conclusions and sound research • Adequate product is accurate, in-depth, neat, organized; few grammar or spelling errors • Few technical problems; consistent navigation and formatting; five or less graphics from outside sources • Use of some advanced features or enhancements such as video, transitions, sounds, animations (appropriate to software or project), or all of the above • Includes essential information with most sources properly cited in APA format. Information is mostly clear, appropriate, correct, and suited to the specified purpose and audience; and encourages some readers to know more • Uses a good persuasive technique to convince key decision makers	• Excellent, original, unique product; art or photos, color, and space used in original ways that carry theme, tone, or concept • Professional look with an overall graphical theme that appeals to the audience, compliments the information, and based upon logical conclusions and sound research • Accurate, in-depth, neat, organized product and information; no grammar or spelling errors • No technical problems; consistent navigation and formatting; seven or more graphics from outside sources; use of several advanced features or enhancements such as video, transitions, sounds, animations (appropriate to software or project), or all of the above • Covers topic completely and in depth; information is clear, appropriate, correct, and suited to the specified purpose and audience; encourages readers to know more; sources cited in proper APA format • Uses the best persuasive technique to convince key decision makers

Sample Student Work

The following is an analysis of a news article.

A LOOK AT WHAT IS HAPPENING IN OUR WORLD TODAY	
Title of Article	"Obama proposes new rule for immigrant families"
Format	Online news article
Reference	Bennett, B. (1986, March 13). Obama proposes new rule for immigrant families. *Los Angeles Times*. Accessed at http://articles.latimes.com/2012/mar/30 /nation/la-na-immigration-residency-20120331 on May 29, 2013.
What events are happening that constitute oppression?	Young illegal immigrants enrolled in college or enlisted in the military do not have an efficient or effective path to citizenship. When illegal immigrants do apply for legal status, they often receive a *hardship waiver*, which means an illegal immigrant who has overstayed a visa for more than six months is barred from reentering the U.S. for three years and those who overstay more than a year are barred for ten years. Consequently, families are separated for extended periods of time. The *discretion policy* encouraged immigration agents to focus on the removal of illegal immigrants who pose a threat to public safety or are repeat immigration law violators.
What kinds of discrimination appear to be present?	Policies such as the "discretion policy" discriminate unjustly on the basis of race. Such discrimination violates internationally protected rights. This policy brings up questions of ethnic and racial profiling. Illegal immigrants are being improperly treated as a result of a conflict in state and federal laws. For instance, in 2011, 396,906 people were deported, a record number for the third consecutive year, and many of the deportees were relatives of U.S. citizens.
What kinds of social movements have addressed this problem or could address this problem?	American Civil Liberties Union (ACLU): This organization defends and preserves the individual rights and liberties that the Constitution and laws of the United States guarantee everyone in this country. Mexican American Legal Defense and Educational Fund (MALDEF) This is the nation's leading Latino legal civil rights organization which promotes social change through advocacy, communication, education, and through the law.

English Language Arts Projects

This student group selected the issue of rights to wear hoods or hats in school as their focus for step 3 of the student directions.

Intended Audience

How will you spread the word?
We will use the Tinker standard (Tinker v. Des Moines) as the basis on which to construct our arguments. We can outline the court case and its ruling in a pamphlet or via a web 2.0 tool that people can access using a QR code.

Intended Audience

How will you spread the word?
To get others aware of our movement and to possibly join, we could create a slogan that would be displayed on banners in and around the school as well as on buttons for people to wear.

Intended Audience

How will you spread the word?
Social networking sites would be very effective in spreading the word to a variety of people. We could create Facebook pages that would meet the needs of different people (one for friends our age and one for adults).

Brainstorming graphic organizer: Social movement.

This group of students created the website http://lms-we-stand.wikispaces.com/Welcome%21 to support their project. It is their product for objective 2.

Create Excellence Framework Rating

CREATE ANALYSIS		
CREATE COMPONENT	**LEVEL**	**JUSTIFICATION**
Real-World Learning	4: Integrating	Learning impacts the students' classroom or school when their social-movement campaign informs or persuades its targeted audience of taking action. Learning is integrated across subject areas: social studies and language arts. Students are creating a product (the social movement) with an authentic purpose to present to an authentic audience (key decision makers) that corresponds to certain criteria developed by past movements. The students could potentially make a strong impact on our school as well as our community in persuading the administrators to support the key aspects of their movement's campaign. When students write the specifics of their movement, they must apply writing and language skills from language arts in order to effectively communicate their campaign to an audience. Students' learning provides real-world tasks, which can be integrated across subject areas. Learning has a classroom or school emphasis and impact.
Cognitive Complexity	4: Integrating	Produce level of Bloom's revised taxonomy when students create a social-movement campaign for fellow classmates and a targeted audience (Create level) that illustrates the important aspect(s) of their movement, which is based on an issue in the classroom or school that constitutes oppression (Evaluate level). This project requires aspects of each of the earlier cognitive-process categories to some extent to ensure the creation of a successful product which persuades key decision makers to support a specific cause (Apply level). This assignment also promotes inquiry-based learning through teamwork and decision making via student-generated questions and clarifications.
Student Engagement	4: Integrating	Teacher directions guide students' projects and learning. Students use an inquiry-based learning approach by working in teams, making decisions, and making revisions through collaboration. Students collaborate with the students in their group when creating their social-movement campaign as well as other students for the means of revising their campaign. Students choose their own project topic and type of multimedia software to use. Students are engaged in projects based on preferred learning styles, interests, or passions. Students employ multiple instructional strategies.
Technology Integration	3: Investigating	The students use the Internet for research. Students' technology use is an add-on. Students' technology is used to present information (their campaign) to other students and targeted decision makers for the purpose of evaluation (students judge the social movement based on the criteria for a successful social movement as well as the potential for positive and negative consequences). Technology use is integrated and essential to task or project completion. Technology use encourages collaboration among students for planning, implementing, evaluating, or all of these in their work. Technology is used as an instrument to help students identify and solve higher-order thinking and authentic issues relating to an overall theme or concept.

A WORD OF ADVICE

Source: Erica Cassady. Used with permission.

Content: English language arts

Learning Objectives:

1. Students will create a narrative addressing a conflict in their life and how it was resolved.
2. Students will publish their work using online technologies.
3. Students will present their work to an audience.

Standards:

Common Core English Language Arts—

- W.8.3 Write narratives to develop real or imagined experiences or events using effective technique, relevant descriptive details, and well-structured event sequences (NGA & CCSSO, 2010a).
- W.8.5 With some guidance and support from peers and adults, develop and strengthen writing as needed by planning, revising, editing, rewriting, or trying a new approach, focusing on how well purpose and audience have been addressed (NGA & CCSSO, 2010a).
- SL.8.4 Present claims and findings, emphasizing salient points in a focused, coherent manner with relevant evidence, sound valid reasoning, and well-chosen details; use appropriate eye contact, adequate volume, and clear pronunciation (NGA & CCSSO, 2010a).

Project Options: Students will use online publishing tools in order to be able to share their work. Suggested technologies include Storybird, StoryJumper, or ZooBurst.

Resources Needed: Computer with Internet access; word processors; access to online publishers

A Word of Advice

Sometimes being in middle school is tough! You are forced to deal with different conflicts every day. This is your chance to share your words of wisdom to help make middle school easier for the younger students who are about to enter the world of junior high.

Project Tasks

1. The entire class should work in groups of three to four to brainstorm a list of conflicts you have dealt with since entering middle or high school. Remember, conflicts are not always with other people; they could also be internal struggles.

2. Choose the conflict you feel like you know the most about. Perhaps it is something you have dealt with personally or something you have helped a friend overcome.

3. Develop a story that focuses on this central conflict and how the conflict was resolved. Your story may be based on real events in your life, but it should be fictional. Do not include real names or places. Be creative! Use a graphic organizer to plan your story. You may want to utilize the story map at www.readwritethink.org/files/resources/interactives/storymap to help you organize your story.

4. After you have created a draft of your story, we will work as a class to develop an editing checklist. Then, work in small groups to edit each other's stories. Be sure your peers' stories match the editing criteria we have developed.

5. Once your story is free of errors, it is time to publish! Use an online story publisher to share your story. The publisher should allow you to add pictures and text, so that you are able to share your story in the best possible way! You may use any free publishing website such as Storybird, StoryJumper, or ZooBurst.

6. You should also design some discussion questions that you may share with the elementary students. Create questions that connect your story to the lives of the elementary students. For example, "How would you handle this situation?" or "What could the character have done differently?"

7. Once your stories are published, we will take a trip to a local elementary school so that you can share your stories and make their transition just a little bit easier!

Real-World Learning Framework for Secondary Schools © 2016 Solution Tree Press • solution-tree.com
Visit **go.solution-tree.com/instruction** to download this page.

Scoring Rubric

	1 SIGNIFICANT REVISION NEEDED	2 SOME REVISION NEEDED	3 PROFICIENT	4 EXCEEDS EXPECTATIONS
Objective 1: Students will create a narrative addressing a conflict in their life and how it was resolved.	• Story lacks in creativity. • Conflict is irrelevant. • Resolution does not occur. • There are several errors in spelling, grammar, or mechanics.	• Story is slightly creative. • Conflict is vague. • Resolution is unclear. • There are a few errors in grammar, spelling, or mechanics.	• The story is unique and creative. • Conflict is apparent. • Resolution is logical and clear. • There are one or two errors in spelling, grammar, or mechanics.	• The story is highly creative and unique to the student's own mind. • Conflict is relevant and obvious in the story. • Resolution is clear and logical. • There are no errors in grammar, spelling, or mechanics.
Objective 2: Students will publish their work using online technologies.	• Student work is not published. • Work that may be published is very messy and unorganized.	• Student work is published. • Published work is messy or appears incomplete.	• Student work is published. • Published work is neat and organized.	• Student work is published. • Published work is exceptionally neat and organized.
Objective 3: Students will be able to present their work to an audience.	• Student needs improvement in their speaking skills.	• Student uses somewhat appropriate eye contact, adequate volume, and clear pronunciation when speaking.	• Student uses appropriate eye contact, adequate volume, and clear pronunciation when speaking.	• Student excels at using appropriate eye contact, adequate volume, and clear pronunciation when speaking.

Real-World Learning Framework for Secondary Schools © 2016 Solution Tree Press • solution-tree.com
Visit **go.solution-tree.com/instruction** to download this page.

Sample Student Work

The following is a sample resembling student work created in Storybird.

Create Excellence Framework Rating

CREATE ANALYSIS		
CREATE COMPONENT	**LEVEL**	**JUSTIFICATION**
Real-World Learning	4: Integrating	Students will share these stories with children in the community. Students will use their speaking skills to present their story.
Cognitive Complexity	3: Investigating	Students will collaborate to brainstorm ideas for the assignment. They will then select a question or problem that they wish to address and create a story that resolves this problem. This is the Create level of the revised Bloom's taxonomy.
Student Engagement	4: Integrating	Students collaborate from the beginning, brainstorming ideas and developing conflicts. The students also collaborate to create an evaluation method and work with their peers to help edit and revise each other's work.
Technology Integration	3: Investigating	Technology is used to design their story. The technologies provide pictures that are necessary for the story books. Students also could use an online graphic organizer to plan their ideas. To make this a stronger project, students could enter their books in a children's literature competition.

THE DO-SOMETHING CHALLENGE

Source: Jennifer Gonzalez. Used with permission.

Content: English language arts and social studies

Learning Objectives:

1. After thoroughly researching a school problem, students will create a detailed plan for solving that problem.

2. Students will create a three-to-five minute video to promote their solution.

Standards:

Common Core English Language Arts—

- W.8.1 Write arguments to support claims with clear reasons and relevant evidence (NGA & CCSSO, 2010a).
- W.8.2 Write informative/explanatory texts to examine a topic and convey ideas, concepts, and information through the selection, organization, and analysis of relevant content (NGA & CCSSO, 2010a).
- W.8.6 Use technology, including the Internet, to produce and publish writing and present the relationships between information and ideas effectively as well as to interact and collaborate with others (NGA & CCSSO, 2010a).

The College, Career, and Civic Life (C3) Framework for Social Studies State Standards—

- D2.Civ.7.6–8 Apply civic virtues and democratic principles in school and community settings (NCSS, 2013).
- D4.3.6–8 Present adaptations of arguments and explanations on topics of interest to others to reach audiences and venues outside the classroom using print and oral technologies (e.g., posters, essays, letters, debates, speeches, reports, and maps) and digital technologies (e.g., Internet, social media, and digital documentary) (NCSS, 2013).

Project Options: Students will work in groups based on interest. They will have a choice of technology options for producing video. Although Windows Movie Maker and iMovie are the default programs, students may seek approval for other video-production tools.

Resources Needed: Desktop or laptop computers with Internet access; Windows Movie Maker, iMovie software, or comparable teacher-approved software; Audacity software and internal or external microphones for voice recording; digital cameras for still photography and video recording; Freeplay Music for background music

The Do-Something Challenge

Like most schools, your school has its share of problems. In this challenge, you and your group are going to (1) choose one problem in your school, (2) create a plan for solving that problem, (3) create a promotional video to sell your idea to your principal, and (4) obtain the principal's permission to put your plan into action.

Project Tasks

Once you and your group of up to three other students identify your problem, use the following steps to complete this assignment.

1. Carefully research that problem until you fully understand it. This should involve interviewing key people in the school who understand the problem, and doing online research that supplies you with any facts to help you get a clear picture of the problem outside of your school. Take notes as you do your research, and get all the necessary information to provide American Psychological Association (APA)– or Modern Language Association (MLA)–style references (whichever your teacher prefers) at the end of your video. You should research until you can:

    *   Clearly explain what the problem is
    *   Identify the root cause(s) of the problem
    *   Explain the impact this problem has on students, teachers, administrators, school staff, or community members

2. Write a script for a video presentation, where you present your solution to a school problem that can be conducted in the building during regular school hours. The script will be scored according to the rubric and must receive a *proficient* rating before you have permission to create your video.

3. Use Audacity software and Freeplay Music (www.freeplaymusic.com) to record the voice-over and background music for your video.

4. Use Windows Movie Maker, iMovie, or another program to produce a video to go with the sound file created in step 3.

5. When your movie is complete, upload it to YouTube and send your teacher the link. After your group has gotten approval from the administration, you may begin implementing your solution.

Real-World Learning Framework for Secondary Schools © 2016 Solution Tree Press • solution-tree.com
Visit **go.solution-tree.com/instruction** to download this page.

Scoring Rubric

Objective	1 SIGNIFICANT REVISION NEEDED	2 SOME REVISION NEEDED	3 PROFICIENT	4 EXCEEDS EXPECTATIONS
Objective 1: After thoroughly researching a school problem, students will create a detailed plan for solving that problem.	• Ineffective or missing lead or closing statement.	• Lead or closing are unclear or off message.	• Lead establishes clear purpose; clear closing statement.	• Captivating lead and powerful closing statement.
	• Problem, cause, and impact are unclear or have minimal development.	• Some aspects of problem, cause, and impact are unclear or underdeveloped.	• Problem, cause, and impact are presented and developed with sufficient facts, definitions, concrete details, or quotations.	• Problem, cause, and impact are thoroughly explained and developed with well-chosen facts, definitions, concrete details, and quotations.
	• Solution is unclear or is not *sustainable,* does not *build capacity,* or does not demonstrate *partnership.*	• Solution is somewhat unclear or is either not *sustainable,* does not *build capacity,* or does not demonstrate *partnership.*	• Clear claim is made proposing a solution that is *sustainable* (can be maintained even after the work is done), *builds capacity* (helps recipients become self-sufficient), and demonstrates *partnership* (shows that you have consulted with those affected).	• Clear claim is made proposing a solution that is strong in *sustainability, capacity building, and partnership.*
	• Description of solution, timetable, or both have many lapses in clarity.	• Description of solution or timetable have some lapses in clarity.	• Solution is clearly described, including a clear timetable of events.	• Solution is thoroughly described, including a detailed timetable of events.
	• Claim lacks sufficient or relevant support.	• Claim is supported with reasoning or evidence; more support is needed.	• Claim is supported with logical reasoning, evidence, or both.	• Claim is supported with logical reasoning and powerful evidence.
	• Opposing claims are not adequately addressed or refuted.	• Opposing claims are somewhat addressed and refuted.	• Opposing claims are addressed and refuted.	• Opposing claims are effectively addressed and refuted.
	• Description of how success will be measured is unclear, or inadequately measures the factors described in the original problem.	• Description of how success will be measured is somewhat unclear, or incompletely measures the factors described in the original problem.	• Clear description of how success will be measured, which directly addresses the original problem.	• Thorough description of how success will be measured, which clearly and thoughtfully addresses all aspects of the problem.
	• One or no resources listed at the end. Source formatting is incorrect. Personal interview, if included, does not provide support for claim.	• Two resources listed at the end. Source formatting is inconsistent or incorrect. Personal interview, if included, does not provide strong support for claim.	• Three or more resources listed at the end in APA or MLA style. At least one is an interview with a real person with connections to the problem.	• Four or more resources listed at the end in APA or MLA style. At least two are interviews with real people with strong connections to the problem.
	• Errors in spelling, usage, capitalization, or punctuation interfere with the message.	• Some errors in spelling, usage, capitalization, or punctuation.	• Minimal errors in spelling, usage, capitalization, or punctuation.	• Control of spelling, usage, capitalization, and punctuation.
	• No resources listed.	• Resources are listed but not in APA or MLA style.		

Real-World Learning Framework for Secondary Schools © 2016 Solution Tree Press • solution-tree.com
Visit **go.solution-tree.com/instruction** to download this page.

	1 SIGNIFICANT REVISION NEEDED	2 SOME REVISION NEEDED	3 PROFICIENT	4 EXCEEDS EXPECTATIONS
Objective 2: Students will create a three- to five- minute video to promote their solution.	• Many visuals off topic, do not fit overall message, or are low quality.	• Some visuals off topic, do not fit overall message, or are low quality.	• Good-quality visuals that add information and fit the message.	• High-quality visuals that add information and enhance the message.
	• Ineffective layout of visual elements. Animation is ineffective or not used.	• Some visual clutter or ineffective layout choices. Animation does little to enhance visual impact.	• Balanced, attractive layout of visual elements. Animation enhances visual impact.	• Exceptionally effective visual layout. Advanced use of animation enhances visual impact.
	• Inconsistencies in colors, fonts, or both are distracting and convey a lack of professionalism.	• Some inconsistencies in colors, fonts, or both.	• Style of colors and fonts are harmonious throughout video.	• Sophisticated use of colors and fonts, resulting in a professional feel.
	• Uses no music, nonroyalty-free music, or music that is inappropriate to audience or message.	• Incorporates royalty-free music that is somewhat effective for the audience or message.	• Incorporates royalty-free music that enhances message and is audience-appropriate.	• Royalty-free music is exceptionally well-chosen and placed to motivate viewer.
	• Volume of music and voice-over are inconsistent and ineffective.	• Some inconsistencies in volume of music and voice-over.	• Music and voice-over are set at an appropriate volume.	• Music and voice-over are set at an appropriate volume.
	• Narration is hard to understand and adds minimal information or ideas.	• Narration is sometimes unclear; adds some new information or ideas.	• Includes clear narration that adds new information or ideas.	• Narration is effective and captivating, and adds significant new information or ideas.
	• Problems with navigation, animations, transitions, sound or final product-delivery system create a poor user experience and interfere with the message.	• Some problems with navigation, animations, transitions, sound, or final product-delivery system.	• Navigation, animations, transitions, and sound are smooth and well-timed.	• Navigation, animations, transitions, sound, and final product-delivery system provide a highly satisfying user experience.
			• Final product-delivery system functions properly.	

Real-World Learning Framework for Secondary Schools © 2016 Solution Tree Press • solution-tree.com
Visit **go.solution-tree.com/instruction** to download this page.

Sample Student Work

To address the problem of poor eating habits in the student population, eighth graders at Main Street Middle School (MSMS) launched "The Veggie Games," a two-part competition that includes a recipe contest and a contest between classes to eat more fruits and vegetables at lunchtime. Visit http://youtu.be/nFV cuwJLyT8 to view the promotional video.

Video Script: The Veggie Games—Fighting for Our Health

Teenagers are not the healthiest eaters. The USDA guidelines for healthy eating tell us that half of our plate at every meal should be filled with fruits and veggies. But according to the Centers for Disease Control and Prevention, adolescents are not getting nearly that much.

And Main Street Middle Schoolers are no better. Our team spent three days studying typical lunches of the 8th graders at MSMS. What we discovered is that most eighth graders here eat very little fruit and almost no veggies. Half of the people who brought a packed lunch had some kind of fruit, but most of the time that was canned fruit or a fruit juice, rather than fresh fruit, which is much healthier. And the people who bought lunch? Well, even though our cafeteria provides lots of fruit and vegetable choices, about half of students in our study didn't even take a vegetable from the line, and many more of those threw them away untouched. Sharon Crosby, the cafeteria manager, has noticed this problem for years. "We keep telling them to pick a fruit or pick a vegetable, but most of the kids just don't want it." In three days, we watched as students threw away 173 whole apples, 416 baby carrots, 244 cups of untouched cooked vegetables, and 150 grape tomatoes. And that was just during 8th grade lunch.

Apart from this horrible waste of food, we need these nutrients! A poor diet can cause all kinds of problems, such as obesity, type 2 diabetes, iron deficiency, dental issues, impaired brain development, and poor school performance. (Cali, CDC)

But because we are young, many of us don't think much about the future. So even though the school lunch is healthy, we still aren't eating healthy. Why aren't MSMS eighth graders eating more fruits and veggies? Jane Wilson said, "I just don't like the taste of most vegetables." Petey Travis added, "They're nasty. Bananas are alright, but everything else is nasty." When asked what it would take to get her to eat more fruits and vegetables, Mackenzie Cattrell said, "I guess just make them taste better."

So here's what we're going to do about it.

Part 1: The "Make it Taste Better" Competition

First, to address the "bad taste" problem, we are going to start by holding a contest to see who can come up with the best new recipes for school lunch veggies. Home cooks, pay attention! If you have a way of making fruits or vegetables taste better, write up your recipe, and submit it—more details on that will be posted outside Mr. Jackson's room. The cafeteria staff will read the recipes, choose the six best ones, and cook them for "Make it Taste Better" day, when the eighth grade will try the samples and vote for their favorites. The top three recipes will be incorporated into our regular school menu, and will be featured on our local TV midday program, where the cooks will demonstrate how to prepare their recipes.

Part 2: The "Just Eat More" Competition

Sometimes, to get more fruits and veggies into your diet, you just have to eat more. We know that nothing motivates people like a challenge, so we're going to set up a competition between all eighth grade fifth-period classes. Since fifth period is when we go to lunch, this is the group we sit with in the cafeteria. Fifth-period classes will compete to be the class that eats the most total servings of fresh fruits and veggies. Every day, a pair of student monitors will tally the total number of fruit and veggie servings eaten, minus the servings that are thrown away. And don't worry about cheating: The student monitors will watch a different class from their own! After two weeks, the class with the greatest average servings per students will win a gourmet vegetarian lunch prepared for them, generously donated and catered by Lanie's Garden Bistro.

During this time, to help motivate students, we will also offer one-minute tips on the MSMS morning news to help students get more fruits and vegetables into their daily diet.

Won't all this veggie and fruit eating cause rowdy lunchtime behavior?

We have already recruited enough teacher volunteers to serve as table monitors for the two-week competition. They will keep track of servings eaten and make sure no one gets too crazy with the spirit of competition.

How will you know if this makes a difference?

We have established a few criteria to measure whether this will really have an impact on the health of student diets:

1.   On three different secret days before announcing the Veggie Games, we will tally the number of fruit and vegetable servings actually put on students' trays or that comes from their packed lunches, subtract the number that is thrown away, and end up with a total number of fruit and veggie servings eaten.

2.   Several weeks after the Games are over, we will repeat this activity. If the total number of servings eaten has gone up, we'll know we have succeeded.

Will it cause the students running the project to miss class?

The project coordinators and student monitors will need to be excused from some of fifth period on some days in order to eat their own lunches, because the work of measuring our project's success will make us miss our own eating time. Fifth period teachers have already agreed to either dismiss these students for fifteen minutes on these days, or allow them to eat lunch in class.

It's a student solution for a student problem. We know we can get MSMS on track for healthier eating. Let the games begin!!

References

Cattrell, M. (2013). Personal interview.

Centers for Disease Control and Prevention. (2013). *Adolescent and school health: Nutrition and health of young people.* Accessed at www.cdc.gov/healthyyouth/nutrition/facts.htm on January 23, 2015.

Centers for Disease Control and Prevention. (2013). *Adolescent and school health: Childhood obesity facts.* Accessed on January 23, 2015.

Crosby, S. (2013). Personal interview.

Sillescu, T. (2009). Strike eagle. *On action and adventure volume* 1 [mp3]. Accessed at http://freeplaymusic.com/search /category_search.php?t=v&i=1202 on January 23, 2015.

Travis, P. (2013). Personal interview.

United States Department of Agriculture, Center for Nutrition Policy and Promotion. (2010). *Dietary guidelines for Americans.* Accessed at www.cnpp.usda.gov/DGAs2010-PolicyDocument.htm on January 23, 2015.

Create Excellence Framework Rating

CREATE ANALYSIS		
CREATE COMPONENT	**LEVEL**	**JUSTIFICATION**
Real-World Learning	2: Practicing	The students' solutions ultimately impact the classroom, school, or community by directly addressing and attempting to solve a school-based problem; their video's effectiveness is a necessary step toward implementing those solutions. The lesson integrates learning across several subject areas to some degree: language arts, social studies (historical perspective, social change), and technology.
Cognitive Complexity	5: Specializing	Students develop their own projects by identifying a problem, developing a solution, and carrying out that solution. Solutions can take many forms and can involve a variety of tasks, all generated by the students themselves. No two solutions will look the same. Creating the solution and the video are all at the Create level of Bloom's. Finally, because students essentially create their own mini-charity and develop products that build administrator confidence the same way a public relations department would, they are thinking like content experts.
Student Engagement	5: Specializing	Students partner with the teacher to define the content (problem and solution). Each group does its own inquiry-based research on the problem, from doing online research to conducting personal interviews. Students will collaborate within their groups and between groups to evaluate each other's videos. Students will also collaborate with community members to solve their problems, which will be pupil-initiated (level 5). Some groups may need more teacher help and structure, which would put them at a 4, while others may take more initiative themselves, which would be at level 5.
Technology Integration	3: Investigating	The videos are not essential to project completion: It could be argued that the same information could be conveyed to the administration in a live presentation. However, videos would allow students to prepare and edit their presentations until they convey their message precisely, and they circumvent the logistical complications of arranging a live presentation. Students produce the videos in groups, which naturally builds in collaboration, and their teacher, advising and supporting that work, serves as a partner. Finally, because the videos are a tool for getting the solutions implemented, students are using them to solve authentic problems at the Create level.

Mathematics Projects

DO-IT-YOURSELF (DIY) LANDSCAPING

Source: Shannon Lay. Used with permission.

Content: Mathematics

Learning Objectives:

1. Students will create a landscape design for their school, which includes geometric shapes, and the area and circumference of each shape.
2. Students will present their landscape design to the class and principal.

Standards:

Common Core Mathematics—

- 6.G.A.1 Find the area of right triangles, other triangles, special quadrilaterals, and polygons by composing into rectangles or decomposing into triangles and other shapes; apply these techniques in the context of solving real-world and mathematical problems (NGA & CCSSO, 2010b).
- 7.G.B.4 Know the formulas for the area and circumference of a circle and use them to solve problems; give an informal derivation of the relationship between the circumference and area of a circle (NGA & CCSSO, 2010b).
- 7.G.B.6 Solve real-world and mathematical problems involving area, volume and surface area of two- and three-dimensional objects composed of triangles, quadrilaterals, polygons, cubes, and right prisms (NGA & CCSSO, 2010b).

Project Options: Students are free to design their yard however they choose, as long as the basic requirements are met. Computer programs can also vary.

Resources Needed: Computer with landscaping software (like SmartDraw) downloaded; pencils; paper; graphing paper; rulers; calculators

Do-It-Yourself (DIY) Landscaping

Our school's landscaping is way too dull. The principal needs some ideas for a new design. I want you to come up with a yard design that would make our school look amazing!

Project Tasks

Work in teams of three to design and present the plans. Make sure that you come up with a name for your landscaping company. First, you will create your own design. Then, you will share it with your group and decide which plan would be the best. Afterward, present the chosen design to the class. Next, you will use SmartDraw to create your design. The principal wants to make sure that the school will have unique landscaping, so you have to include at least four different geometric shapes in your design. After the plan is complete and you have recorded all data, create a technology presentation for the principal to convince him or her that your plan is the best. The total presentation should be about five minutes. Finally, the class gets to implement the plan that the principal selects. In other words, the class will help plant the shrubs and flowers as your class designed it!

The principal will come to class and tell us what our budget is, and he or she will return on presentation day to see all your hard work come together!

1. The principal presents your class with the idea. He or she requests your help in redesigning the school landscape, but you must remain within a given budget.

2. Complete the "Redesign Worksheet" with your group of three. State the problem in a question format and list the project's restraints and criteria.

3. Walk around the building and decide which area you would like to redesign.

4. Begin working individually to create a preliminary design with the graphing paper and rulers provided.

5. After the initial plans are complete, present your ideas to the other members in your group. They will decide among themselves which plan looks the best, seems to be the least expensive, and includes four or more geometric shapes.

6. You decide on a model and begin researching the types of plants you wish to use in the plan. Use computers to fill out the "Idea Sheet." The "Idea Sheet" will help you not only keep track of the cost of each plant but also any other important information about the plants.

7. If you decide to use other objects, such as benches or gazebos, include those items in the "Idea Sheet" as well.

8. Once the "Idea Sheet" is completed and the teacher approves it, transfer your plans onto SmartDraw. You have a day to get acquainted with SmartDraw, and you will have a checklist to complete that day to understand the basics of the program.

9. Use the information in the "Idea Sheet" and the design from SmartDraw to present your plan to the class. Classmates will give constructive feedback on the presenting group's plan.

10. Modify your landscape design to address the class's critiques.

page 1 of 3

11.   Once the group finishes its final SmartDraw landscape plan, create a presentation of your proposal using any teacher-approved web 2.0 presentation tool (such as SlideRocket, Smilebox, Prezi, and so on). Other options could be to create a model of their design or design a printed pamphlet.

12.   Your group and the others will then present your proposals to the class and the principal.

13.   Finally, after the principal selects one or more designs, the class will get to assist with implementing their designs. You can plant the shrubs or flowers yourself!

Redesign Worksheet

Use the following sentences to summarize the task.
1. How can I design a __ _____ that will _____?
2. What criteria must be met?
3. What are possible restraints?
4. Use the back of the page for your ideas.

Idea Sheet

SHAPES	AREA FORMULA AND CALCULATIONS

PLANT	SHAPE	PRICE	OTHER INFORMATION (INCLUDE GROWING RESTRICTIONS, THE BEST CLIMATE TO GROW IN, AND SO ON)

Scoring Rubric

	1 SIGNIFICANT REVISION NEEDED	2 SOME REVISION NEEDED	3 PROFICIENT	4 EXCEEDS EXPECTATIONS
Objective 1: Students will create a landscape design for their school, which includes geometric shapes, and the area and circumference of each shape.	• Student design only uses two different shapes. • Student miscalculates area and circumference for all of the shapes in the design. • The landscape design is unclear, poorly designed, or is not different from the current design.	• Student design only uses three different shapes. • Student miscalculates area and circumference for some of the shapes in the design. • The landscape design is unclear or does not improve the school property.	• Student design uses four different shapes. • Student correctly calculates area and circumference for each of the shapes in the design. • The landscape design is clear, logical, and improves the school property.	• Student design uses five or more different shapes. • Student correctly calculates area and circumference for each of the shapes in the design. • The landscape design is clear, logical, well thought-out, and significantly improves the school property.
Objective 2: Students will present their landscape design to the class and principal.	• Student-presentation design presents only a small part of the landscape plan. • Students do not participate equally in the presentation.	• Student-presentation design does not clearly present the entire landscape plan. • Students do not participate equally in the presentation.	• Student-presentation design is adequate and clearly presents the landscape plan. • Students participate equally in the presentation.	• Student-presentation design is excellent and clearly presents the landscape plan. • Students participate equally in the presentation.

Real-World Learning Framework for Secondary Schools © 2016 Solution Tree Press • solution-tree.com
Visit **go.solution-tree.com/instruction** to download this page.

Sample Student Work

The following student work shows samples of landscape design, budget information, and area calculations.

DIY Landscaping
Sample Student 1, 2, 3

Budget Information

From Home
Improvement Store
- Gardenias—$12.98
- Spruce—$6.98
- Bench—$433.04
- Rose of
  Sharon—$6.98
- Rosemary—$5.98

Other
- In-ground lights—$180.81
  + From searchinglight
    ing.com
- Already on grounds:
  + Bird bath
  + Birdcage
- Pond
  + Will vary depending
    on company used

Subtotal: $1,764.48

The Design

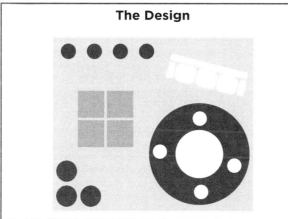

Areas

- Total area: 924.67 ft.²

ITEM (SHAPE)	AREA (FT²)
2 Gardenia boxes (Squares)	50
2 Spruce trees (Circles)	39.26
Bench (Rectangle)	12
Bench area (Circle)	78.54
7 lights (Circles)	5.50
Bird bath (Circle)	3.14
Pond (2 Trapezoids)	346.62
2 Rosemary bushes (Circles)	14.14
Total	549.20

Mathematics
Projects

Create Excellence Framework Rating

CREATE ANALYSIS		
CREATE COMPONENT	**LEVEL**	**JUSTIFICATION**
Real-World Learning	4: Integrating	This project will have an impact on the landscape of the school. Art, science, and economics are also topics in this project, so the task/project is interdisciplinary.
Cognitive Complexity	3: Investigating	The students are creating their own designs, planning the budgeting of the design, and producing a presentation. Therefore, this is at the Create level of the revised Bloom's taxonomy.
Student Engagement	3: Investigating	Students work in teams for the designing process. The task/project is teacher-directed since the teacher designed the task and worksheet plans, chose the software, and approves the student work throughout the task.
Technology Integration	4: Integrating	Students will work in teams to utilize the technology to create the final landscaping plan, research the plants used in the design, and make sure they do not exceed the budget.

MYTHBUSTERS: STATISTICS EDITION

Source: Shannon Lay. Used with permission.

Content: Mathematics

Learning Objectives:

1. Student will create a survey to test common statistics.
2. Student will analyze the survey results, calculate the statistics, and present findings to the class.

Standards:

Common Core Mathematics—

- 7.SP.A.1 Understand that statistics can be used to gain information about a population by examining a sample of the population; generalizations about a population from a sample are valid only if the sample is representative of that population. Understand that random sampling tends to produce representative samples and support valid inferences (NGA & CCSSO, 2010b).
- 7.SP.A.2 Use data from a random sample to draw inferences about a population with an unknown characteristic of interest. Generate multiple samples (or simulated samples) of the same size to gauge the variation in estimates or predictions (NGA & CCSSO, 2010b).

Project Options: Students are free to design their survey however they choose, as long as the basic requirements are met.

Resources Needed: Pencils and paper for data collection; computer with Internet access and Microsoft Office (specifically Word, Excel, and PowerPoint) installed to create survey and charts; SurveyMonkey or Google Forms

Mythbusters: Statistics Edition

Your task, should you choose to accept it, is to find a statistic and to test it. We all hear statistics on the news or read them in magazines, but how true are they? Your job is to act as mythbusters and find out!

Project Tasks

1. We will watch an episode of *MythBusters*, so you can see how the hosts test the myths submitted.

2. After watching the episode, begin your research. Find a statistic that you think is interesting or could be inaccurate using any tools available to you (Internet, magazines, newspapers, and so on).

3. In groups of three, compare the statistics you found and vote on which statistic the group would like to investigate.

4. As a group, create a simple survey to distribute among classmates and then collect the data. Use SurveyMonkey or Google Forms to create your data. It is easier to collect the data using a tablet that you can just hand to random students to take your survey.

5. Once the data are collected, one group member will create a chart and print the results. The other team members will begin outlining the presentation. Don't forget to cite your sources!

6. Conclude the project with a class presentation of your research. While a team is presenting, the other classmates will evaluate each presentation using the following chart. Include the original statistic, your survey, your findings, and a new statistic. The new statistic will be for the class to evaluate and should come from your findings. It can be true or false, but you must reveal whether it's true or false information at the end of the presentation. So did you bust a myth, or was the original statistic correct?

CHECKLIST	POOR	FAIR	EXCELLENT
Stated statistic	The team did not tell the class the original statistic or the source.	The team summarized the original statistic and mentioned the source.	The team presented the original statistic word for word and cited the source.
Created survey	The team did not create a survey, or the survey was incomplete.	The team created a survey that was a list of questions.	The team created a survey that included questions divided into categories for analysis.
Stated accuracy	The team did not tell the class the results of the survey.	The team presented a chart, but did not explain it.	The team presented a chart and explained its findings.

CHECKLIST	POOR	FAIR	EXCELLENT
Presented findings	The team had a presentation that included one to two of the following criteria: • 10 minutes in length • Statistics • Chart and findings • Survey results	The team had a presentation that included all but one to two of the following criteria: • 10 minutes in length • Statistics • Chart and findings • Survey results	The team had a presentation that included all of the following criteria: • 10 minutes in length • Statistics • Chart and findings • Survey results

Scoring Rubric

	1 SIGNIFICANT REVISION NEEDED	2 SOME REVISION NEEDED	3 PROFICIENT	4 EXCEEDS EXPECTATIONS
Objective 1: Student will create a survey to test common statistics.	• Student shows little effort in finding a statistic.	• Student does some research, and finds a statistic from a questionable source.	• Student researches and finds a statistic from a credible source.	• Student finds a statistic from a credible source and is able to cite the source correctly.
Objective 2: Student will analyze the survey results, calculate the statistics, and present findings to the class.	• Student does not create a survey or does not address the original question. • Statistic calculations and conclusions are incorrect. • Student does not present any data collected. • Student does not participate in the presentation.	• The survey created only has one question or does not clearly address the original question. • Statistic calculations and conclusions have some mistakes. • Student summarizes data collected. • Student participates little in the presentation.	• Student creates a survey that asks two to three questions and addresses the original question. • Statistic calculations and conclusions are correct. • Student presents the data collected well. • Student participates equally in the presentation.	• Student creates a survey that has more than three questions and clearly addresses the original question. • Statistic calculations and conclusions are outstanding. • Student presents the data collected well and analyzes them. • Student participates equally in the presentation and has good presentation skills.

Sample Student Work

The following work shows a presentation of data from a student that shares results from a survey about their shopping habits. The data are shown in bar graph and pie graph formats.

Online Shopping
Sample Student 1, 2, 3

How we surveyed
Our survey had three questions:

- Q1: Do you go shopping on a regular basis (once or more a week)?
- Q2: Do you use your computer or other electronic devices that can connect to the Internet to shop on a regular basis?
- Q3: How often do you use an electronic device to shop online?

According to
***The Independent* newspaper . . .**

- 83 percent of people admit to have shopped online once in their lifetime. (found on wiki.answers.com)

We found that . . .
We found that 75 percent of people shop online regularly.

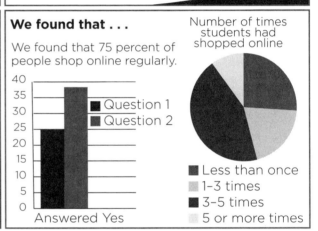

Number of times students had shopped online

Believe it or not . . .
Most people do all their shopping online.
- Do you believe it?
  - ◆ You shouldn't. We misinterpreted our data.
  - ◆ Many people answered the survey that they shop online regularly, but looking at the question of how often, a majority of people answered they only do it one to five times a week.

Create Excellence Framework Rating

CREATE ANALYSIS		
CREATE COMPONENT	**LEVEL**	**JUSTIFICATION**
Real-World Learning	3: Investigating	This project is a simulation of an investigative team. Students act as statisticians and use the scientific method to prove or disprove the statistic.
Cognitive Complexity	3: Investigating	It is a student-generated project at the Evaluate level of the revised Bloom's taxonomy. Students are researching statistics to check and critique the accuracy of the statements.
Student Engagement	4: Integrating	Students work in teams to develop the testing process. The teacher oversees the investigations and assists when needed.
Technology Integration	4: Integrating	Students use technology by creating a survey, researching their statistics, creating a chart, and making a presentation of their findings.

WHY DO WORLD ECOSYSTEMS MATTER?

Source: Marge Maxwell. Used with permission.

Content: Mathematics and science

Learning Objectives:

1. Students will create statistical questions and data charts that represent those statistical questions.

Standards:

Common Core Mathematics—

*   7.SP.B.3 Informally assess the degree of visual overlap of two numerical data distributions with similar variabilities, measuring the difference between the centers by expressing it as a multiple of a measure of variability (NGA & CCSSO, 2010b).
*   7.SP.B.4 Use measures of center and measures of variability for numerical data from random samples to draw informal comparative inferences about two populations (NGA & CCSSO, 2010b).

Next Generation Science Standards—

*   MS-LS2–2 Construct explanation that predicts patterns of interactions among organisms across multiple ecosystems (Achieve, 2013).

Resources Needed: Computer with Internet access; Gapminder

Why Do World Ecosystems Matter?

Use the website Gapminder (www.gapminder.org), which is an excellent resource that provides data about over three hundred indicators for all of the countries in the world, to create data charts and maps. It lets you visualize and track all countries' progress on many different measures of health, education, and so on. What's really great is how Gapminder World converts dry numbers into fun, animated, interactive graphs, which show patterns and relationships in stunning ways.

Project Tasks

1. Select any ecosystem that you have studied (for example, desert, arctic tundra, mountains, temperate forests, rainforests, savannah, grasslands, and so on).

2. Identify the countries around the world where this ecosystem exists.

3. Use Gapminder to compare data from these countries. Data to compare could include population, imports, exports, crops, and any other relevant data.

4. Develop research questions you would like to explore. Questions could include:

   ◆ Which data indicators are most affected by this ecosystem? Explain.

   ◆ When you compare the countries in this ecosystem for any three data indicators that you select, evaluate inconsistencies in these data. Do some of the data not really make sense for this ecosystem? Hypothesize other factors that could be causing these inconsistencies.

Real-World Learning Framework for Secondary Schools © 2016 Solution Tree Press • solution-tree.com
Visit **go.solution-tree.com/instruction** to download this page.

Scoring Rubric

OBJECTIVE	1 SIGNIFICANT REVISION NEEDED	2 SOME REVISION NEEDED	3 PROFICIENT	4 EXCEEDS EXPECTATIONS
Objective 1: Students will create statistical questions and data charts that represent those statistical questions.	• Much difficulty in selecting an ecosystem of the world	• Needed assistance in selecting an ecosystem of the world	• Selected an ecosystem of the world	• Selected an ecosystem of the world
	• Incorrectly identified few of the countries that contain that ecosystem	• Identified half of the countries that contain that ecosystem	• Correctly identified most countries that contain that ecosystem	• Correctly identified *all* countries that contain that ecosystem
	• The question posed is not a statistical question and not really related to the ecosystem	• Inappropriate statistical question or not related to the ecosystem	• Appropriate statistical question related to the ecosystem	• Creative, insightful statistical questions (two to three questions) related to the ecosystem
	• Much difficulty in selection of data indicators and graph and not related to question	• Selection of data indicators and graph are not related to question	• Selection of data indicators and graph are relevant, accurate, and specific to question	• Selection of data indicators and graph are relevant, accurate, and specific to question; used the best possible data indicators
	• Discussion very short; not really an interpretation of the chart and data indicators; discussion is not logical	• Interpretation of the chart and data indicators are incorrect or not logical	• Interpretation of the chart and data indicators is logical	• Interpretation of the chart and data indicators is creative, insightful, logical
	• Product, information, or both are not related to the discussion; many grammar or spelling errors	• Product, information, or both are inaccurate or not related to the discussion; several grammar or spelling errors	• Accurate product and information; few grammar or spelling errors	• Accurate, in-depth, neat, organized product and information; no grammar or spelling errors
	• No real inconsistencies discussed; no evidence of understanding	• One inconsistency discussed; poor evidence of understanding	• One to two inconsistencies discussed; evidence of understanding	• More than one inconsistency discussed; several hypotheses presented to explain inconsistency; evidence of deep insight and understanding; well-developed ideas, complex
	• Information used in the discussion is inappropriate, incorrect, and not suited to the specified inconsistency and question	• Information used in the discussion is inappropriate, incorrect, or not suited to the specified inconsistency and question	• Information used in the discussion is appropriate, correct, and suited to the specified inconsistency and question	• Information used in the discussion is clear, appropriate, correct, and suited to the specified inconsistency and question
				• Accomplished all of the above on the first attempt

page 2 of 2

Sample Student Work

The following are two student work samples demonstrating selection of an ecosystem, the countries that contain that ecosystem, creation of a statistical question, creation of a Gapminder chart and video to demonstrate visual data, and a discussion answering the statistical question with the data.

Ecosystem = Desert

Countries in the world with a desert: Australia; Northern Africa (Egypt, Niger, Libya, Sudan, Tunisia, etc); Chile; The Middle East (especially Saudi Arabia, Yemen, Iraq, Kuwait and UAE); Mexico; South Africa; Namibia; Somalia; Central Asia (Afghanistan, Turkmenistan, Uzbekistan, etc); United States; China

Statistical Question: How is the percentage of agricultural land related to the total surface area of countries that contain a desert?

Images of Chart and Map:

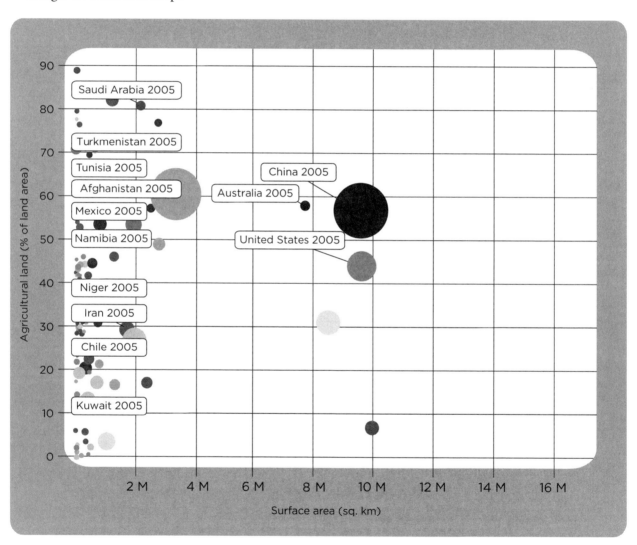

Video: http://youtu.be/MmKD1jTWPY8

Discussion and inconsistencies: It can be seen from the chart that most countries have less than four million square kilometers of total surface area. It would be expected that a desert country would have little agricultural land as you see in Egypt, UAE, Kuwait, and Libya. However, all but eight of the countries listed above have more than 45 percent agricultural land. Therefore, it can be concluded that not all of the country is desert (has another ecosystem in the country that can be farmed) or the country has learned ways to develop the desert land into agricultural land.

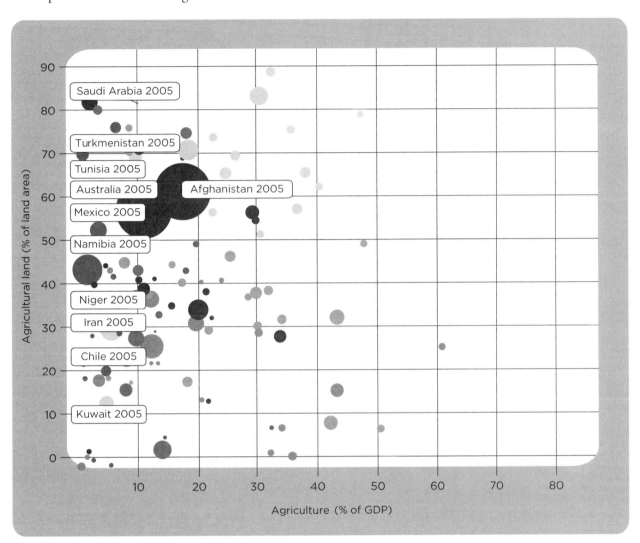

Statistical question: How is the percentage of agricultural land related to the percentage of money made on agriculture to the total Gross Domestic Product (GDP)?

Video: http://youtu.be/rEAqmbMzzIs

In only four countries does agriculture contribute more than 15 percent to the GDP: Afghanistan 39 percent, Sudan 32 percent, Uzbekistan 28 percent, and Turkmenistan 19 percent. Therefore, even in countries that have a higher percentage of agricultural land, agriculture does not contribute much to total GDP. One explanation could be that agriculture sales do not make much money. Food does not bring much money compared to selling wood or manufactured products. The people could be eating the food rather than selling it. There could be environmental conditions that cause damage to the crops. The countries may not know of research that makes crops grow better and faster. These countries are making most of their money in methods other than agriculture.

Map of these countries:

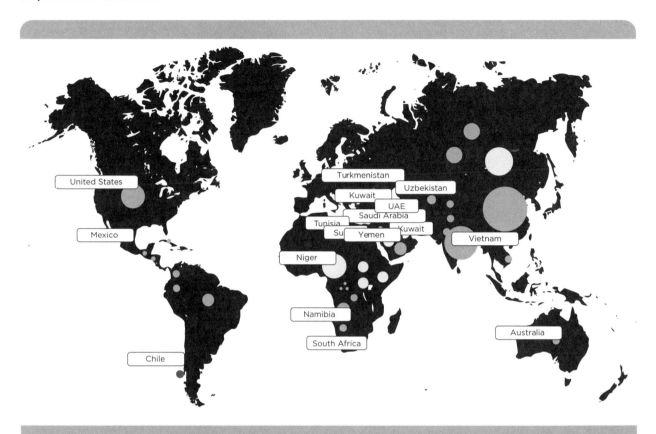

Create Excellence Framework Rating

CREATE ANALYSIS		
CREATE COMPONENT	**LEVEL**	**JUSTIFICATION**
Real-World Learning	2: Practicing	The project does not get into the realm of the simulation, but rather connects to real-world topics. This could be improved to a level 3 task or project projecting real-world learning by simulating a country in need, or a level 4 by actually communicating and contacting a school and students in a country in need.
Cognitive Complexity	3: Investigating	This is a level 3 as the students are investigating various research questions. This project is profiled as students are investigating research questions and analyzing data. This task is on the Analyze level of Bloom's taxonomy.
Student Engagement	3: Investigating	Students have some choice by selecting an ecosystem, data, and research questions. The project is very teacher directed, which could be bumped up considerably to a level 4 overall if the students could have the opportunity to generate their ideas of how the Gapminder information could be used.
Technology Integration	2: Practicing	Students are using Gapminder at the application level and for gathering information. The technology integration could be enhanced with another media component added.

A DAY IN THE LIFE OF AN HISTORIAN

Source: Kelli Ralston. Used with permission.

Content: Social studies

Learning Objectives:

1. Students will evaluate multiple philosophical views of the Enlightenment Period and critique those philosophies using historical facts from that period.
2. Students will analyze research on a specific time period by using their research to support or critique a primary source achieving at least three out of four on a rubric.

Standards:

The College, Career, and Civic Life (C3) Framework for Social Studies State Standards—

- D2.His.7.9–12 Explain how the perspectives of people in the present shape interpretations of the past (NCSS, 2013).
- D2.His.8.9–12 Analyze how current interpretations of the past are limited by the extent to which available historical sources represent perspectives of people at the time (NCSS, 2013).

Project Options: This activity can be done with any historical period being studied.

Resources Needed: Computer with Internet access; Padlet (www.padlet.com) or another web board tool; library; social studies textbook

A Day in the Life of an Historian

Historians are interpreters of the past. One of the ways in which they interpret history is by evaluating primary sources and the point of view of the author. Historians contrast points of view and try to connect those viewpoints to what was happening during the time. This assignment will give you the chance to act as a mini-historian.

Project Tasks

1. You are a present-day historian who is interested in studying Western European history. Find a primary source from the Enlightenment Period (17th to 18th centuries) in European history. Look in online databases or in the library to find your source. This could be a speech, document, letter, personal diary entry, philosophical work, and so on. Anything that was published by historians during this time period in Western European history is acceptable.

2. Carefully read your primary source document. Think about the perspective of the author. What point of view is this person taking?

3. Evaluate your source using the following questions.

   * Does the author's perspective connect to what was happening during the Enlightenment?
   * Is the author's point of view similar to or different than others' from the Enlightenment Period?
   * Are there consistencies between what the author said in your source and a specific event that took place or an improvement that was made during the Enlightenment?

4. Now you will research to find support for your evaluation. You may use articles, credible websites, library books, textbooks, and online primary sources.

5. Post your research on the class Padlet (www.padlet.com) wall. Post events or facts from your research and explain how those help to support your evaluation of the primary source.

   * The teacher will post tips and guiding questions on the wall to guide your research.
   * Comment on other students' work. If you disagree with someone's evaluation, support your own evaluation with evidence.
   * Make sure to post the link to your sources or mention the source of your information.

6. Look for an expert on the subject of the Enlightenment.

   * Pick one of the secondary sources you have used that has been particularly helpful in answering your questions. Use a mind-map tool like Bubbl.us to compare and contrast your primary and secondary sources.
   * Research the source's author. Is the author still living? If so, continue. If not, look for a historian that you can contact. It should be fairly easy to find an email address for the author. (Most likely she or he will be working at a university, and you can contact the author through her or his university email).
   * Write an email explaining your research, findings, and any questions you have. You can ask for any suggestions the author may have for completing your research.

page 1 of 2

- You *must* allow the teacher to read and approve your email message before sending it to the historian.
7. With your claims made on the class wall, be prepared to defend your evaluation in a class debate. If you find that you and another student agree on an evaluation, work together to form an argument and defense of that argument.

Scoring Rubric

	1 SIGNIFICANT REVISION NEEDED	2 SOME REVISION NEEDED	3 PROFICIENT	4 EXCEEDS EXPECTATIONS
Objective 1: Students will evaluate multiple philosophical views of the Enlightenment Period and critique those philosophies using historical facts from that period.	The student does not use historical facts to evaluate two perspectives from the Enlightenment. Opinion is used but is not backed up with evidence.	The student's critique of the philosophical views of the primary and secondary sources using historical facts from the Enlightenment Period is somewhat incorrect and poorly written. The facts are irrelevant to the perspectives but there is still some effort shown.	The student's critique of the philosophical views of the primary and secondary sources using historical facts from the Enlightenment Period is correct. Some facts may be somewhat irrelevant to the perspectives but do show a clear assertion.	The student's critique of the philosophical views of the primary and secondary sources using historical facts from the Enlightenment Period is insightful, correct, and well-written.
Objective 2: Students will analyze research on a specific time period by using their research to support or critique a primary source achieving at least three out of four on a rubric.	One source is used in student research. Source represents little to no credibility. The student only summarizes the source.	At least two sources are used in student research. At least one of the sources is credible, and the student only summarizes the sources.	At least three sources are used in student research. Sources are credible, and the student correctly summarizes and analyzes some elements of the sources and what they represent about that time period.	At least three sources are used in student research. Sources are credible, and the student correctly analyzes what the sources represent about that time period.

Real-World Learning Framework for Secondary Schools © 2016 Solution Tree Press • solution-tree.com
Visit **go.solution-tree.com/instruction** to download this page.

Sample Student Work

Following is a student work sample for this project. Several students correspond via email with the teacher about the philosophers.

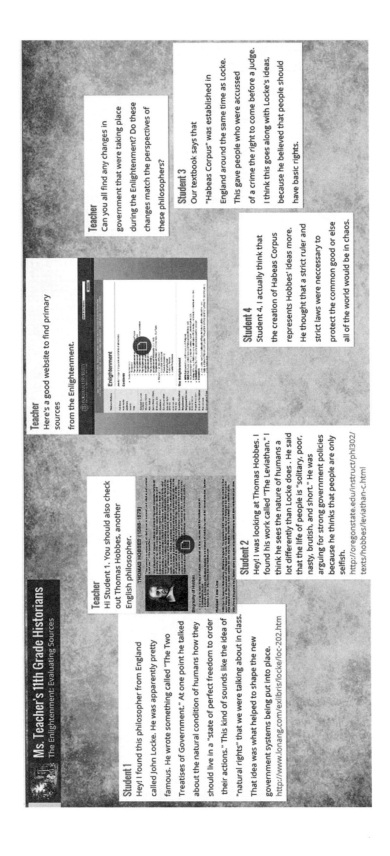

Create Excellence Framework Rating

CREATE ANALYSIS		
CREATE COMPONENT	**LEVEL**	**JUSTIFICATION**
Real-World Learning	3: Investigating	Students are also collaborating with experts in this field. They are asked to email the author of one of their sources to talk about the research they are conducting. They are simulating the analysis of a source.
Cognitive Complexity	3: Investigating	They are working at an Evaluate level, as they are judging quality and philosophical viewpoints of a variety of sources and comparing them to historical facts of the period.
Student Engagement	3: Investigating	Students read primary sources and then search for facts to back up their own evaluations of those sources.

Students are collaborating with other students to improve their finished product. By using an online class wall, students are sharing ideas, offering suggestions, and keeping each other updated on their own work.

Students also collaborate with historians who are in the field to discuss their research. |
| **Technology Integration** | 3: Investigating | Students interact with technology to share their research in this assignment. They are using multiple online sources, and also utilizing Padlet to collaborate with other students and record their findings and evaluations. Students are collaborating with field experts as well by communicating with the authors of their sources. |

HOW CAN WE IMPROVE OUR TOWN?

Source: Kelli Ralston. Used with permission.

Content: Geography

Learning Objectives:

1. Students will evaluate a map based on their knowledge of the five themes of geography.
2. Students will propose a community improvement and create a presentation to persuade community leaders.

Standards:

The College, Career, and Civic Life (C3) Framework for Social Studies State Standards—

- D2.Geo.2.9–12 Use maps, satellite images, photographs, and other representations to explain relationships between the locations of places and regions and their political, cultural, and economic dynamics (NCSS, 2013).
- D2.Geo.5.9–12 Evaluate how political and economic decisions throughout time have influenced cultural and environmental characteristics of various places and regions (NCSS, 2013).

Project Options: This assignment could also be done at a country-wide or global level. Have students look at a country or world map and think of improvements that can be made between states or countries.

Resources Needed: Computer with Internet access; brainstorming tools such as Scribble Maps, Mind-Meister, or Bubbl.us; projector screen; Edublogs (www.edublogs.com); multimedia-presentation tools such as Animoto or PhotoPeach; other student suggestions for online technologies

How Can We Improve Our Town?

Have you ever wondered why towns were built where they are, or have you ever wondered what geography has to do with your own town? In this activity you analyze your own town in geographical terms and think about ways in which your town can improve itself to make the most out of its geography.

Project Tasks

1. You will be investigating the town that we live in as if you were a geographer. Look at the online map of our town using Scribble Maps (www.scribblemaps.com).

    *   Look for and circle any geographical patterns on the map (such as, where streets are placed, where homes are located, and so on).
    *   Look at and circle the physical features on the map (such as grassy areas, hills, rivers, and so on).
    *   Circle and label one feature on the map for each theme of geography (location, movement, region, and human-environment interaction).

2. You will be put into peer groups. Each group will be assigned one of the five themes of geography to focus on for this project. Look again at the town map. Look for and label all ways in which that map represents your theme of geography. Look for improvements that can be made to the town, based on your theme of geography. The following are some questions to think about.

    *   What can the town do to improve its appeal to tourists and potential residents?
    *   How can the town use the human and physical characteristics of its place on the map to provide a better place to live for its citizens?
    *   How can the town encourage more people to move there?
    *   How can the town interact with the environment to create a healthier atmosphere for its citizens?
    *   How can the town work with other areas within its region to improve its citizens' quality of life?
    *   Use a web-based mind map like MindMeister (www.mindmeister.com) or Bubbl.us (www.bubbl.us) to brainstorm ideas and connections as a group. Other groups can give you feedback and make comments on your mind-map ideas.

3. Come to a consensus on a definite improvement that can be made in your town. Use your theme of geography for justifying why that improvement should be made.

4. In your groups, create a way to persuade your town to make this improvement. Decide on who you should talk to about your idea. The following are some ideas for connections to make:

    *   Authority figures like the police
    *   Town officials like the mayor
    *   Residents
    *   Community organizations like the local historical board

5. Create a product to communicate your idea to the targeted audience.

6. Explain the improvement that needs to be made.

7. Justify why that improvement should be made using your theme of geography.

8. Develop a plan to implement your improvement in the community.

   - Create an estimated list of expenses, and include where the funding of the project should come from.
   - Create an outline that lists the detailed steps to be taken to implement your improvement in the community.

9. Use technology for creating your final product, such as:

   - A blog that includes input from the mayor or community leaders
   - A multimedia presentation to give at a town council meeting; you could choose tools like Animoto or PhotoPeach
   - An online pamphlet or brochure to email to community officials
   - Other ideas students suggested

10. Give your presentation to community leaders, and note their response. Were they in favor of your ideas? Do you think that they will implement your plan?

Real-World Learning Framework for Secondary Schools © 2016 Solution Tree Press • solution-tree.com
Visit **go.solution-tree.com/instruction** to download this page.

Scoring Rubric

	1 SIGNIFICANT REVISION NEEDED	2 SOME REVISION NEEDED	3 PROFICIENT	4 EXCEEDS EXPECTATIONS
Objective 1: Students will evaluate a map based on their knowledge of the five themes of geography.	Little to no themes are labeled on the online town map, and those that are show little accuracy. Online mind map only summarizes the town map and shows little effort to evaluate it and use relevant details to brainstorm an improvement.	Not all themes are labeled on the online town map, but the themes labeled are generally accurate. Online mind map shows an effort to evaluate the town map, but many details are irrelevant in the brainstorming process.	All five themes of geography are labeled on the online town map and are generally accurate. Online mind map shows an adequate evaluation of the town map, but some details are irrelevant in the brainstorming process that is used to decide on an improvement.	All five themes of geography are accurately labeled on the online town map. Online mind map shows deep evaluation of the town map and uses relevant details to brainstorm an improvement.
Objective 2: Students will propose a community improvement and create a presentation to persuade community leaders.	Online technology is used. A proposed improvement and two-part implementation plan are lacking description. The improvement does not show a generation of new knowledge, but merely repeats the theme in a general and unauthentic manner. The theme is not used to effectively justify the improvement, and therefore no understanding or application of the theme is present.	Online technology is used. A proposed improvement and two-part implementation plan are described and outlined, but lack detail and are unclear. The improvement is questionable on whether or not it has generated new knowledge. Justification of the improvement uses the theme of geography but does not show a deep understanding and application of that theme.	Online technology is used and explains the proposed improvement and outlines a two-part implementation plan. The improvement illustrates a clear generation of new knowledge. Justification of the improvement uses the theme of geography but may lack on showing a deep understanding and application of that theme.	Online technology is used and clearly explains the proposed improvement and outlines a two-part implementation plan. The improvement is creative and illustrates a clear generation of new knowledge. Justification of the improvement uses the theme of geography and shows deep understanding and application of that theme.

Real-World Learning Framework for Secondary Schools © 2016 Solution Tree Press • solution-tree.com
Visit **go.solution-tree.com/instruction** to download this page.

Sample Student Work

The following is a Scribble map of the town in this project. The mind map that follows demonstrates the student thinking prior to creating the blog website.

Online Town Map

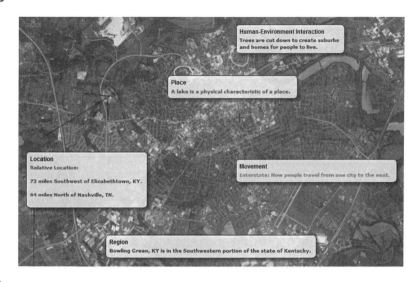

Online Mind Map

Human-Environment Interaction in our hometown.

Student 1: So, we're supposed to think about human-environment interaction in this town. And then think of an improvement that can be made in our town.

Student 4: Human-environment interaction means the ways in which people interact with the world around them. Buildings, bridges, industrial factories, farming. These are all examples.

Student 3: Improvement. How about improving farming equipment to ensure that the environment is not being harmed by pesticides, animals, waste, etc.?

Student 2: On the map, I circled suburbs that were created. This shows human-environment interaction because trees had to be cut down in order to build those houses.

Student 5: Industrial factories . . . there are a few of those in our town, I saw them on the map. There's one right beside a lake called "Limestone Lake."

Student 1: That seems like a very broad goal. Maybe something specific?

Student 3: How can we argue an improvement for that? It's hard to protest the building of houses

Student 3: Industrial factories obviously affect the environment. Think of the pollution they put off. Could we do something about this? I think this is more attainable than my farming suggestion.

Student 2: Well Student 5 said that there is a lake right beside of the factory. I'm sure that is easily affected by industrial pollution.

Student 4: We could ask the town to move the factory?

Student 5: Yeah! That would help to preserve the lake.

Student 1: And better yet, we could say that Limestone Lake should be made into a park so that citizens in our town can enjoy it.

The blog *Community Improvement: Make Limestone Lake a Place for Everyone* (http://kelliralston20 .edublogs.org) documents and publicizes the proposal to improve the town. This blog is the final product of this project.

Create Excellence Framework Rating

CREATE ANALYSIS		
CREATE COMPONENT	**LEVEL**	**JUSTIFICATION**
Real-World Learning	4: Integrating	Students are looking for ways to improve their community in this assignment. Since they will present their results to community leaders, they are having an impact on the community. Learning is integrated across subject areas since writing, geography, technology, and mathematics skills are involved.
Cognitive Complexity	4: Integrating	While this lesson begins as teacher directed, it moves to a student-directed approach where students propose a community plan based on geography. Students choose how they will communicate that idea to others and devise their own procedures to accomplish a task. Students are learning at the Create level of the revised Bloom's taxonomy since they are generating ideas and solutions for their community.
Student Engagement	4: Integrating	Students are partnering with the teacher and other students to define their solution and what their final product will be. They arrive at this point by initiating their own analysis of the map and then by creating their own improvement and plan. The entire assignment revolves around the students' application of their own research and implementation of their own idea. Students are initiating collaborations within the community. Depending on the product they create, students will in some way have to interact with authority figures or citizens in the community.
Technology Integration	4: Integrating	Students are constantly using technology throughout this assignment in order to produce their own ideas from content. There are three different technologies used by the students. Technology is embedded in the content and activities, promotes collaboration among group members, and helps students to create their solution and presentation.

AMENDING SCHOOL RULES: THE POWER OF INTERPRETATION

Source: Kelli Ralston. Used with permission.

Content: U.S. government or civics course

Learning Objectives:

1. Students will evaluate the freedoms and limits of a constitutional amendment.
2. Students will argue for a revision of a school rule by creating persuasion materials.

Standards:

The College, Career, and Civic Life (C3) Framework for Social Studies State Standards—

- D2.Civ.10.9–12 Analyze the impact and the appropriate roles of personal interests and perspectives on the application of civic virtues, democratic principles, constitutional rights, and human rights (NCSS, 2013).
- D2.Civ.12.9–12 Analyze how people use and challenge local, state, national, and international laws to address a variety of public issues (NCSS, 2013).

Resources Needed: Copy of the U.S. Constitution; computer with Internet access; online-presentation tool like PhotoPeach, iMovie, Animoto, or PechaKucha; schoolwide polling system or online survey

Amending School Rules: The Power of Interpretation

Interpretation is perhaps the largest issue concerning written rules and laws. Words can have different meanings to different people. This activity allows you to become an interpreter of rules and gives you an opportunity to persuade others to adopt your interpretation. You also see how national rules and laws connect to your school's rules and laws.

Project Tasks

For this assignment, you will look at U.S. Constitutional amendments and how they affect your freedom as a student in this school.

1. Browse the U.S. Constitution. In your group, select an amendment that affects the freedom you have while in school.

   - Paraphrase the amendment in your own words.
   - What rights does the amendment give to U.S. citizens and in particular to you?
   - What limitations does the amendment place on your freedom at schools?

2. Record other people's interpretations of that amendment. Walk around the classroom and interview at least five of your classmates. Consider, "What rights do your classmates think that the amendment gives to students?"

3. Debate the U.S. amendments with your classmates. As a group, argue your case of which amendment is most limited at school.

4. After thinking about your classmates' interpretations of the amendment, decide what *your own* interpretation is of *one* amendment. Record your answers to the following on your paper.

   - What freedoms does the amendment give to you as a high school student, and what are the limits on those freedoms?
   - How does the amendment affect teens in your school?
   - What is your take on the amendment?

5. Once you decide on your position, act as a lawyer searching for court cases online or in the library that support your interpretation.

6. Propose a positive revision to a school rule to align with the amendment. Brainstorm several good options and then evaluate which option is the best. Explain the following in your paper.

   - How will this revision connect to the amendment, and how will it make students in this school better off?
   - How does this rule revision align with your interpretation of the U.S. amendment?

7. Form another group with classmates and review their revisions and chart out the positive and negative aspects of each revision. Come to an agreement on the best revision proposed.

8. After deciding on your interpretation and revision, initiate a campaign in your school to gather support for your interpretation and revision.

page 1 of 2

- Record and justify your interpretation of the amendment. The purpose of this is to persuade others to adopt your viewpoint.
- Create a presentation using an online-presentation tool of your choice to convince the student body and school administrators to adopt your viewpoint and to agree with your revision. Presentations will be posted online for classmates to review. Possible presentation platform options include PhotoPeach (www.photopeach.com), iMovie, Animoto (www.animoto.com), or PechaKucha (www.pechakucha.org).
- Focus on how your interpretation or revision improves student lives within the school and the school atmosphere in general.

9. Finally, our school will have a schoolwide vote to decide on which revision to the rules should be presented to the administration.

Scoring Rubric

	1 SIGNIFICANT REVISION NEEDED	2 SOME REVISION NEEDED	3 PROFICIENT	4 EXCEEDS EXPECTATIONS
Objective 1: Students will evaluate the freedoms and limits of a constitutional amendment.	Online presentation shows little to no evaluation of the U.S. amendment and no clear connection to a school rule.	Online presentation lacks in the evaluation of a U.S. amendment but shows its connection to school rules.	Online presentation shows some evaluation of the U.S. amendment and its connection to school rules.	Online presentation shows complete evaluation of the U.S. amendment and its connection to school rules.
Objective 2: Students will argue for a revision of a school rule by creating persuasion materials.	A revision to a school rule is proposed, but the benefits the revision will have on students in the school are not explained.	A revision to a school rule is proposed, but it is not clearly explained as to how the revision will benefit students in the school.	A revision to a school rule is proposed, and the presentation somewhat explains how the revision benefits students in the school.	A revision to a school rule is proposed, and the presentation clearly explains how the revision will benefit students in the school.

Real-World Learning Framework for Secondary Schools © 2016 Solution Tree Press • solution-tree.com
Visit **go.solution-tree.com/instruction** to download this page.

Sample Student Work

Visit http://animoto.com/play/Ba3LJm0ZGlEa5q4kgBOPxQ to view the sample project. In this project, the student is explaining how the Bill of Rights connects to school rules and student rights. The student proposes a change to the school dress code to be more aligned to the rights for freedom of expression.

Create Excellence Framework Rating

CREATE ANALYSIS		
CREATE COMPONENT	**LEVEL**	**JUSTIFICATION**
Real-World Learning	3: Integrating	In this task, students are reviewing their school policies or rules and recommending a change.
Cognitive Complexity	4: Integrating	At the beginning students are determining which amendment affects most high school students. Students do this by developing their own interpretations of specific amendments and brainstorming the freedoms and limitations each amendment offers. Students then work at the Evaluate level as they consider the positive and negative aspects of each revision. Finally, students work at the Create level as they brainstorm possible options, select the best one, and initiate their own campaign to persuade the school to adopt their rule revision.
Student Engagement	3: Investigating	While teachers are guiding students toward appropriate actions, students are largely defining the content and process. Students select the amendment and propose a revision to the school rules. Students collaborate with other students in a way that helps them to think about differing perspectives to help them determine their own perspective.
Technology Integration	3: Investigating	Student technology is embedded in the completion of the final products for this assignment. The student presentations that are intended to inform other students and teachers are done so using unique online technologies. This use of technology depicts a culmination of their efforts to problem solve, evaluate various interpretations and points of view, and design effective solutions.

BAKIN' IN THE SUN: ENGINEERING A SOLAR OVEN

Source: Shelton Fisher. Used with permission.

Content: Science

Learning Objectives:

1. Students will design and construct an efficient solar oven.
2. Students will modify their solar oven to optimize temperature and calculate its power output.

Standards:

Next Generation Science Standards—

- MS-PS3 Apply scientific principles to design, construct, and test a device that either minimizes or maximizes thermal energy transfer (Achieve, 2013). Clarification Statement: Examples of devices could include an insulated box, a solar cooker, and a Styrofoam cup.

Common Core English Language Arts—

- RST.6–8.3 Follow precisely a multistep procedure when carrying out experiments, taking measurements, or performing technical tasks (NGA & CCSSO, 2010a).

Project Options: Throughout this project, students will have numerous opportunities to be autonomous during the designing, engineering, and testing process. Students will be able to:

- Research designs, select materials that will be needed, and engineer their own solar oven
- Document, display, and present their design, data collected, and their solar oven's power output

Resources Needed: For the successful completion of this project, students will need various materials (for example, boxes, aluminum foil, glue, duct tape, plastic wrap, picture frame glass, measuring devices, and so on). Students will be able to select the materials they will need to engineer their solar oven design. Therefore, as part of this assignment, students will be expected to scavenge for materials or buy them on a budget. This restriction is in place to require students to think critically about materials they could use in order to create an innovative solar oven.

After designing and constructing a solar oven, students will be able to test their projects. Students will need access to digital thermometers in order to record the temperature change over a time interval of sixty minutes. Moreover, students will need to utilize technology (computers, tablet computer, Data Analysis app, Internet, and so on) to research solar oven designs and present their projects.

Bakin' in the Sun: Engineering a Solar Oven

Yesterday, a terrible thunderstorm traversed through your community. It left several thousand people without power and absolutely no way to prepare meals. The community has been told it could take up to two weeks to repair the damaged power lines. Despite this news, families are proactively brainstorming ways in which they can engineer an oven that utilizes an alternative energy source in order to provide food for their families and the community during this time. They have concluded the best energy source for this project is solar energy and have asked middle school science students to help them.

Project Tasks

Develop a team of two other fellow scientists to research, engineer, and test an innovative and efficient solar oven for the people in your community. Your oven will need to efficiently heat large amounts of soup or broth in order to provide food for the community until the power is restored. Moreover, they have challenged you to only use scavenged materials found around your home or in your community. If needed, you have a budget of five dollars which you may spend on the project, and all expenses must be reported in your presentation.

1. Throughout this project, your group will maintain an online blog with daily entries that discuss your thought process, ideas, solutions, and steps taken each day. Reflect on what worked and what did not work and why. Share your blog with your teacher so that she or he can track your group's progress and thought processes. You could use Blogger, Weebly, LiveJournal, or WordPress to create your blog. Don't forget to take digital pictures (yes, you can use your cell phone camera!) to upload to your blog.

2. With your group, brainstorm ideas or features you need to consider or incorporate into your design in order to create an efficient solar oven. Use the following questions to discuss and inspire original ideas; outline answers to the following questions to guide your thinking throughout the engineering process. Think outside the box!

   - How can I optimize temperature and power output of my oven?
   - What factors will influence the solar oven's performance?
   - How will the sun's energy be captured and trapped inside of the oven?
   - How can the sun's energy be transferred as a heat source to cook food, and how can I design the oven to concentrate this energy into a specific place?
   - What materials would be excellent for this project, and where can they be found? How will these specific materials be helpful in this process?
   - What materials possibly needed to be purchased? Is this a necessity to the overall design and performance of my oven? Why or why not?

3. Research solar oven designs and analyze the materials used, the engineering process, and how it works. Select two designs that would be most effective and briefly describe them in the appropriate section of the "Solar Oven Project Sheet" table.

4. Using your knowledge about energy and ideas collected from your research, design a solar oven. Utilize drawings, pictures, scales, measurements, and other pieces of information to communicate your design plan efficiently and effectively. This design plan must be neatly organized and included in your final presentation.

5. Begin gathering your materials and construct an efficient solar oven. Be sure to document the process along the way by taking digital pictures (by any technology device the teacher approves) and developing a procedure, which you'll title "How to Engineer a Solar Oven," to include in your presentation.

6. Test your solar oven's power using the following procedures:

   ◆ Set up your oven as intended in order to collect as much sunlight as possible.
   ◆ Measure and record the temperature (in Celsius) of a 500 milliliter sample. Place the water sample in your oven.
   ◆ After ten minutes, measure and record the soup or broth's temperature (in Celsius) in your data table. Continue to collect data every ten minutes over the course of one hour (sixty minutes).
   ◆ Using your data, determine the total energy absorbed by the water. Show all of your work and circle your final answer.
   ◆ Now, calculate the power output of your solar oven.

7. Reflect on the design and power output of your solar oven. Brainstorm ways in which you can collect as much energy as possible to improve your oven in order to optimize temperature and power output in the "Solar Oven Project Sheet" table. Document these ideas, and improve, adjust, or modify your solar oven design.

8. Perform the solar oven test again and record your results in the appropriate section of the "Solar Oven Project Sheet" table.

9. Utilizing technology (advertisement video, Prezi, student webpage, animation, infographic, and so on), prepare a presentation outlining your engineering process. You will present your solar oven design to the community and help community members prepare soup for the families without power. Incorporate all of the following components into your presentation.

   ◆ Detailed solar oven design plan
   ◆ List of materials used for the construction of the solar oven and material cost, if necessary
   ◆ Procedure followed to construct the solar oven
   ◆ Data tables (for test one and test two)
   ◆ One graph to compare time and temperature (include data from both tests on one graph)
   ◆ Energy and power calculations for test one and test two (show all calculations)
   ◆ Include any modifications you made and your project conclusions. Answer the following questions:
     ▴ "What possible factors influenced the performance of the solar oven?"
     ▴ "What modifications or adjustments did you make to the oven before the second test? Why?"

- ⬆ "How did these modifications influence the performance of your solar oven?"
- ⬆ "What other modifications could be made to the solar oven to optimize temperature and power output?"
- ◆ During your presentation, demonstrate how your solar oven works by heating up a soup or broth sample for at least two families of four.

Solar Oven Project Sheet

1. Brainstorm Ideas and Features

2. Possible Solar Oven Designs (include source)

3. Our Solar Oven Design and Procedures

4. Data

TEST 1		TEST 2	
Time (minutes)	Temperature (°C)	Time (minutes)	Temperature (°C)
0		0	
10		10	
20		20	
30		30	
40		40	
50		50	
60		60	

5. Energy and Power Output

6. Modifications

Real-World Learning Framework for Secondary Schools © 2016 Solution Tree Press • solution-tree.com
Visit **go.solution-tree.com/instruction** to download this page.

Scoring Rubric

	1 SIGNIFICANT REVISION NEEDED	2 SOME REVISION NEEDED	3 PROFICIENT	4 EXCEEDS EXPECTATIONS
Objective 1: Students will design and construct an efficient solar oven.	• The learner attempts to design and construct a solar oven. The product does not meet the assignment specifications. The solar oven is not efficient and takes more than five minutes to assemble. • The group's blog outlines little of the group's thoughts, ideas, and processes in creating the solar oven.	• The learner designs and constructs a solar oven that meets some of the assignment specifications. Some parts of the solar oven are built according to the design plan; collects some light. The learner needs more than two minutes to assemble the solar oven. • The group's blog outlines some of the group's thoughts, ideas, and processes in creating the solar oven.	• The learner designs and constructs a solar oven that meets the assignment specifications. Most of the solar oven is built according to the design plan, collects the light, and attempts to concentrate it to the container inside the oven. The learner also assembles the oven in two minutes or less. • The group's blog outlines most of the group's thoughts, ideas, and processes in creating the solar oven.	• The learner designs and constructs a solar oven that meets the assignment specifications and is built according to the plan. The solar oven collects light efficiently and concentrates it toward the container inside the oven. The learner also can assemble the oven in two minutes or less. • The group's blog clearly outlines all of the group's thoughts, ideas, and processes in creating the solar oven.
Objective 2: Students will modify their solar oven to optimize temperature and calculate its power output.	• After testing the solar oven, the learner does not attempt minor modifications to the oven to optimize temperature and power output. The learner does not increase power output and does not attempt to calculate it or does so inaccurately. The presentation does not effectively communicate components to the community.	• After testing the solar oven, the learner makes a minor modification to the oven to optimize temperature and power output. The learner does not increase the power output and calculates it with several errors. The presentation outlines a few components to community members.	• After testing the solar oven, the learner attempts to modify the solar oven to optimize temperature and power output. The learner increases power output by one to two watts and is able to calculate this with few or minor errors. The presentation outlines and demonstrates some components to community members.	• After testing the solar oven, the learner demonstrates his or her ability to modify the design to optimize temperature and power output. The learner increases power output by three watts or more and is able to calculate this correctly. The presentation clearly outlines and demonstrates all components to community members.

page 4 of 4

Sample Student Work

The following provides sources for solar oven research and step-by-step instructions for how to design the actual solar oven.

Sources for Solar Oven Research

- http://solarcooking.org/plans/
- www.instructables.com/id/Cardboard-and-Duct-tape-Solar-Oven/
- www.instructables.com/id/Cardboard-Foil-Glue-The-Solar-Funnel-Cooker/
- www.instructables.com/id/Solar-Cooking-With-A-Cardboard-Oven-10/

The following is the Solar Oven Design and Procedures

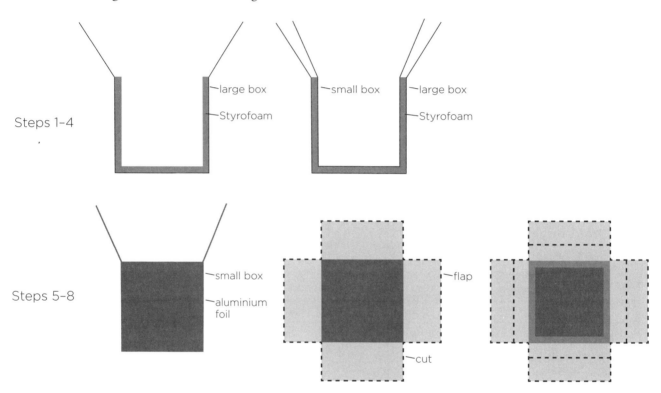

1. Take the small box (with removed flaps) and place inside the large box. Determine the amount of Styrofoam needed to secure the smaller box.
2. Cut pieces of Styrofoam block. The shape/size of Styrofoam will depend on the amount of space between the small box inside the larger box (around the edges and underneath the small box). Whatever the depth of that space is how thick the Styrofoam should be.
3. Place the bottom piece into the box and insert the small box.
4. Insulate the sides of the box with the remaining Styrofoam pieces (make sure there is a clean level).
5. Remove the small box and line the inside with aluminum foil. Glue in sections and use a stiff straight edge to create a smooth surface. Insert small box inside the large one.
6. Fold over large flaps and determine how much is needed to cover the Styrofoam and meet the edge of the small box.
7. Cut the excess flaps off.
8. Take duct tape and secure the smaller flaps down. Make sure the Styrofoam is covered and the tape is tight and secure.

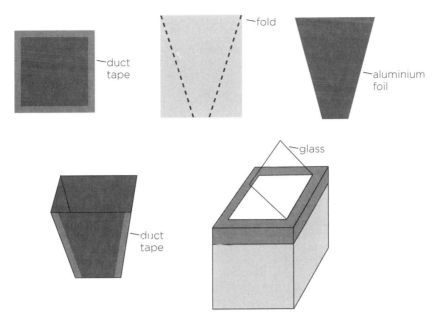

9. Take a large piece of cardboard to cut four trapezoid reflectors.
10. Create a template and cut reflectors.
11. Line the reflectors using glue and aluminum foil. Wrap the foil around the backside and secure with duct tape. (This should not interfere with the reflective foil because it should be on the outside.) Use a stiff straight edge to make a smooth clean surface while gluing.
12. Repeat step 11 for all four reflectors.
13. Take strips of duct tape and secure the reflectors together on the outside corners.
14. Take the piece of picture frame glass and place over opening of the small box.
15. Secure the glass on the box along one of the longest sides with duct tape.
16. Now, place the reflector piece (from step 13) and place on top of the solar oven box.
17. Adjust the reflectors in order to be able to lift the glass up.
18. Tape the reflectors onto the oven box with duct tape.
19. Spray paint a medium-sized metal can black.
20. After the can dries, place it inside the solar oven.
21. Place water sample inside the can and adjust the oven to collect the maximum amount of sunlight.

Data

TEST 1		TEST 2	
Time (minutes)	Temperature (°C)	Time (minutes)	Temperature (°C)
0	23.2	0	11.3
10	32.5	10	23.0
20	35.9	20	42.3
30	49.7	30	42.2
40	43.1	40	50.5
50	54.7	50	50.7
60	55.4	60	51.9

Science Projects

Solar Oven Calculations Test 1

The following solar oven calculations show how to find the Power (P) for each test.

Test # 1	**Test # 2**
$T_0 = 11.3\ °C$ Δ temperature = $(55.4°\ C{-}23.2°\ C)$	$T_0 = 11.3\ °C$ Δ temperature = $(51.9°\ C{-}11.3°\ C)$
$T_6 + 51.9\ °C$ $= 32.1°\ C$	$T_6 + 51.9\ °C$ $= 40.6°\ C$
$(4180 J)(.5L)(32.2°\ C) = 67{,}298\ J$	$(4180 J)(.5L)(40.6°\ C) = 84{,}854\ J$
$P = \dfrac{Work\ (Joules)}{Time\ (Seconds)}$	$P = \dfrac{Work\ (Joules)}{Time\ (Seconds)}$
$P = \dfrac{67,298\ J}{3600\ sec}$	$P = \dfrac{84,854\ J}{3600\ sec}$
$P = 18.7\ watts$	$P = 23.6\ watts$

Modifications: To optimize temperature and power output of my solar oven, I adjusted its ability to capture more sunlight. I did this by creating a wedge that could be placed underneath the box to angle it more toward the sun. As my results indicate, my solar oven power output increased almost five watts after I made this change to my design.

Create Excellence Framework Rating

CREATE ANALYSIS		
CREATE COMPONENT	**LEVEL**	**JUSTIFICATION**
Real-World Learning	3: Investigating	Students are creating a model of a solar oven and testing it for efficiency. However, they are not making an impact on their school or community.
Cognitive Complexity	3: Investigating	While this is a teacher-directed lesson, students are designing a solar over at the Create level of the revised Bloom's taxonomy. Students are researching solar ovens and combining ideas to generate their own plan.
Student Engagement	4: Integrating	Students will work in teams to define the process of this project, it is inquiry-based, and students are collaborating.
Technology Integration	3: Investigating	Students are using technology to document their progress in the solar oven project and create a presentation at the end about their findings. Therefore, this is an add-on and the lesson could have been done without these technology products.

ENERGY IN MOTION: KINETIC ENERGY

Source: Lydia Renfro. Used with permission.

Content: Science

Learning Objectives:

1. Students will create a bar graph to compare the relationship between mass and velocity of three or more animals and create a line graph to show one or more animal's kinetic energy over time.
2. The students will create a proposal to the zoo and share with the class through a short presentation.

Standards:

Next Generation Science Standards—

- MS.PS3.A Construct and interpret graphical displays to describe the relationships between the kinetic energy of an object and its mass, and between the kinetic energy of an object and its speed, in order to better define a real world problem (Achieve, 2013).

Common Core English Language Arts—

- W.6.1 Write arguments to support claims with clear reasons and relevant evidence (NGA & CCSSO, 2010a).
- W.6.1a Introduce claim(s) and organize the reasons and evidence clearly (NGA & CCSSO, 2010a).

Project Options: This activity can span into other areas. Students can create a proposal to a zoo of their creation. Students will use the app Graphs (for iPad or any tablet) to create a bar graph comparing the animals' mass and velocity (speed). Students will also create a line graph to compare an animal's kinetic energy over the course of its life. The students will be given the chance to place their graphs and proposal into a technology program of their choice.

Resources Needed: Access to a computer or tablet with Internet access; technology to research an online encyclopedia for the chosen animals as well as to create presentations and graphs

Energy in Motion: Kinetic Energy

When you think about animals running, what do you see? Do you see the fastest animal, the cheetah, running across the African plains? Do you see your dog or cat running across your backyard? All animals and humans use energy to do everything, every day. We will be finding out how much energy an animal uses when they are in motion, or their kinetic energy.

Project Tasks

A local zoo wants to open a new exhibit focusing on animals with high kinetic energy. Write a proposal to the zoo for the animals you want to see in the exhibit. Research animals of your choice and compare the animals' mass and the animals' velocity (speed) to find the animals' kinetic energy. After your research, create a bar graph that represents your animals' kinetic energy. Also pick one or two of your animals to create a line graph showing the animal's kinetic energy over its life span. Present this to the class through a persuasive presentation, and your classmates will act as the zoo representatives.

1. Review the rubric provided before completing the graph and proposal.

2. Research three or more animals of your choice. Be sure to collect information on the animal's mass and the velocity (speed). You will need this for the graphs.

3. To find kinetic energy, use the following formula: $E_k = 1/2m(v*v)$

4. Using the app *Graphs* or something comparable, input your data into the correct area for either your x axis or your y axis. Create a bar graph representing your animals' kinetic energy you calculated from their mass and velocity. Create a line graph to represent an animal's kinetic energy over its lifespan. Be sure to include a title and label for each part of your graph.

5. You will create a short presentation using an approved technology program of your choice. Think about the following questions as you create your presentation.

   ◆ What do the zoo representatives need to know about my animals?
   ◆ How can I make my graph easy to follow?
   ◆ Do I have my bar graph and line graph included?
   ◆ Do my graphs include mass, velocity, and kinetic-energy calculations?
   ◆ Is my proposal organized?
   ◆ Is my proposal persuasive?
   ◆ Does the proposal include all of my information?

6. Use the graphic organizer to collect your thoughts.

Real-World Learning Framework for Secondary Schools © 2016 Solution Tree Press • solution-tree.com
Visit **go.solution-tree.com/instruction** to download this page.

Zoo Proposal

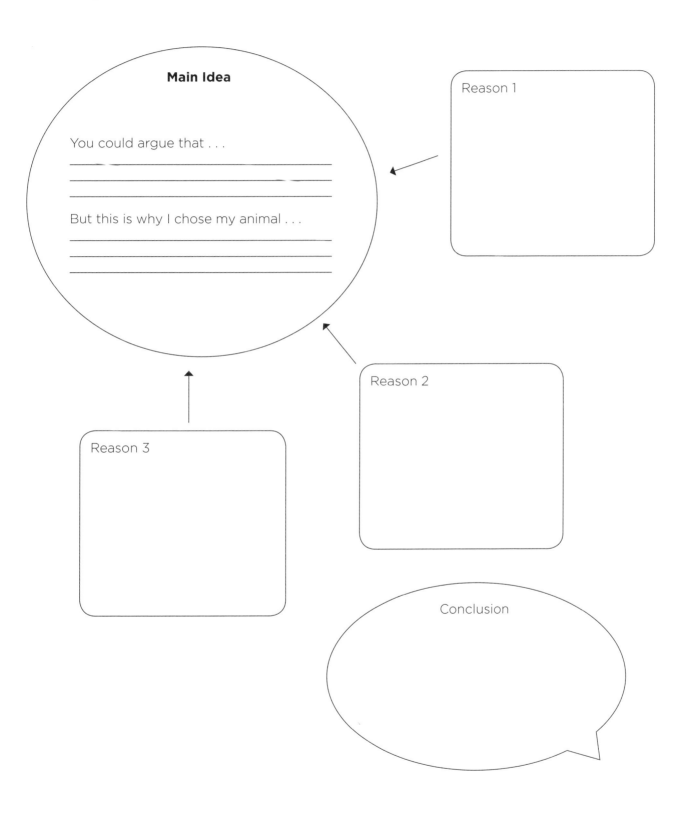

Scoring Rubric

	1 SIGNIFICANT REVISION NEEDED	2 SOME REVISION NEEDED	3 PROFICIENT	4 EXCEEDS EXPECTATIONS
Objective 1: Students will create a bar graph to compare the relationship between mass and velocity of three or more animals and create a line graph to show one or more animal's kinetic energy over time.	• Student creates a graph, but not about animals. • Student inputs incorrect or inappropriate data. • There are no labels on x or y axis. • There is no title on graph. • Animal data are not labeled. • If the student uses colors, a key is not included.	• Student creates a graph about animals. • Animal data do not include mass or speed of animal(s). • Labels on either x or y axis, but not both. • Title on graph is incomplete. • Not all of animal data are labeled. • If the student uses colors, key only labels a few, not all colors.	• Student creates an organized bar graph and line graph about animals. • Graph includes animals' mass and speed. • x and y axes are correctly labeled. • Graph is titled. • All animal data are labeled. • If the student uses colors, each color is correctly labeled on the key.	• Student creates an organized bar graph and line graph. • Graph includes animals' mass and speed. • Both the x and y axis are labeled correctly. • Clever and accurate titles are present. • All animal data are labeled. • The student uses colors and labels each color correctly on the key. • Pictorial representation of the animals researched is present.
Objective 2: The students will create a proposal to the zoo and share with the class through a short presentation.	• Student does not create presentation.	• Student creates a presentation, but does not include graph or all of the information.	• Student creates a proposal that includes graphs and the majority of the information about their animals.	• Student creates an effective and persuasive proposal on their animals' kinetic energy and specifies what animal should be chosen.

Sample Student Work

Visit www.smore.com/m1q5-zoo-proposal to view a sample project. Here you will find information about the animals researched, graphs comparing the kinetic energy of the animals, and a case for which animal would be the best choice with accompanying videos.

CREATE ANALYSIS		
CREATE COMPONENT	**LEVEL**	**JUSTIFICATION**
Real-World Learning	3: Investigating	Students create a proposal about animals to include at a local zoo. The students research different animals they would like to see in their zoo. Since they are not really making the proposal to the zoo, it is considered a simulation.
Cognitive Complexity	2: Practicing	The students generate their own bar graph and line graph to create their proposal to the zoo over their animals' kinetic energy. As stated on the Create Excellence Framework, the teacher is directing the students to create these graphs and presentations and at the Apply level of Bloom's revised taxonomy.
Student Engagement	3: Investigating	Students will be engaged in this project as they are given a choice between animals to research and technology to use when presenting their findings. The task or project is differentiated by choice of interests and ability levels.
Technology Integration	3: Investigating	The technology in this lesson is an add-on to this lesson. In other words, the lesson could have been completed without technology. The technology for the graphs and the presentation enhanced the lesson but were not necessary.

TAKING FLIGHT HIGH INTO THE SKY

Source: Shelton Fisher. Used with permission.

Content: Science

Learning Objectives:

1. Students will construct a series of rockets to determine the optimal length and mass in order to obtain maximum flight time.
2. Students will determine factors that influence flight time by creating a graphical representation of data.

Standards:

Next Generation Science Standards—

*   MS-PS3–1 Construct and interpret graphical displays of data to describe the relationships of kinetic energy to the mass of an object and to the speed of an object (Achieve, 2013).
*   MS-PS3–5 Construct, use, and present arguments to support the claim that when the motion energy of an object changes, energy is transferred to or from the object (Achieve, 2013).
*   MS-PS3–3 Analyze data from tests to determine similarities and differences among several design solutions to identify the best characteristics of each that can be combined into a new solution to better meet the criteria for success (Achieve, 2013).

Project Options: Throughout this project, students will have opportunities to be autonomous during the construction and testing process. Students will be able to:

*   Select the length of rockets they would like to construct and test
*   Document, display data, and present their series of rockets to demonstrate the optimal length and mass needed in order to obtain maximum flight time

Resources Needed: For the successful completion of this project, students will need various materials to construct rockets—drawing pad paper, duct tape, foam craft sheets, clear packing tape, foam nose cones, PVC pipe (quarter inch), pipe insulation, cardboard scissors, hot glue gun and hot glue sticks, and meter stick or ruler. After constructing a series of four rockets, you will be able to test them. Therefore, students will need access to a launch pad, launch box, and stopwatch. Finally, students need to utilize technology (computers, iPads, Data Analysis app, Microsoft Excel, and so on) to organize their data and graph the results.

Taking Flight High Into the Sky

Prepare for takeoff! Next week marks the annual rocket competition, and NASA needs your help! As stakes are higher this year, so is the competition. Last year, our team, the Rocketeers, was runner up and we would like to take home the top prize this year. However, we need your help to construct a series of rockets that will travel the highest altitude!

Project Tasks

Develop a team of three other junior astronauts to construct a series of four rockets of different lengths. You will be using the blueprint and procedures last year's team developed in order to design your rockets. It is in your best interest to modify the design plans in order to construct a rocket that goes even higher than last year's winning team! After testing your team's rocket series, you will use the data to create another rocket in order to achieve the maximum altitude possible. However, because this is a competition, you must meet the parameters of this event. These specifications and restrictions are:

- The diameter of your rocket must be a quarter inch.
- It must be made of raw materials including: duct tape, scotch tape, packing tape, cardboard, paper, foam nose cones, foam sheets, pipe insulation, glue, and so on.
- Students competing must construct it.

To do this project, complete the following steps.

1. Reflect and discuss the following questions within your group before you construct a rocket. Brainstorm your ideas in the appropriate space in the "Brainstorm Ideas" table to guide your thinking throughout the process.

    - What factors influence the altitude a rocket travels?
    - How can this experiment be controlled so some variables do not skew data? Remember that you will be constructing four different rockets, so how can you control this process in order to control variables you do not want to influence the results?
    - In what ways can you construct a series of rockets that are exactly the same, except for the mass and length?
    - How do you think mass and length will affect the altitude and time of flight of the rocket?

2. Develop a series of four different rockets with your group (see Building a Rocket steps in this document).

3. Measure and record the mass and length of each rocket on one of its respective fins and in your data tables.

4. Test each of your rockets three times and record the time of flight of each one in the appropriate column in the data table.

5. On graphing paper, graph your results to analyze and compare the length of the rocket to the mass of the rocket.

6. On graphing paper, graph your results to analyze and compare the length of the rocket to the average time of flight for the rocket.

7. Input your data onto a classroom Microsoft Excel spreadsheet (or graph) or onto the *Data Analysis* app on the classroom iPad.

8. Using the classroom data, compare the two graphs to draw conclusions about the rockets and answer the following questions.

   - What factors influenced the altitude each rocket traveled? Justify your answer.
   - In this experiment, it was not feasible to measure the altitude the rocket traveled. How could you determine which rocket traveled the highest?
   - What factors influence the flight time for a rocket?
   - Identify the outliers in your data set, if necessary, and describe what you think occurred during the testing of each groups' rockets. How could these factors be addressed to change our results if you were to perform this experiment again?
   - Analyze the length versus mass graph. What is the correlation between length and mass? Explain your reasoning. How can you develop a mathematical equation to fit the data?
   - Analyze the length versus time graph. What is the correlation between length and mass? Explain your reasoning. How can you develop a mathematical equation to fit the data? What does this tell you about the relationship between length of the rocket and the flight time?

9. Using your team's data and the classroom's data, modify the original procedures to optimize the length and mass of a rocket to achieve the maximum altitude possible. This will be the rocket you carry to the NASA competition next week! Good luck!

10. Lastly, prepare a brief presentation documenting the data you collected during your original tests. In addition, include a brief description of how you modified the original design to optimize the length and mass of the rocket to achieve the highest altitude possible. Be sure to display your final rocket to the class! You may utilize any approved type of technology to present this portion of the assignment to the class.

BRAINSTORM IDEAS			
Data			
ROCKET NUMBER	**MASS OF ROCKET**	**LENGTH OF ROCKET**	**TIME OF FLIGHT (SECONDS)**
Attach your two graphs to this document.			
Conclusions			

Real-World Learning Framework for Secondary Schools © 2016 Solution Tree Press • solution-tree.com
Visit **go.solution-tree.com/instruction** to download this page.

Building a Rocket

1. Cut a sheet of drawing paper to meet the length specifications of your rocket. You will need to create a rocket that is 45 cm.

2. Using a quarter-inch PVC pipe, roll a sheet of drawing paper into a tube to make the paper more flexible.

3. Unroll the paper, and perform step two again.

4. Place the sheet of paper onto the table and place the quarter-inch PVC pipe onto the edge of the paper (the width side). Roll one time, and place glue on the edge of the backside (this edge will be able to stick to the side of your paper that is facing up as you roll the rest of the paper into a tube).

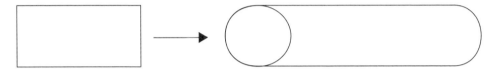

5. Put glue all over the upward-facing side of the paper.

6. Carefully begin to roll your paper into a tube, making sure the ends are even as you do so. Also, make sure that you roll the paper tightly to make a snug fit around the pipe.

7. At one end of your rocket, take a six-inch strip of duct tape and place it around the end of the tube (line the duct tape up with the end of the paper, and do not cover the end of the rocket).

8. Repeat step 7 on the other end of your rocket.

9. Starting at half of the width of the duct tape on one end of your rocket, use clear packing tape to secure the ends of the paper along the length of the rocket (or roll, where the paper ends), stopping at midway on the piece of duct tape at the other end of the roll.

10. Repeat step 9 until your rocket is completely wrapped in clear packing tape. Smooth out any wrinkles or air bubbles.

11. Next, cut a small foam circle that is the same diameter as your rocket.

12. Cut a one-inch square piece of duct tape and place the foam piece in the middle of it.

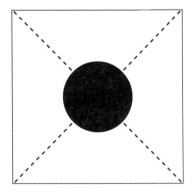

13. Using a pair of scissors, cut a slit from the corner of the tape square to the foam circle (do this for all four corners).

14. Place this piece of tape and foam on the rocket to cap off one end. At the slits you cut in the corners of the tape, fold the tape down onto the rocket body.

Real-World Learning Framework for Secondary Schools © 2016 Solution Tree Press • solution-tree.com
Visit **go.solution-tree.com/instruction** to download this page.

15. Take the foam nose cone and place it on top of the end of your rocket you just capped off.

16. Then, take a piece of duct tape and tape half of the rocket body to half of the foam nose-piece.

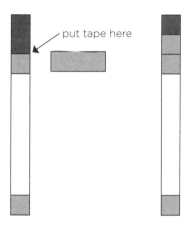

put tape here

17. Place your fins at the other end of your rocket.

18. Using the foam sheet of paper, cut four fins like the bold shape below. Make sure you measure each fin.

19. Using the hot glue gun, glue the four fins on the bottom of the rocket (the longest side of the fin should be glued to the rocket body). Try to use the same amount of glue on each fin and be consistent among the construction of your other rockets. Also, leave a little space (see picture) between the bottom of your fin and the bottom of the rocket.

Real-World Learning Framework for Secondary Schools © 2016 Solution Tree Press • solution-tree.com
Visit **go.solution-tree.com/instruction** to download this page.

Scoring Rubric

	1 SIGNIFICANT REVISION NEEDED	2 SOME REVISION NEEDED	3 PROFICIENT	4 EXCEEDS EXPECTATIONS
Objective 1: Students will construct a series of rockets to determine the optimal length and mass in order to obtain maximum flight time.	The learner does not attempt to construct a series of rockets or develop mathematical models to determine the optimal length and mass in order to obtain maximum flight time. In addition, the learner does not create a new rocket for this project.	The learner constructs a series of rockets, with several errors or flaws, *or* the learner does not construct a full series of rockets. The learner does not or inaccurately uses mathematical models (graphs) to determine the optimal length and mass of a rocket to obtain maximum flight time. The learner does not attempt to use his or her graphs to build a new rocket.	The learner constructs a series of rockets. The learner also develops mathematical models (graphs) to determine the optimal length and mass in order to obtain maximum flight time. The learner creates a new rocket, but does not do so according to the specifications determined from his or her graph.	The learner constructs an outstanding series of rockets and uses mathematical models (graphs) to determine the optimal length and mass in order to obtain maximum flight time. The learner also creates a new rocket according to these specifications.
Objective 2: Students will determine factors that influence flight time by creating a graphical representation of data.	The learner does not identify factors that may have influenced flight time. Likewise, the learner does not display a graphical representation of data, includes an irrelevant or inaccurate data display, and does not attempt to discuss its content during the presentation.	The learner identifies at least one factor that may have influenced flight time. The learner also displays a graphical representation of data with errors and somewhat attempts to discuss its content during the presentation.	The learner communicates at least two factors that may have influenced flight time. The learner also displays or discusses a graphical representation regarding the data collected during the presentation.	The learner clearly and effectively communicates at least three factors that may have influenced flight time. The learner also supplements a correct graphical representation of data to demonstrate, communicate, and support her or his reasoning during the presentation.

Sample Student Work

This student work sample gives the information of the mass, length, and time of flight of four rockets launched.

ROCKET NUMBER	MASS OF ROCKET (GRAMS)	LENGTH OF ROCKET (CENTIMETERS)	TIME OF FLIGHT (SECONDS)
1	12.8 g	14.25 cm	4.6 s 4.8 s avg: 4.63 sec 4.5 s
2	25.3 g	35.0 cm	5.6 s 5.7 s avg: 5.6 sec 5.5 s
3	43.4 g	60.5 cm	4.0 s 4.2 s avg: 4.2 sec 4.4 s
4	63.0 g	96.0 cm	2.5 s 2.7 s avg: 2.7 sec 2.9 s

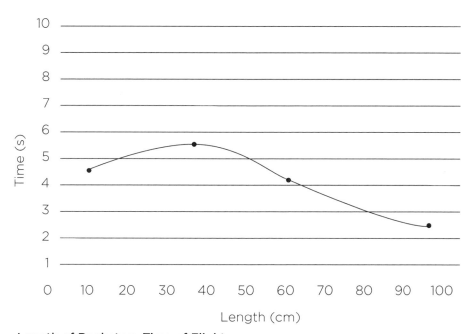

Length of Rocket vs. Time of Flight

Create Excellence Framework Rating

CREATE ANALYSIS		
CREATE COMPONENT	**LEVEL**	**JUSTIFICATION**
Real-World Learning	3: Investigating	Students are participating in a simulation of rocket design and competing in the rocket launches.
Cognitive Complexity	3: Investigating	Students create a series of rockets and test the rockets. This learning is at the Create level of the revised Bloom's taxonomy.
Student Engagement	3: Investigating	Students have choice in their design of the rocket. Task or project is differentiated by allowing for students to choose how they build their rocket.
Technology Integration	3: Investigating	Technology is an add-on as students are using a spreadsheet to enter the data for time and the mass for the rocket launch. Students also use the graphing app to graph the data to see how close they are to their graphs.

References and Resources

Abrami, P. C., Lou, Y., Chambers, B., Poulsen, C., & Spence, J. C. (2000). Why should we group students within-class for learning? *Educational Research and Evaluation, 6*(2), 158–179.

Achieve. (2013). *Next generation science standards.* Accessed at www.nextgenscience.org on January 26, 2015.

Anderson, L. W., & Krathwohl, D. R. (Eds.). (2001). *A taxonomy for learning, teaching, and assessing: A revision of Bloom's taxonomy of educational objectives.* New York: Longman.

Antonetti, J. V., & Garver, J. R. (2015). *17,000 classroom visits can't be wrong: Strategies that engage students, promote active learning, and boost achievement.* Alexandria, VA: Association for Supervision and Curriculum Development.

Baron, K. (2010). *Six steps for planning a successful project.* Accessed at www.edutopia.org/stw-maine-project-based-learning -six-steps-planning on January 26, 2015.

Barton, K., & Smith, L. (2000). Themes or motifs? Aiming for coherence through interdisciplinary outlines. *The Reading Teacher, 54*(1), 54–63.

Berliner, D. C. (1990). What's all the fuss about instructional time? In M. Ben-Peretz & R. Bromme (Eds.), *The nature of time in schools: Theoretical concepts, practitioner perceptions* (pp. 3–35). New York: Teachers College Press.

Bloom, B. S. (1956). *Taxonomy of educational objectives, book I: Cognitive domain.* New York: McKay.

Blumenfeld, P. C., & Meece, J. L. (1988). Task factors, teacher behavior and students' involvement and use of learning strategies in science. *Elementary School Journal, 88,* 238–249.

Briggs, C. L., & Keyek-Franssen, D. (2010). Clickers and CATs: Using learner response systems for formative assessments in the classroom. *Educause Review.* Accessed at www.educause.edu/ero/article/clickers-and-cats-using-learner-response -systems-formative-assessments-classroom on January 26, 2015.

Brookhart, S. M. (2013). Assessing creativity. *Educational Leadership, 70*(5), 28–34. Accessed at www.ascd.org/publications /educational-leadership/feb13/vol70/num05/Assessing-Creativity.aspx on June 3, 2015.

Bruner, J. (1960). *The process of education.* Cambridge, MA: Harvard University Press.

Buck Institute for Education. (n.d.). *What is project based learning (PBL)?* Accessed at http://bie.org/about/what_pbl on February 26, 2015.

Buck Institute for Education. (2013a). *Collaboration rubric for PBL.* Accessed at https://bie.org/object/document/6_12 _collaboration_rubric_ccss_aligned on June 3, 2015.

Buck Institute for Education. (2013b). *Creativity and innovation rubric for PBL.* Accessed at https://bie.org/object /document/6_12_creativity_innovation_rubric_non_ccss on June 3, 2015.

Buck Institute for Education. (2014). *Designing your project.* Accessed at http://bie.org/ on January 15, 2014.

Bulger, M., Mayer, R. E., & Almeroth, K. C. (2006, June). *Engaged by design: Using simulations to promote active learning.* Paper presented at the World Conference on Educational Multimedia, Hypermedia and Telecommunications, Chesapeake, VA.

Certo, J. L., Cauley, K. M., Moxley, K. D., & Chafin, C. (2008). An argument for authenticity: Adolescents' perspectives on standards-based reform. *High School Journal, 91*(4), 26–39.

Chao, E. (2001). *Report on the American workforce: Message from the Secretary of Labor.* Washington, DC: Department of Labor.

City, E., Elmore, R., Fiarman, S., & Teitel, L. (2009). *Instructional rounds in education: A network approach to improving teaching and learning.* Cambridge, MA: Harvard Education Press.

Common Cents New York, Inc. (2013). *About the penny harvest.* Accessed at http://pennyharvest.org/penny-harvest/about-penny-harvest on May 29, 2015.

Crie, M. (2005). *Inquiry-based approaches to learning.* New York: Glencoe.

Cronin, J. F. (1993). Four misconceptions about authentic learning. *Educational Leadership, 50*(7), 78–80.

Danielson, C. (2014). *The framework for teaching: Evaluation instrument.* Princeton, NJ: Danielson Group. Accessed at *www.danielsongroup.org/userfiles/files/downloads/2013EvaluationInstrument.pdf* on January 26, 2015.

Dewey, J. (1913). *Interest and effort in education.* Boston: Houghton Mifflin.

Dewey, J. (1938). *Experience and education.* New York: Collier Books.

Dwyer, D. (2009). *End-user design: Creating schools for today and tomorrow* (part V). Accessed at http://21stcenturyscholar.org/2009/10/30/end-user-design-creating-schools-for-today-and-tomorrow-part-iv/ on January 26, 2015.

Ennis, R. H. (1987). A taxonomy of critical thinking dispositions and abilities. In J. B. Baron & R. J. Sternberg (Eds.), *Teaching thinking skills: Theory and practice* (pp. 9–26). New York: Freeman.

Forkosh-Baruch, A., Mioduser, D., Nachmias, R., & Tubin, D. (2005). "Islands of innovation" and "school-wide implementations": Two patterns of ICT-based pedagogical innovations in schools. *Human Technology, 1*(2), 202–215.

Gabel, D. L. (Ed.). (1994). *Handbook of research on science teaching and learning.* New York: Macmillan.

Gavin, M. K., Casa, T. M., Adelson, J. L., Carroll, S. R., & Sheffield, L. J. (2009). The impact of advanced curriculum on the achievement of mathematically promising elementary students. *Gifted Child Quarterly, 53*, 188–202.

Gordon, D. (2011). Return to sender: Schools continue to deliver new graduates into the workplace lacking the tech-based "soft skills" that businesses demand—Experts blame K–12's persistent failure to integrate technology. *Technological Horizons in Education Journal, 38*(3), 30–35.

Gray, L., Thomas, N., & Lewis, L. (2010). *Teachers' use of educational technology in U.S. public schools: 2009* (NCES 2010–040). Washington, DC: National Center for Education Statistics.

Greaves, T. W., Hayes, J., Wilson, L., Gielniak, M., & Peterson, E. L. (2010). *The technology factor: Nine keys to student achievement and cost-effectiveness.* Chicago: Market Data Retrieval.

Greaves, T. W., Hayes, J., Wilson, L., Gielniak, M., & Peterson, E. L. (2012). *Revolutionizing education through technology: The Project RED roadmap for transformation.* Eugene, OR: International Society for Technology in Education.

Gregory, G., & Chapman, C. (2007). *Differentiated instructional strategies: One size doesn't fit all* (2nd ed.). Thousand Oaks, CA: Corwin Press.

Grow, G. O. (1991). Teaching learners to be self-directed. *Adult Education Quarterly, 41*(3), 125–149.

Harris, G. (2010, June 11). *A new model for inquiry in the school library program* [PowerPoint]. Accessed at www.slideshare.net/GregoryHarris/inquiry2010 on January 26, 2015.

Hart County School District. (2011). *Create task/project template.* Hart County, KY: Author.

Herrington, J., Oliver, R., & Reeves, T. C. (2003). Patterns of engagement in authentic online learning environments. *Australian Journal of Educational Technology, 19*(1), 59–71.

Hung, D., Tan, S. C., & Koh, T. S. (2006). Engaged learning: Making learning an authentic experience. In D. Hung & M. S. Khine (Eds.), *Engaged learning with emerging technologies* (pp. 29–48). Dordrecht, Netherlands: Springer.

Illinois Mathematics and Science Academy. (2011). *IMSA's PBL teaching and learning template.* Accessed at http://pbln.imsa.edu/model/template on January 26, 2015.

International Society for Technology in Education. (2007). *The national educational technology standards for students (NETS-S).* Eugene, OR: Author. Accessed at www.iste.org/docs/pdfs/nets-s-standards.pdf?sfvrsn=2 on January 26, 2015.

International Society for Technology in Education. (2008). *ISTE NETS-T standards: Advancing digital age teaching.* Eugene, OR: Author. Accessed at www.iste.org/docs/pdfs/nets-t-standards.pdf?sfvrsn=2 on January 26, 2015.

International Society for Technology in Education, Partnership for 21st Century Skills, & State Educational Technology Directors Association. (2007). *Maximizing the impact: The pivotal role of technology in a 21st century education system.* Accessed at www.p21.org/storage/documents/p21setdaistepaper.pdf on January 26, 2015.

Jacobs, H. H. (2010). *Curriculum 21: Essential education for a changing world.* Alexandria, VA: Association for Supervision and Curriculum Development.

Jenkins, H. (2006). *Confronting the challenges of participatory culture: Media education for the 21st century.* Chicago: The MacArthur Foundation.

Jones, B. F., Valdez, G., Nowakowski, J., & Rasmussen, C. (1995). *Plugging in: Choosing and using educational technology.* Oak Brook, IL: North Central Regional Educational Laboratory.

Jukes, I., McCain, T., & Crockett, L. (2010). *Understanding the digital generation: Teaching and learning in the new digital landscape.* Thousand Oaks, CA: Corwin Press.

Krathwohl, D. R. (2002). A revision of Bloom's Taxonomy: An overview. *Theory Into Practice, 41*(4), 212–218.

Kwit, H. C. (2012). *Making the Common Core come alive! e-newsletter.* Accessed at www.prweb.com/releases/2012/11/prweb10080978.htm on January 26, 2015.

Learn and Serve America's National Service-Learning Clearinghouse. (2007). *Why districts, schools, and classrooms should practice service-learning.* Accessed at www.communityschools.org/assets/1/AssetManager/A7_Howard_Why%20Districts.pdf on January 26, 2015.

Lemke, C., Coughlin, E., & Reifsneider, D. (2009). *Technology in schools: What the research says—An update.* Culver City, CA: Cisco.

Licensed Geriatric Resources for Education and Learning. (2013). *What's new with Let's Get Real?* Accessed at www.lgreal.org/index.shtml on February 19, 2015.

Lin, L. (2006). Cultural dimensions of authenticity in teaching. *New Directions for Adult and Continuing Education, 111,* 63–72.

Lombardi, M. M. (2007, May). *Authentic learning for the 21st century: An overview.* Accessed at https://net.educause.edu/ir/library/pdf/ELI3009.pdf on January 26, 2015.

Martinez, M. (2014). *Deeper learning: The new normal.* Accessed at www.advanc-ed.org/source/deeper-learning-new-normal on January 26, 2015.

Marzano, R. J. (2007). *The art and science of teaching: A comprehensive framework for effective instruction.* Alexandria, VA: Association for Supervision and Curriculum Development.

Maxim, G. W. (2014). *Dynamic social studies for constructivist classrooms: Inspiring tomorrow's social scientists* (10th ed.). New York: Pearson.

Maxwell, M. (2012). *Designing instruction using revised Bloom's taxonomy.* Accessed at https://itunes.apple.com/us/book/designing-instruction-using/id536339837?mt=11 on August 17, 2015.

Maxwell, M., Constant, M., Stobaugh, R., & Tassell, J. (2011). Developing a HEAT framework for assessing and improving instruction. In C. Maddux (Ed.), *Research highlights in technology and teacher education 2011* (pp. 13–20). Chesapeake, VA: Society for Information Technology and Teacher Education.

Maxwell, M., Stobaugh, R., & Tassell, J. (2011). Analyzing HEAT of lesson plans in pre-service and advanced teacher education. *Journal of the Research Center for Educational Technology, 7,* 16–29.

McGinnis, J. (2006). Age of the empirical. *Policy Review, 137,* 47–58.

Meece, J. L., Blumenfeld, P. C. & Hoyle, R. H. (1988). Students' goal orientations and cognitive engagement in classroom activities. *Journal of Educational Psychology, 80*(4), 514–523.

Miller, A. (2011, June 28). *Assessing the Common Core standards: Real life mathematics.* Accessed at www.edutopia.org/blog/assessing-common-core-standards-real-life-mathematics on January 26, 2015.

Moersch, C. (2002). Measures of success: Six instruments to assess teachers' use of technology. *Learning and Leading With Technology, 30*(3), 10–18.

National Council for the Social Studies. (2013). *College, Career, & Civic Life C3 Framework for Social Studies State Standards.* Silver Spring, MD: Author. Accessed at www.socialstudies.org/system/files/c3/C3-Framework-for-Social-Studies.pdf on June 11, 2015.

National Governors Association Center for Best Practices & Council of Chief State School Officers. (2010a). *Common Core State Standards for English language arts and literacy in history/social studies, science, and technical subjects.* Washington, DC: Authors.

National Governors Association Center for Best Practices & Council of Chief State School Officers. (2010b). *Common Core State Standards for mathematics.* Washington, DC: Authors.

National Governors Association Center for Best Practices & Council of Chief State School Officers. (2012). *Common core state standards initiative: Preparing America's students for college and career.* Accessed at www.corestandards.org on January 26, 2015.

National Research Council. (2012). *A framework for K–12 science education: Practices, crosscutting concepts, and core ideas* (Committee on a Conceptual Framework for New K–12 Science Education Standards). Washington, DC: The National Academies Press.

November, A. (2012). *Who owns the learning? Preparing students for success in the digital age.* Bloomington, IN: Solution Tree Press.

Oblinger, D. (2003). Boomers, gen-xers, and millennials: Understanding the "new students." *Educause Review, 38,* 37–47.

Ohler, J. (2013). The uncommon core. *Educational Leadership, 70*(5), 42–46.

Partnership for 21st Century Skills. (2009). *Curriculum and instruction: A 21st century skills implementation guide.* Accessed at www.p21.org/storage/documents/p21-stateimp_curriculuminstruction.pdf on January 26, 2015.

Partnership for 21st Century Skills. (2011). *Framework for 21st century learning.* Accessed at www.p21.org/our-work/p21-framework on January 26, 2015.

Pence, H., & McIntosh, S. (2010). Refocusing the vision: The future of instructional technology. *Journal of Educational Technology Systems, 39*(2), 173–179.

Pink, D. H. (2005). *A whole new mind: Moving from the information age to the conceptual age.* New York: Riverhead Books.

Pink, D. H. (2009). *Drive: The surprising truth about what motivates us.* New York: Riverhead Books.

Prensky, M. (2001). Digital natives, digital immigrants. *On the Horizon, 9*(5), 1–6.

Prensky, M. (2010). *Teaching digital natives: Partnering for real learning.* Thousand Oaks, CA: Corwin Press.

Raphael, L. M., Pressley, M., & Mohan, L. (2008). Engaging instruction in middle school classrooms: An observational study of nine teachers. *Elementary School Journal, 109*(1), 61–81.

Rasicot, J. (2006). Learning in the classroom by reaching out to others. *Washington Post.* Accessed at www.washingtonpost.com/wp-dyn/content/article/2006/03/01/AR2006030101181.html on January 27, 2015.

Raths, J. (2002). Improving instruction. *Theory Into Practice, 41,* 233–237.

Ray, B. (2012). *Design thinking: Lessons for the classroom.* Accessed at www.edutopia.org/blog/design-thinking-betty-ray on January 26, 2015.

Reeves, T. C. (2006). How do you know they are learning? The importance of alignment in higher education. *International Journal of Learning Technology, 2*(4), 302–304.

Renzulli, J. S., Gentry, M., & Reis, S. M. (2004). A time and a place for authentic learning. *Educational Leadership, 62,* 73–77.

Richardson, W. (2013). Students first, not stuff. *Educational Leadership, 70*(6), 10–14.

Richardson, W., & Mancabelli, R. (2011). *Personal learning networks: Using the power of connections to transform education.* Bloomington, IN: Solution Tree Press.

Roberts, J. L., & Inman, T. F. (2009). *Strategies for differentiating instruction: Best practices for the classroom* (2nd ed.). Waco, TX: Prufrock Press.

Robinson, K. (2009). *The element: How finding your passion changes everything.* New York: Penguin.

Schamel, D., & Ayres, M. P. (1992). The minds-on approach: Student creativity and personal involvement in the undergraduate science laboratory. *Journal of College Science Teaching, 21*(4), 226–229.

Schools We Need Project. (2013). *An engaging program of real world learning.* Accessed at http://schoolsweneed.wikispaces .com/Real+World+Learning on January 26, 2015.

Schwartzbeck, T. D. (2012). *The digital learning imperative: How technology and teaching meet today's education challenges.* Washington, DC: Alliance for Excellent Education.

Simpson, R. (2008). Visualizing technology integration: A model for meeting ISTE Educational-Technology Standards. *Edutopia.* Accessed at www.edutopia.org/ferryway-school-saugus-ironworks on June 11, 2015.

Skinner, E. A., & Belmont, M. J. (1993). Motivation in the classroom: Reciprocal effects of teacher behavior and student engagement across the school year. *Journal of Educational Psychology, 85*(4), 571–581.

Sousa, D. (2006). *How the brain learns* (3rd ed.). Thousand Oaks, CA: Corwin Press.

Stewart, A., & Rivera, Y. (2010). *Inquiry-based learning* [PowerPoint]. Accessed at www.slideshare.net/teeneeweenee/inquiry -based-learning1 on May 29, 2015.

Stobaugh, R. (2013). *Assessing critical thinking in middle and high schools: Meeting the Common Core.* Larchmont, NY: Eye on Education.

Sulla, N. (2011). *Students taking charge: Inside the learner-active, technology-infused classroom.* New York: Routledge.

Swartz, R. J., & Parks, S. (1994). *Infusing critical and creative thinking into content instruction: A lesson design handbook for the elementary grades.* Pacific Grove, CA: Critical Thinking Press & Software.

Tassell, J. L., Maxwell, M., & Stobaugh, R. (2013). CReaTE excellence: Using a teacher framework to maximize STEM learning with your child. *Parenting for High Potential, 3*(2), 10–13.

Tucker, M. S. (Ed.). (2011). *Surpassing Shanghai: An agenda for American education built on the world's leading systems.* Cambridge, MA: Harvard Education Press.

U.S. 21st Century Workforce Commission. (2000). *A nation of opportunity: Building America's 21st century workforce.* Accessed at http://digitalcommons.ilr.cornell.edu/cgi/viewcontent.cgi?article=1003&context=key_workplace on January 27, 2015.

UNESCO (2004). *Integrating ICTs into education: Lessons learned—A collective case study of six Asian countries.* Accessed at www.unescobkk.org/fileadmin/user_upload/ict/e-books/ICTLessonsLearned/ICT_integrating_education.pdf on January 26, 2015.

van Opstal, D. (2008). *Compete 2.0: Thrive. The skills imperative.* Washington, DC: Council on Competitiveness.

Virginia Board of Bar Examiners. (2006). *Law reader memorandum: A memorandum on the concept of reading law under an attorney's supervision.* Accessed at www.vbbe.state.va.us/reader/readermemo.html on January 26, 2015.

Willingham, D. T. (2009). *Why don't students like school? A cognitive scientist answers questions about how the mind works and what it means for the classroom.* San Francisco: Jossey-Bass.

Wolf, M. A. (2012). *Culture shift: Teaching in a learner-centered environment powered by digital learning.* Washington, DC: Alliance for Excellent Education.

Wood, D. (2003). ABC of learning and teaching in medicine: Problem based learning. *British Medical Journal, 326*(7384), 328–330.

Yazzie-Mintz, E. (2010, June). *Charting the path from engagement to achievement: A report on the 2009 high school survey of student engagement.* Bloomington: Indiana University Center for Evaluation and Education Policy.

Zhao, Y. (2012). *World class learners: Educating creative and entrepreneurial students.* Thousand Oaks, CA: Corwin Press.

Index

Unstoppable Learning
Douglas Fisher and Nancy Frey
Discover how systems thinking can enhance teaching and learning schoolwide. Examine how to use systems thinking—which involves distinguishing patterns and considering short- and long-term consequences—to better understand the big picture of education and the intricate relationships that impact classrooms.
BKF662

Personal Learning Networks
Will Richardson and Rob Mancabelli
Follow this road map for using the web for learning. Learn how to build your own learning network. Use learning networks in the classroom and make the case for schoolwide learning networks to improve student outcomes.
BKF484

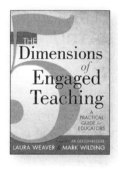

The Five Dimensions of Engaged Teaching
Laura Weaver and Mark Wilding
Engaged teaching recognizes that educators need to offer more than lesson plans and assessments for students to thrive in the 21st century. Equip your students to be resilient individuals, able to communicate effectively and work with diverse people.
BKF601

Deeper Learning
Edited by James A. Bellanca
Education authorities from around the globe draw on research as well as their own experience to explore deeper learning, a process that promotes higher-order thinking, reasoning, and problem solving to better educate students and prepare them for college and careers.
BKF622

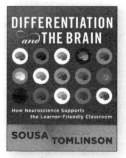

Differentiation and the Brain
David A. Sousa and Carol Ann Tomlinson
Examine the basic principles of differentiation in light of educational neuroscience research that will help you make the most effective curricular, instructional, and assessment choices. Learn how to implement differentiation so that it achieves the desired result of shared responsibility between teacher and student.
BKF353

Visit solution-tree.com or call 800.733.6786 to order.

Wait! Your professional development journey doesn't have to end with the last pages of this book.

We realize improving student learning doesn't happen overnight. And your school or district shouldn't be left to puzzle out all the details of this process alone.

No matter where you are on the journey, we're committed to helping you get to the next stage.

Take advantage of everything from **custom workshops** to **keynote presentations** and **interactive web and video conferencing**. We can even help you develop an action plan tailored to fit your specific needs.

Let's get the conversation started.

Call 888.763.9045 today.

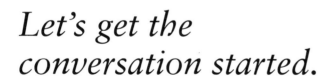

 solution-tree.com